Courtyards

Courtyards

AESTHETIC, SOCIAL, AND THERMAL DELIGHT

John S. Reynolds

JOHN WILEY & SONS, INC.

This book is printed on acid-free paper. ∞

Copyright © 2002 by John Wiley & Sons, Inc., New York. All rights reserved.

Published simultaneously in Canada.

No part of this publication may be reproduced, stored in a retrieval system or transmitted in any form or by any means, electronic, mechanical, photocopying, recording, scanning or otherwise, except as permitted under Sections 107 or 108 of the 1976 United States Copyright Act, without either the prior written permission of the Publisher, or authorization through payment of the appropriate per-copy fee to the Copyright Clearance Center, 222 Rosewood Drive, Danvers, MA 01923, (978) 750-8400, fax (978) 750-4744. Requests to the Publisher for permission should be addressed to the Permissions Department, John Wiley & Sons, Inc., 605 Third Avenue, New York, NY 10158-0012, (212) 850-6011, fax (212) 850-6008, E-mail: PERMREQ @ WILEY.COM.

This publication is designed to provide accurate and authoritative information in regard to the subject matter covered. It is sold with the understanding that the publisher is not engaged in rendering professional services. If professional advice or other expert assistance is required, the services of a competent professional person should be sought.

Interior design and layout: Jeff Baker, BookMechanics

Library of Congress Cataloging-in-Publication Data:

Reynolds, John, 1938-
Courtyards: aesthetic, social, and thermal delight / John S. Reynolds
        p.   cm.
Includes bibliographical references and index.
ISBN 0-471-39884-5 (cloth : alk. paper)
1. Courtyard houses. 2. Courtyard gardens. 3. Architecture and climate. I. Title.
NA7523.R49 2001
712'.6—dc21

Printed in the United States of America.

10 9 8 7 6 5 4 3 2 1

FOR LEN, WITH MANY THANKS

Contents

Courtyards are special places that are outside yet almost inside, open to the sky, usually in contact with the earth, but surrounded by rooms. The courtyard is closely related to its surrounding rooms, serving them as both a conduit and a filter of daylight, night darkness, wind, rain, and sound. Courtyards provide people with daily contact with nature. And a courtyard is often the most beautiful place in a building.

While courtyards bring nature within a building, they also moderate nature's extremes. They are rarely as hot at summer's mid-afternoon, or as cold just before dawn, as the temperatures in the countryside, or even in the street outside.

Any exterior space surrounded by walls might be called a courtyard, but this book is about those with openings to interior spaces on nearly all sides, offering many opportunities for inside-outside exchange. Thus the walled garden, bordered but not surrounded by a building, is not included here.

At their best, courtyards are exquisite landscapes, worthy centers of attention and activity within a building. In Hispanic cultures, they offer carefully framed views designed to attract the passerby. They offer a pleasant contrast to the environment of the street.

Occasionally, courtyards draw all the owner's attention to themselves, discouraging any investment in the public streetscape. They then become examples of private-space care, but public-space neglect. At their worst, courtyards are meager holes in buildings, concerned solely with the technical role of bringing light and air—however paltry and unpleasant—down to spaces below.

There are courtyards in many parts of the world, in varying climates, in differing cultures. The courtyard is at least as old as ancient Sumeria, and this building type was widely used for housing throughout the ancient Mideast. In China, courtyard houses abound. In the colder north the courtyards are larger (to admit winter sun); in the warmer south, courtyards are smaller (to exclude summer sun). Pit dwellings utilize central courtyards to bring light and air to underground housing, with cultivated fields above. There are buildings clustered around courtyards in rural Japan, Europe, Africa, and America. Contemporary architects incorporate courtyards when a semicontrolled outdoor space is appropriate, although the glass-covered, air-conditioned "atrium" is seen more frequently at present.

Earlier books about courtyard buildings have looked at examples worldwide, notably *Atrium: Five Thousand Years of Open Courtyards*, by Werner Blaser. I began my fascination with Hispanic courtyards because of their climate modifying characteristics, as I describe in Chapter 7. Their beauty, accessibility, and social centrality within their buildings added enormously to their appeal. Here within a broad Spanish-speaking culture are a wide variety of courtyard proportions, degrees of formality, and usages, through a wide variety of climates. Here are courtyards that a stranger can ask to visit and probably be warmly received. Here are spaces that delight the senses, that make obvious why architecture is such a life-affirming art. Therefore, this book concentrates on my explorations of Hispanic courtyards, old and new—those in Spain and Latin America.

These chapters consider the Hispanic courtyard—or *patio*—in three roles within buildings: aesthetic pleasure, social centrality, and technical modification of the climate. Unlike the North American patio, which typically faces a much larger walled garden or lawn, the Hispanic patio or courtyard discussed here is a space enclosed by, and closely related to, a building.

Acknowledgments

The Graham Foundation for Advanced Studies in the Fine Arts provided major support for my work in 1996. Sabbatical leaves in 1981–82, 1988, and 1995–96 and a faculty grant in summer 1995 were funded by the University of Oregon; this work would not have been possible without them. A Fulbright teaching grant in 1988 took me to Argentina, supporting my South American courtyard observations.

I am grateful for production assistance from Stephanie Thompson, Matthew Wilson, and Walter Biddle. Amanda Miller has given freely of her editorial advice. It is always welcome; several parts of this book exist because of her suggestions.

In Mexico, several people in Colima were especially helpful, beginning with architect Umbierto Martinez Baez during my first visit some twenty years ago. I also thank Maria Emilia Rangel Brun, archivist Irma Lopez Razgado, and University of Colima Professors Leandro Sandoval Alvarez, Francisco Cárdenas Munguía, and Dr. Ignacio Galindo Estrada. I am grateful to Hector Arturo Velaso Villa, Presidente Municipal; and Jesús Rios Aguilar, Director, Obras Públicas, who cooperated with my monitoring. Measuring of several courtyards was assisted by University of Colima architecture students Sergio Mendoza Gutiérrez and Angélica Muñoz Martin. In Oaxaca, University of Minnesota Professor Lance LaVine generously shared his knowledge of his favorite courtyards.

In Andalucía, my interviews with inhabitants and physical measurements of courtyards were made much easier by the considerable help of Leonard Delgado Siqueiro. Thanks to his social skills (and superior Spanish), I was free to roam with camera in hand through many courtyard buildings.

For permission to measure and monitor their courtyards in Córdoba, I thank Alejandro López Obrero of Meryn Leathers, and Giovanni Miceli Baglioletti of the Taberna Santa Clara. Similar thanks to homeowners Blanca Ciudad, Angela García Cobos and Paco Jiménez, Mr. and Mrs. Manuel Ruíz Guzman, Victoria Molina and Luis Mateo Lunar, Maria Rodríguez Soto, Julia Alonzo Velarde, and caretaker Manuel Sánchez Colmenero of Los Amigos de los Patios Cordobeses.

I am grateful to Professor Pedro Domínguez Bascón, professor of geography at the University of Córdoba, for many insights into Córdoba's microclimates and courtyards. A plan of the old section (*Casco Histórico*) of Córdoba was furnished by José González Maddorán, City Manager. University of Oregon professor Al Urquhart's gift of *Arquitectura Civil Sevillana* provided valuable historical perspective. Professor Kenneth Helphand encouraged my writings.

I owe architect Victor Carrasco a great debt for his work in describing and thermally monitoring his home in Bornos. Other help in Spain came from architectural photographer Jane Lidz; weather data at Campo de Villamartin is from the Junta de Andalucía, Consejería de Agricultura y Pesca. Professor Jaime Lopez de Asiain contributed many observations on courtyards in Seville.

Elsewhere, Professor Guillermo Gonzalo, in Tucumán, advised me on Argentine courtyards, and Professor Renato Peralta Chappell conducted me through many of his favorite courtyards of Córdoba, Argentina. William Lowry (1927–1999) was a valued colleague with whom I could discuss biometeorology in general and courtyards in particular; he is missed. Many colleagues' insights have helped me appreciate the interconnection between comfort, energy, and culture; in particular, I thank Edward Allen, G.Z. Brown, Virginia Cartwright, Jeffrey Cook, Baruch Givoni, Ralph Knowles, Murray Milne, and Rob Peña.

Several former students at the University of Oregon helped shape my interest in Hispanic courtyards, notably Liliana Olga Beltrán (Peru), Isabel Torrealba Ramos (Venezuela), and Alfredo Fernández Gonzales (Mexico). My interest in Islamic courtyards was nourished by former students Can Elmas (Turkey), whose work appears in Chapter 13, and Aydan Ilter (Turkey), and Fatih Rifki (Cyprus). Courtyards in China were brought to my attention by former student David P. Y. Lung. Michael Cockram has contributed several drawings to this book. Finally, my students in my yearly seminars on passive cooling, with their enthusiasm and probing questions, have encouraged me to investigate and explain. This book is one result.

PART ONE

Courtyard Characteristics

El Sur

Desde uno de tus patios haber mirado	*To have watched from one of your patios*
las antiguas estrellas,	*the ancient stars,*
desde el banco de sombra haber mirado	*from the bench of shadow to have watched*
easas luces dispersas	*those scattered lights*
que mi ignorancia no ha aprendido a nombrar	*that my ignorance has learned no names for*
ni a ordenar en constelaciones,	*nor their places in constellations,*
haber sentido el círculo del agua	*To have heard the note of water*
en el secreto aljibe,	*in the cistern,*
el olor del jazmín y la madreselva,	*known the scent of jasmine and honeysuckle,*
el silencio del pájaro dormido,	*the silence of the sleeping bird,*
el arco del zaguán, la humedad	*the arch of the entrance, the damp*
—easa cosas, acaso, son el poema.	*—these things, perhaps, are the poem.*

Jorge Luis Borges

(translation, W. S. Merwin)

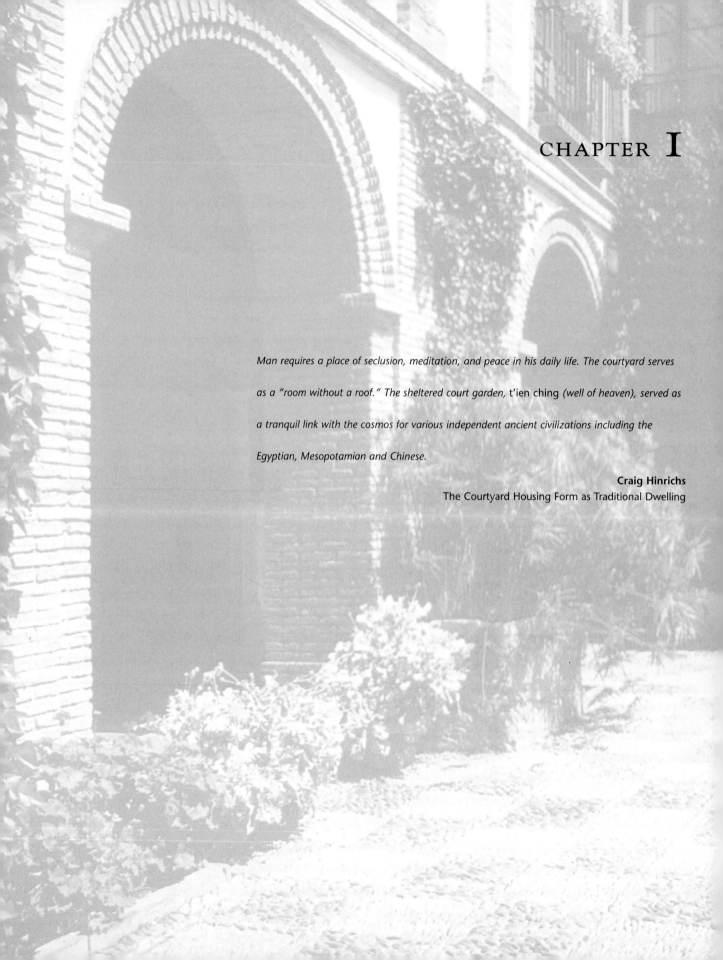

CHAPTER **I**

Man requires a place of seclusion, meditation, and peace in his daily life. The courtyard serves

as a "room without a roof." The sheltered court garden, t'ien ching (well of heaven), served as

a tranquil link with the cosmos for various independent ancient civilizations including the

Egyptian, Mesopotamian and Chinese.

Craig Hinrichs
The Courtyard Housing Form as Traditional Dwelling

Classifying Courtyards

Courtyards serve buildings of nearly every imaginable function. Residences are particularly likely to be designed around courtyards, because courtyards offer both privacy and access to nature. Commercial activities also benefit. For example, restaurants offer shaded courtyards as escapes from oppressive small offices and the midday heat. Hotels use flowering courtyards as the first impression for their guests, and the surrounding arcades for lobby functions. A courtyard might surround the hotel swimming pool. Colleges organize their offices and classrooms around formal courtyards that host informal gatherings between classes. Public buildings maintain courtyards as examples of civic pride, much as the courthouse lawn serves the North American town. Hospitals and clinics use the arcades around their quiet courtyards as waiting areas, and better yet as visiting places, a momentary escape for the patient from the confinement of the hospital bed.

With so many possible functions and endless variations in size and shape, there are many ways of classifying courtyards. The following approaches could be taken in any order, but entry sequence is first, because it presents the courtyard as experienced on first contact.

Entry Sequence

Contrast is an essential ingredient of courtyard aesthetics, beginning with the first transition from the heat, noise, stench, and glare of the street to the cool dark quiet of the *zaguán* (covered entranceway from street to courtyard). A verdant cluster of light and shadow is framed by a dark tunnel and decorative iron gate. In the second transition, one emerges into the courtyard with its contrasts of light and shadow, made rich by patterns formed by leaves. The splash of water and the sound of canaries replaces the quiet of the *zaguán*. Shadows from the movement of the leaves and water, and reflected sparkle from water surfaces, play off the massive immobile walls, reinforcing the contrast between soft plants and hard structure, between green leaves, vivid blossoms, and white stucco. In a hot and dry climate, wet surfaces are rare: their darker hue and shining texture are made even more attractive by adding the motion of flowing water. The more unpleasant the street, the more appealing is the courtyard in contrast.

The "axial" path from the street to the courtyard (prominent on the north side of the Mediterranean and throughout Hispanic cultures) allows direct passage and direct views from the street, often leading straight to the courtyard's center (Figure 1.1a). A walk down the narrow sidewalks of Spanish colonial cities is enlivened at each *zaguán* by this darkly framed view of the courtyard's sunny center.

Some courtyards place the *zaguán* in a way that leads directly to one arcade along the courtyard, rather than the center; an example is shown in Figure 1.1b. While this compromises the privacy of that one arcade, it provides more privacy for the center.

FIG. 1.1 VARIATIONS ON ENTRY
(a) A typical Hispanic arrangement places the *zaguán* pointing to the courtyard's center.
(b) Less-direct courtyard entry examples from Venezuela, Egypt, Greece, and Morocco (From Rapoport 1969. Reprinted by permission of Prentice-Hall, Inc., Upper Saddle River, N.J.)
(c) The arcade is the only transition from street to courtyard at Bustos Tavera 25, Seville (from Collantes de Terán Delorme and Gómez Estern, 1976.).
(d) A typical "four-in-one" courtyard house in Beijing. Entry is at southeast corner, and a "hanging flower gate" separates the smaller front courtyard from the more private, larger main courtyard. (From Lung 1991).

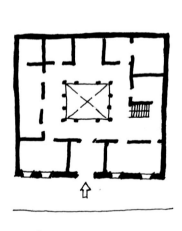

a

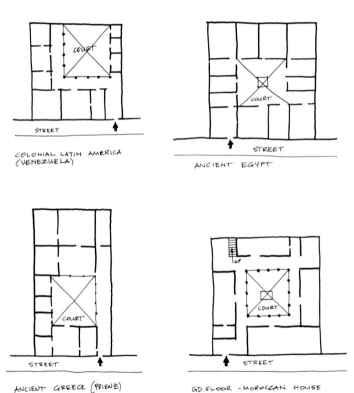

b

Variations on the "bent" path are more typical of Islamic cultures (Figure 1.1b). Its indirectness ensures visual privacy from the street. An abrupt departure is a direct gate from street to courtyard, where the courtyard and street are adjacent (Figure 1.1c). This style of courtyard may take on the role of the walled garden, or even the front yard of a well-fenced home, depending on the number of openings in the street facade.

In China, the typical "four in one" courtyard house in Beijing (Figure 1.1d) allows public access to the first, smaller courtyard, but a "hanging flower gate" screens the second, larger and private courtyard (Lung 1991).

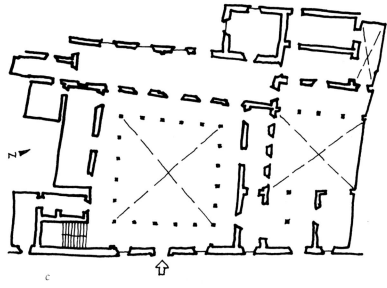

c

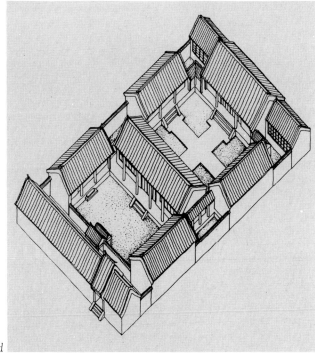

d

The main hall and the courtyard are the two most significant parts of a courtyard house, complementing each other. After entering at the main gate, one comes across the first courtyard which is the long and narrow front yard that runs from east to west. It contains a front block that faces north with bedrooms for male servants or for miscellaneous purposes. Through the front yard, one comes to the second gate which is situated on the central axis. It is sometimes elaborately decorated and is called the "hanging flower gate." After passing this gate, one comes to the main courtyard. To the north of this important courtyard is the main block, with chambers on the east and the west. The central part of the main block is the main hall. The rooms on either side are the parents' bedrooms, while the chambers on the east and west are the guest rooms or bedrooms for the children or junior members of the household.

David Lung
Chinese Traditional Vernacular Architecture

Placement Within a Building

We usually think of the courtyard as physically at the center of a building. But courtyards might have one, perhaps two walls that form barriers to a neighboring building or street, and still "qualify" as courtyards (rather than walled gardens) because of their degree of interaction with the building on the remaining sides. The Palacio de Viana in Córdoba, Spain, known as the Patio Museum, shows the difficulty of neatly classifying such outdoor spaces (Figure 1.2). Clearly, five of its thirteen "patios" are true courtyards, surrounded by rooms or arcades of the building. Several more are clearly walled gardens, with but one wall of the building adjacent. But several others could be in either category.

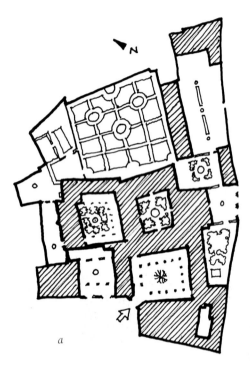

a

b

FIG. 1.2 CÓRDOBA, SPAIN
The Palacio de Viana is known as the patio museum for its thirteen "patios." (*a*) Many of these outdoor spaces are really walled gardens, as is evident from the plan. (*b*) The museum's main entrance is a rare example of a patio corner entry. A very tall palm tree rises from the courtyard center. (*c*) Another true courtyard displays a fountain, potted plants, vines, and a small tree. (*d*) Along the edges of the museum are several spaces called patios, but they actually are large walled gardens.

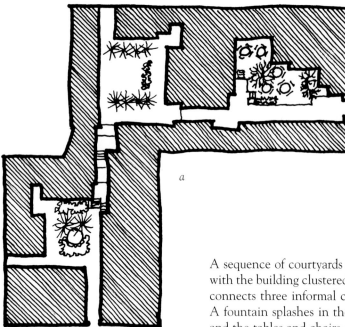

a

FIG. 1.3 OAXACA, MEXICO
The Hotel Las Golondrinas is a sequence
(*a*) of three courtyards linked (*b*) by
narrow passages with dense plantings.
(See also Figure 3.10.)

A sequence of courtyards and connecting passages may wander through a site,
with the building clustered around them. The Hotel Las Golondrinas in Oaxaca
connects three informal courtyards with open stairs and passages (Figure 1.3).
A fountain splashes in the first courtyard, a hammock beckons in the second,
and the tables and chairs of a small dining area brighten the third courtyard.

b

Orientation

In most cases, the orientation of the courtyard's walls depends upon that of the street outside. At least one wall will usually be roughly parallel to the street (see again Figure 1.1). Thus for a rectangular site the orientation is straightforward. For a distinctly nonrectangular site, there are some intriguing variations. In Figure 1.4a, a triangular block in Seville contains one major courtyard, with its four sides managing to be parallel to each of the streets. In Figure 1.4b, a very irregular site surrounds a square courtyard oriented to the cardinal points of the compass, without regard to the edges of its site. The resulting awkward transitions between building walls and courtyard opening are made within the wildly trapezoidal (and highly unusual) plans of the arcades.

FIG. 1.4 ORIENTATION OF COURTYARDS
While rectangular sites usually contain rectangular courtyards placed parallel to the street front, the Hospital de los Viejos, Seville (a) occupies a triangle between Calles Amparo, Viriato, and Viejos. The off-center, trapezoidal-plan courtyard has a wall parallel to each street. One wall runs nearly due north-south.

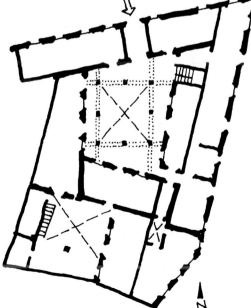

(b) A residence at the corner of Calles Verónica and Valle, Seville, seems determined to orient its courtyard to the compass cardinal points. In consequence, the arcades must mediate between the site's orientation and that of the courtyard. (Based on Collantes de Terán Delorme and Gómez Estern, 1976.)

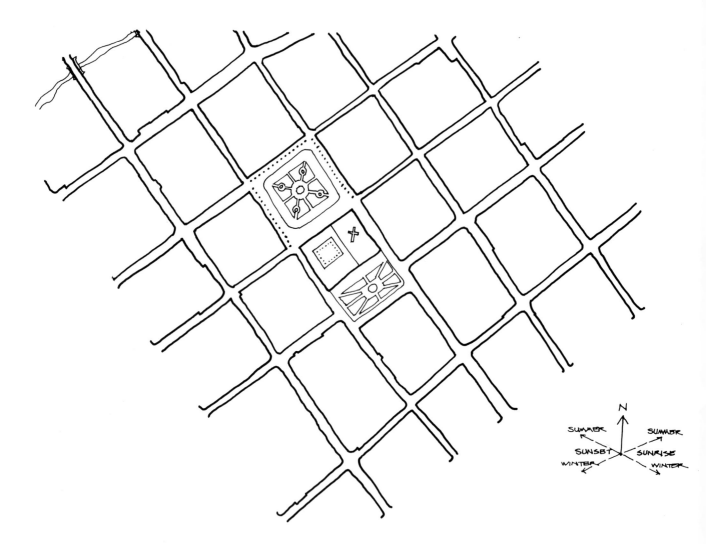

FIG. 1.5 COLIMA, MEXICO
At latitude 19° north, Colima is
a Spanish colonial city of narrow streets
in a grid pattern oriented roughly 45°
to the cardinal points. Each side of a
block has its chance at morning or
evening sun, according to the solstice.

The sun is influential for both people and plants in courtyards; which side receives direct sun and at what time of day determines where and when maximum daylight and optimum thermal comfort is available.

In older cities, with no grid pattern of streets, there is a huge variety of courtyard orientations. In newer gridded cities, the streets—and thus courtyards—are usually either oriented to the cardinal points (north-south, east-west) or set at about 45° off the cardinal points. The latter is typical of many Spanish colonial towns. The result of 45° orientation is a "democratic" distribution of sunlight on the facades through the year (Figure 1.5). At summer solstice, morning sun fills the northeast-facing walls, evening sun fills the northwest-facing walls. At winter solstice, morning sun fills the southeast-facing walls, evening sun fills the southwest-facing walls.

Courtyards oriented to the cardinal compass points are explored in Figure 1.6. For the rectangular but nonsquare courtyard, those that are **elongated east-west** have their longer sides face north and south (Figure 1.6a). At these orientations, direct sun in summer can be prevented from entering the longer sides with shallow overhangs, leaving the openings available for wind. The shorter sides, however, get strong direct sun across the length of the courtyard in the morning or evening. In winter, when strong sun is welcome, it is almost absent (Figure 1.7a).

When plans are **elongated north-south**, the longer walls face east-west (Figure 1.6b). There are difficulties with summer sun in morning or afternoon, but one long wall partially shades the other at the earliest and latest hours. Meanwhile the shorter side (facing the equator) gets direct sun across the length of the courtyard around noon. Again, winter sun is welcome, and in the hours near noon, some walls receive its warmth (Figure 1.7b).

Which orientation is optimal? This depends on which functions inhabit the long or short sides, and whether winter heating or summer cooling is the greater problem. This is explored further in Chapter 12, Figure 12.19, where solar heat gains are considered.

In some cultures the entrance to the courtyard is, where possible, oriented in a propitious direction; in India, as described by Amita Sinha (1989), the Hindus place the entrance passage to the east, while the Muslims face it toward Mecca (west). Sinha also describes the purity-pollution axis that places the kitchen across the courtyard from the latrine.

Observations over time demonstrate a rhythmic measure of space. For example, any architectural space that is oriented from east to west strengthens our experience of seasons. One main wall is nearly always dark; on the other side of the space, a shadow line moves gradually up the wall then down again. To experience the whole cycle takes exactly one year. The basic movement is always the same. As the sun's path drops lower in the sky during late summer and fall, the shadow moves up. As the sun's path rises in the sky during late winter and spring, the shadow moves down. Changing the orientation of the space will evoke a different cycle and rhythm.

Any space that is oriented from north to south sharpens our experience of a day. Both main walls are lighted, but at different hours. Every morning, light from the east will cast a shadow that moves quickly down the opposite wall and across the floor. Every afternoon, light from the west will cast a shadow that crosses the floor and climbs the opposing wall. To experience the whole cycle takes from before sunrise until after sundown.

Where east–west and north–south spaces pierce each other, we can experience both time scales. The common volume intensifies both a seasonal and a daily cycle. It combines them, laying one over the other. The result is a crossing in space that proportions time. Its celebration has often lifted architecture out of the region of fact into the realm of art.

Ralph L. Knowles
Rhythm and Ritual: a Motive for Design

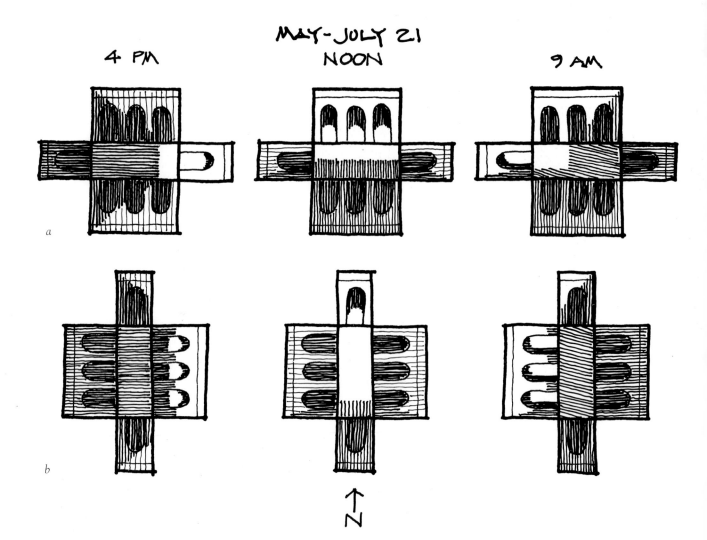

4 PM

MAY-JULY 21 NOON

9 AM

a

b

↑
N

FIG. 1.6 ON MAY 21 AND JULY 21, rectangular courtyards elongated east-west are compared to those elongated north-south at (sun time) 9 AM, NOON, and 4 PM (about an hour past the hottest time of day) at 36° north latitude (near Córdoba, Spain). May is the time of Córdoba's Concurso de Patios, and July is the time of the hottest temperatures, when sun is an enemy. (The shadow lines on the courtyard floor show the sun's direction [azimuth].)

(a) Elongated east-west:
9 AM: About 3/4 of the floor is in shadow. The sun just grazes the north face, leaving its arcade in shadow. But sun fully illuminates the short west face and its arcade.
NOON: Half the courtyard floor is in sun, and the north face is fully illuminated. But the high sun angle leaves much of the north face's arcade in shadow. (The sun, due south, is just grazing the east and west faces.)
4 PM: About 3/4 of the floor is in shadow. The sun, due west, just grazes the north and south faces, leaving their arcades in shadow. The sun fully illuminates the short east face and its arcade.

(b) Elongated north-south:
9 AM: The floor is in shadow. The sun just grazes the short north face, leaving its arcade in shadow. But sun illuminates almost all the long west face and its arcade.
NOON: About 4/5 of the courtyard floor is in sun, and the short north face is fully illuminated. But the high sun angle leaves much of the north face's arcade in shadow. (The sun, due south, is just grazing the long east and west faces, leaving their arcades in shadow.)
4 PM: The floor is in shadow. The sun, due west, just grazes the short north and south faces, leaving their arcades in shadow. The sun illuminates about half the long east facade and its arcade.

Part 1: Courtyard Characteristics

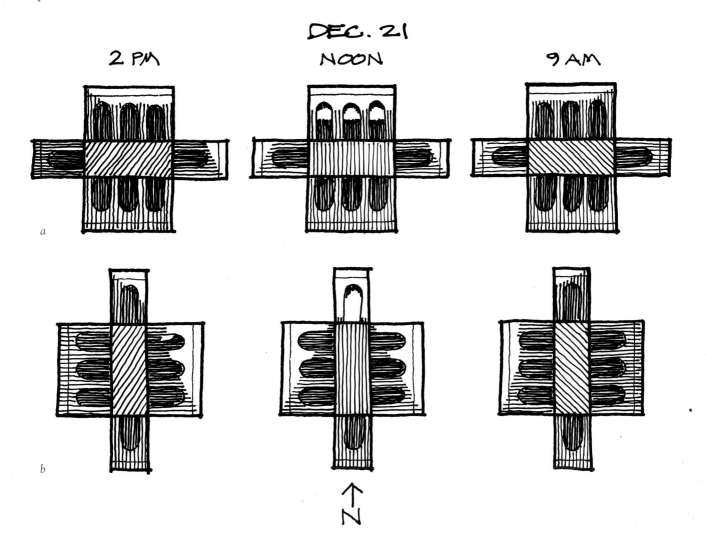

FIG. 1.7. ON DECEMBER 21, rectangular courtyards elongated east-west are compared to those elongated north-south at (sun time) 9 AM, NOON, and 2 PM (about an hour before the warmest time of day) at 36° north latitude (near Córdoba, Spain). December is the time of the coldest temperatures, when sun is a friend. (Note: the shadow lines on the courtyard floor show the sun's direction [azimuth].)

(a) Elongated east-west:
9 AM: Almost all is in shadow. The sun only illuminates the top of the short west face and the long north face.
NOON: Most of the courtyard surfaces are in shadow. The sun only grazes the top of the short east and west faces. The long north face is about half illuminated, with some penetration into the arcade (at about eye level).
2 PM: The sun hits just above the top of the arches of the long north face, and the upper corner of the short east face. All else is in shadow.

(b) Elongated north-south:
9 AM: Almost all is in shadow. The sun only illuminates the top of the short north face and strikes the long west face just above the top of the arches.
NOON: The courtyard floor is in shadow, except for the very back of the short north arcade. The sun only grazes the top of the long east and west faces. The short north face is almost fully illuminated, with deep penetration into the arcade.
2 PM: The sun penetrates more than halfway down the wall in the northeast corner of the courtyard, with a small patch of sun in that corner of both the arcades of the north and east faces. All else is in shadow.

Formality and Symmetry

At the formal extreme, all four sides of a courtyard are identical. At the informal extreme, no two sides are alike. Many courtyards have two sides alike, with the other sides quite different. The most formal courtyards are frequently in institutional buildings such as centers of government. Perhaps this evident visual order symbolizes an orderly (manageable) society? Plants become the subversive element in such courtyards, introducing individual variations within a highly structured surrounding.

A courtyard may at first seem formal and symmetrical, but on closer inspection prove otherwise. The Patio de las Bugambillias in Oaxaca's Hotel Camino Real, a former convent, seems a simple rectangle at first glance (Figure 1.8). But its short north side has two arches, while its opposite short south side has three. Its long east side has four arches; its opposite long west side has five.

Informal courtyards are often the result of change over time; one open arcade is filled in, a second floor is added with a connecting stair within the courtyard, another arcade is filled, the courtyard divided, and so on. This topic is explored in Chapters 6 and 11.

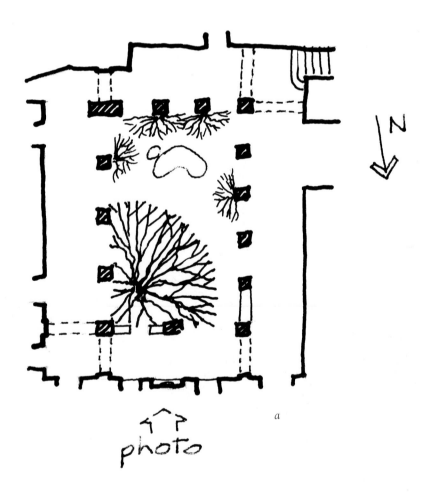

a

FIG. 1.8 OAXACA, MEXICO
At Hotel Camino Real (a former convent), the lobby courtyard has no two sides alike. (*a*) The plan shows one shorter end with two arches; at the other, three. One longer side has four arches, the other five. (*b*) Looking down into this most asymmetrical courtyard, toward the shorter side with three arches.

b

Exposure

If the most important consideration is the courtyard's effectiveness as a conduit of nature, then the **aspect ratio**, or degree of openness to the sky, is paramount; see Figure 1.9*a*.

$$\text{Aspect ratio} = \frac{\text{area of the courtyard floor}}{(\text{average height of surrounding walls})^2}$$

The greater the aspect ratio, the more exposed is the courtyard to the sky. This exposure allows heating by the sun by day, cooling by radiation to the cold sky by night, and some entry to the wind. (Aspect ratio used in daylighting design is found in Baker, Fanchiotti and Steemers [1993].)

Conversely, the **solar shadow index** deals with winter sun exposure (Figure 1.9b).

$$\text{Solar shadow index} = \frac{\text{south wall height}}{\text{north-south floor width}}$$

The greater the solar shadow index, the deeper the well formed by the courtyard, and the less winter sun reaches the floor, or even the north wall, of the courtyard.

Example: Return to the courtyards in Figures 1.6 and 1.7. These courtyards have wall heights that are 1.5 times the shorter floor dimension. The floor length is 2.5 times the floor width. Assume height = 6m, width = 4m, length = 10m.

Both the courtyard elongated east-west and the one elongated north-south have

$$\text{aspect ratio} = \frac{4 \text{ m x } 10 \text{ m}}{[\,6 \text{ m}]^2} = 1.15.$$

However, their solar shadow indices are quite different. For the courtyard elongated east-west,

$$\text{solar shadow index} = \frac{6m}{4m} = 1.5, \text{ not promising of winter sun at noon.}$$

For the courtyard elongated north-south,

$$\text{solar shadow index} = \frac{6m}{10m} = 0.6, \text{ much more winter sun at noon.}$$

While in general a square courtyard with large aspect ratio will have a small solar shadow index, sometimes the south wall is of a height markedly different from the other walls around the courtyard. Thus, this index concerning solar access from the south is important, especially in colder climates.

In Part Two, forty-three courtyards in Mexico and Spain can be compared for both aspect ratio and solar shadow index. See Table 7.1.

In houses that look towards the south, the sun penetrates the portico in winter, while in summer the path of the sun is right over our heads and above the roof so there is shade. To obtain this result, the section of the house facing south must be built lower than the northern section in order not to cut off the winter sun.

Socrates
Xenophon, *Memorabilia*, III, viii, 8f.

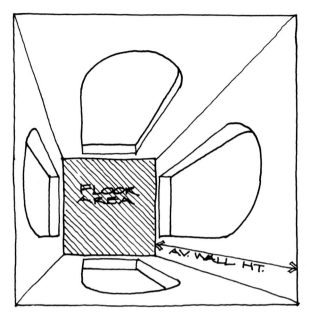

FIG. 1.9 BIRD'S-EYE VIEWS OF A
SQUARE COURTYARD
(a) A high aspect ratio indicates
greater courtyard exposure to the sky.
(b) A high solar shadow index indicates
more winter shadow on the courtyard's
north (most sunny) face.

$$\frac{\text{FLOOR AREA}}{(\text{AV. WALL HT.})^2} = \text{ASPECT RATIO}$$

a

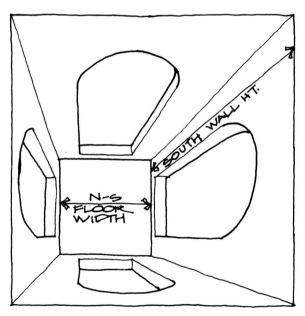

$$\frac{\text{SOUTH WALL HT.}}{\text{N-S FLOOR WIDTH}} = \text{SOLAR SHADOW INDEX}$$

← N

b

FIG. 1.10 COURTYARD LANDSCAPES
Landscapes range from those with very
few or no plants, to those crowded with
them. *(a)* The University of Guanajuato,
Mexico, Faculty of Philosophy is organized around a courtyard nearly barren,
despite its two wells. *(b)* The courtyard
at the Hotel Marisa, Córdoba, Spain,
features many plants and a typical floor
of black and white pebbles.

Plants

Another important variable is the degree to which plants inhabit the courtyard
(Figure 1.10). At one extreme are bare courtyards, at the other full-grown trees
shading the entire courtyard. One might expect that the deeper the courtyard
(smaller aspect ratio), the less likely will be trees in the courtyard, but examples in Part Two provide exceptions. Plants are important to the senses of sight
and smell, can provide food, invite (indeed, demand) caretaking, and thus act
as catalysts for the watering that, through evaporation, can be a major source
of courtyard cooling in hot weather. Chapter 4 and Appendix A explore this
further.

a

b

Open or Closed Facades

Another variable is the transition space between the open courtyard and the surrounding enclosed rooms (Figure 1.11). While some courtyards are surrounded by open facades—arcades or colonnades that separate them from the rooms beyond—others have some walls with doors or windows that open directly into the rooms, or closed facades. Many times, a closed facade is one that was formerly open, a result of building expansion (see Chapter 6).

The arcades of open facades are often well used, serving both as circulation and meeting places. The airiness of the arcades contrasts with the solidity of the building's exterior walls, a kind of unexpected vulnerability at the center of such a defensive enclosure. There is by day much more light in the arcades than in the rooms around them, inviting people to take advantage of both light and fresh air, as well as the pleasant environment within the courtyard.

On the other hand, seated behind the window of a closed facade, one can enjoy the courtyard very close by, but in the thermal comfort of an enclosed room.

Vertical Circulation

At least one stair is included in most courtyard buildings. Even if only one story, such buildings often have extensive roof terraces where laundry or fruit is hung to dry, where one might sleep on particularly hot nights, or where other outdoor activities might occur that would be difficult in the courtyard itself.

Sometimes the courtyard contains this stair, whose strong upward diagonal draws attention (see later Figure 3.5). The stronger the stair's presence, the more it invites visitors up, which may or may not be desirable. The stair might be arrayed along an entire wall; even more frequently, it begins along one wall, with a landing in a corner, then climbs along the adjacent wall. Such an exposed stair might have potted plants on its steps or rails, almost certainly on the landings.

Where a building has three stories, the stair might begin within the arcade, but in the upper stories occupy an interior space rather than continue to take space within the courtyard or its arcades. The higher the stair within a courtyard, the more daylight it might deny to the courtyard floor.

Stairs within arcades are the most common. The roof protects the stair from rain, and the invitation to climb is more restrained than the extrovert stair within the courtyard's space. The stair in an arcade frequently begins at an arch at the courtyard's edge, climbs to an interior landing, then climbs back toward the courtyard. If this invitation to climb needs to be stronger, it can be doubled, as in Figure 1.12.

This overview of physical categories raises many questions that subsequent chapters try to answer. Next to consider: some nonphysical roles of courtyards, those that bring magic to this surrounded oasis.

FIG. 1.11 PLAZA AGUAYAS, CÓRDOBA, SPAIN
From the arcade, an "open facade", we see two "closed" ones; to the left, a doorway in the courtyard wall leads directly to the interior. To the right, a formerly open facade has been enclosed with glass.

a

Part 1: Courtyard Characteristics

b

FIG. 1.12 STAIRS WITHIN ARCADES, OAXACA, MEXICO

(*a*) Two stairs in adjacent arches begin a climb to a single landing, then a single flight between them climbs to the upper arcade. Note the unusual "extra" second-floor arch (at the center of the photograph).

(*b*) Two adjacent stairs climb to a single landing, then turn to continue in separate flights now parallel to the arcade wall. (See also Figure 3.5 for courtyard stair examples.)

CHAPTER 2

Un Patio

Con la tarde

se cansaron los dos o tres colores del patio.

La gran franqueza de la luna llena

ya no entusiasma su habitual firmamento.

Patio, cielo encauzado.

El patio es el declive

por el cual se derrama el cielo en la casa.

Serena,

la eternidad espera en la encrucijada de estrellas.

Grato es vivir en la amistad ocura

de un zaguán, de una parra y de un aljibe.

Jorge Luis Borges

With evening

the two or three colors of the patio grow weary.

The huge candor of the full moon

No longer enchants its usual firmament.

Courtyard, heaven's watercourse.

The patio is the slope

down which the sky flows into the house.

Serenely,

eternity waits at the crossway of the stars.

It is lovely to live in the dark friendliness

of covered entrance way, arbor, and wellhead.

(Translation, Robert Fitzgerald)

Courtyards and Cosmos

In his introduction to *Atrium: Five Thousand Years of Open Courtyards*, Johannes Spalt philosophizes about the courtyard:

> Set in the midst of the universe, man needs a place of peace, seclusion, as part of the greater, hostile, amorphous world outside, a space which, all the same, receives its share of the day and night, sun and moon, heat and cold and rain. This space, which is subservient to the passage of the days and years and to the rules that order existence, is the "courtyard." It is so old that sensations inherited from man's cave-dwelling days have been symbolized in it. It symbolizes femininity in the house and home; it is a spatial symbol of inwardness. Seclusion, the courtyard's artificially created seclusion, makes those who dwell there the inhabitants of an imaginary kingdom.

The courtyard can represent many things: an oasis in the desert of city streets; a fragment of nature (thus a reminder of natural landscapes beyond the city); a center of interest for the building; a concentration of light, sound, and water; a life-sustaining refuge of safety and privacy.

Earth, Water, Air, and Fire

The many plants within the typical courtyard and the fountains that sustain them bring nature within the building's reach. In the densely settled cities of many cultures, with barren, narrow, and noisy streets, this taste of the wild is particularly welcome. It invites the courtyard dweller's imagination out beyond the building and city boundaries. The building's rooms seem more controlled and civilized to the extent that the courtyard seems more savage. A thunderstorm, viewed from the relative safety of the arcade, shows the courtyard swept by wind and rain illuminated with flashes of lightning, and thunder echoes in the hard-surfaced enclosure.

FIG. 2.1 Oaxaca, Mexico
A vine emerges through a restaurant's courtyard floor, a reminder of the earthly zone below.

Since the courtyard was defined by the spaces and structures that surrounded it, it was forced to mediate diverse sets of aesthetic and spatial relationships. The experience of the house was often dominated by the spatial and aesthetic nature of its courtyard(s). The wrapped spatial interval—experienced either by the passage from the main gate to the interior courtyard(s) or by views from an adjacent indoor or outdoor space—is a distinctive characteristic of Korean architecture. The effects created often involved layering open-courtyards, bringing distant views of nature into the house domain. In a sense, the courtyard was a spatial symbol for the introversion that formed a part of a larger tradition in Korean society.

Sang Hae Lee
"Continuity and Consistency of the Traditional Courtyard House Plan in Modern Korean Dwellings"

The earth is evident in nearly every courtyard, wherever a rooted vine, shrub, or tree emerges from the floor (Figure 2.1). The courtyard is almost always somewhat below the level of the floor of the arcades, a reminder that this downward step is from a built surface to one merely paved, another subtle transition from the domestic toward the wild. The aroma of the earth is strongest just after a rain (or a watering), and its surface is slow to dry compared to any pavement. It is the surface most easily manipulated by the courtyard dweller.

Water has a particularly important role; it represents life and coolness, freshness and purity; it collects in the lowest place (emphasizing the courtyard as a resting place),

FIG. 2.2 WATER AS MIRROR
(a) A small basin reflects the sky while standing above a pool of uncertain depth; a recently designed residence in Colima, Mexico.

FIG. 2.2 WATER AS MIRROR
(b) A recent rain shower turns this courtyard floor into a short-lived mirror; University of Guanajuato, Mexico.

and while its surface catches light and reflects the sky, its depth symbolizes the earthly zone below the courtyard floor (Figure 2.2). With fountains, this depth is understood because the shape of the basin reveals its size. With pools in the ground, the depth is more obscure, particularly when algae or other plants conceal the bottom.

Water on the courtyard floor becomes a mirror; after a rain, reflections emphasize the height of the walls.

When sunlight strikes water, it is reflected in a constantly shimmering pattern, even from a surface that appears to be absolutely calm. This shimmering light is intercepted somewhere in a courtyard, unless the sun is directly overhead, or the

FIG. 2.3 OAXACA, MEXICO
The sun strikes this strip of shallow pool at Oaxaca's Photo Museum; its dancing reflection subtly illuminates a strip of the arch's underside.

courtyard very wide and shallow. The dancing light enlivens the surface it strikes, often the underside of an arch or shaded ceiling of an arcade (Figure 2.3). Despite its brightness, it represents coolness, because it is a product of both water and breeze; the stronger the breeze, the faster the dance.

Wells are often centers of attention in courtyards, sources of water for the plants and the people, ornamented with elaborate wellheads (*brocales*). The well represents the deeper zone within the earth, the water table underlying the foundations. It will be the coolest of all places. The well beautifully integrates all three roles: it is an aesthetic object, a social gathering place, and the provider of an essential commodity (Figure 2.4).

FIG. 2.4 CÓRDOBA, SPAIN (OPPOSITE)
This courtyard's well is crudely built, but beautifully framed and often used for watering the plants at this meeting place of Los Amigos de los Patios Cordobeses.

FIG. 2.5 CÓRDOBA, SPAIN
The fireplace in a courtyard wall offers winter warmth, and summer relief from a hot kitchen. Calle Valencia.

Did fire generate the courtyard form? At the center of an ancient dwelling, a fire produced smoke, which was expelled through a hole in the roof. Did this hole widen over many generations, allowing light as well as relief from smoke, eventually becoming the place open to the sky but still at the center of the dwelling?

A fire may accompany a special ceremony in a courtyard. Large fires serve for roasting at feasts. There are fires to symbolize the end of something, such as a mortgage burning. More commonly, when the kitchen is just too hot, cooking moves to the open courtyard, where the heat and moisture are quickly dissipated (Figure 2.5). Some courtyards have permanent cooking facilities such as ovens, sinks, and countertops; one Colima courtyard features a kitchen range, exposed to the cooling sky.

By night the courtyard's fire can become a center of attention, much as did the fountain by day. A single light source in a patio or *zaguán* can make the leaves and the iron grillwork cast beautiful shadows.

Candlelight may illuminate a family shrine on a wall, often in one of the arcades. The shrine is a physical symbol of the spiritual role of this private place that communes with nature and with the cosmos, well beyond a family's boundaries.

A thoroughly darkened courtyard offers a view of the stars. This is quite unlike the opportunity offered by the North American urban yard, where neighbors' lights and street lights easily invade the yards and gardens. The courtyard blocks out such light, throwing a deep shadow over floors and walls that permit the light of moon and stars to be seen from the privacy of one's own garden.

Animal, Vegetable, and Mineral

Against the solid, massive courtyard walls and floor are contrasting arrays of soft and swaying plants. This oasis of cool softness against harsh heat is greatly enhanced by adding animal life. Thus birds in cages, especially canaries and their song, are a common feature of Hispanic courtyards. The sound of birdsong carries beyond the courtyard, along with sounds of running water. When streets are quiet enough, birds and water are a subtle call to people on the sidewalks to enter this oasis. Parrots offer a raucous contrast.

A well-stocked oasis would include domestic animals, such as cats (who stalk the canaries) or dogs who guard the gate and serve as doorbells (Figure 2.6). For a more exotic oasis, a monkey or a peacock may be added. The courtyard serves these smaller animals quite well. Here they are safe from predators and cars on the street. Animal stains are a much less serious issue on the courtyard floor than on rugs or carpets indoors. With the family away, the animals can be isolated from valuables inside, yet kept safe in the courtyard.

There are Hispanic courtyards entirely without vegetation—but such courtyards are rare. Plants bring much to the ambiance; for some investment of care, they pay a very large dividend (Figure 2.7). A courtyard's plants are a sign of its maturity; rather like facial hair that first appears with adolescence and then flourishes. Plants symbolize a courtyard's health and age; they celebrate change. For more about plants, see Chapter 4.

The walls of most Hispanic courtyards are either whitewashed (with *cal*) or painted. The annual application of *cal* is a seasonal ritual, marking the coming of spring. After years of applications, the walls' surfaces take on a multilayered quality (architect Victor Carrasco terms this "phyllo dough") that results in some retarding of the flow of heat into and out of these walls. Walls that are slower to heat in summer are an advantage, but slower to cool a disadvantage. The latter problem can be more quickly overcome by spraying water on the walls in the evening.

Many courtyards are paved with small stones, set in patterns of light and dark colors at times recalling an elaborate rug (Figure 2.8). These stones represent earth, one step removed; objects taken directly from their natural state, then

rearranged. Other paving materials include marble, brick, and concrete. Pavement that absorbs water is a great advantage, because it can slowly release the water through evaporation, cooling all the while. Porous brick and paving stones set in earth are especially good paving materials for this purpose.

FIG. 2.6 CÓRDOBA, SPAIN
A cat basks under a sunny arch in the protection of a courtyard. Calle Augustin Moreno.

FIG. 2.7 Uruapan, Mexico
A North American landscape designer
purchased this courtyard home. (a) The
courtyard, as he began his restoration.
(Photo courtesy of John Mathieson.)
(b) The courtyard a few years later.

FIG. 2.8 CÓRDOBA, SPAIN
Black and white pebbles are arranged in geometric patterns on this courtyard floor. A turtle resides in the right-hand pool of the umbrella stand. The narrow street (Calle Zarco) is visible through the *zaguán*.

(FOLLOWING SPREAD)
FIG. 2.9 CÓRDOBA, SPAIN
A white marble floor reflects and compliments the various plants in this courtyard in Calle Encarnación.

FIG. 2.10
A small residence takes advantage of multiple levels. Below the courtyard is a cistern, where water is kept cool by the earth. The ground level contains all the "living" rooms, including kitchen, dining, bathroom, and bedrooms. At the top of the courtyard stair is a laundry room, opening onto a substantial terrace for hanging clothes. Above this laundry "penthouse" is a small observation terrace; perhaps pigeons could be raised here. (Based on a drawing by Matthew Wilson.)

Below, On, and Above the Ground

White marble is a popular paving material, despite its lack of porosity. It contrasts nicely with dark green leaves and brilliant blossoms, and it reflects maximum daylight from the potentially dark courtyard floor (Figure 2.9).

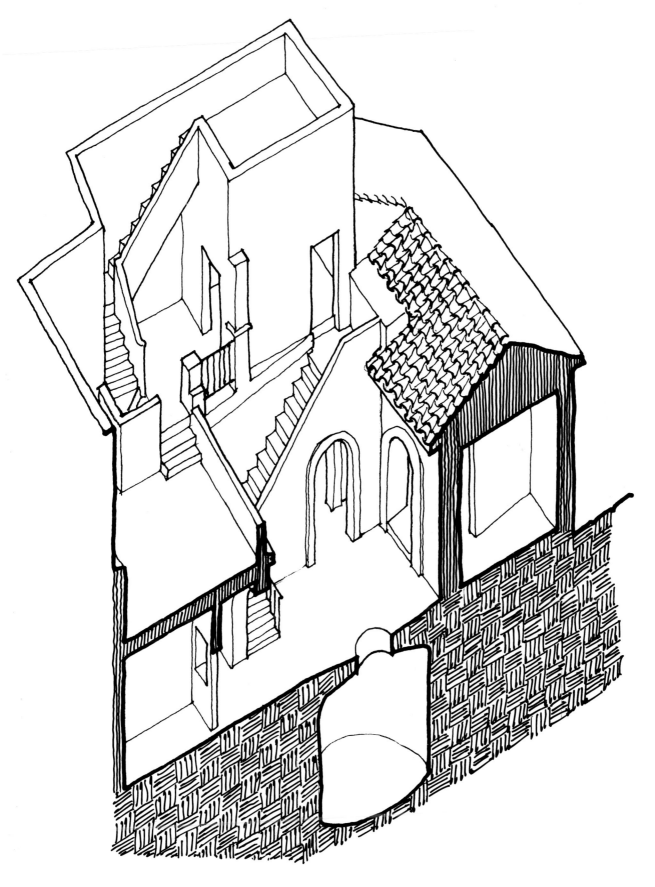

Then, out of the blue, one of them said that the Campillos had buried the English china, the Bohemian crystal, and the Holland linen tablecloths in the patio because they were terrified of being infected by consumption.

Gabriel García Márquez
The General in His Labyrinth

FIG. 2.11 TUCUMÁN, ARGENTINA
Taking advantage of some construction materials, two boys create an imaginary world on the floor of this courtyard.

The floor, with its plants and fountains, is an obvious focus for a courtyard. But below this floor is an environment of darkness, thermal stability, and privacy through isolation. It is the domain of wells and cold water, of roots of plants, where food might be stored and protected against the summer heat (Figure 2.10). This private ground might provide a hiding places for valuables or for contraband, a crude personal vault. Occasionally this most private earth becomes the burial ground for a loved pet.

The maximum interchange of people and nature usually occurs on the level of the courtyard floor. Here is the richest variety of foliage, the damp earth and dry pavement, the still pool or running water, the furniture that invites relaxation, even sleep. Children's imaginations enliven the courtyard floor, a play area both safe and varied (Figure 2.11). Almost any activity within the building can be moved temporarily out into the courtyard, lending a special quality to familiar acts.

The floor levels above the courtyard gain privacy even as they gain a longer-range view. A balcony lets one look out over the courtyard, while partially concealing the viewer (Figure 2.12). It offers a choice: participate, or merely observe. The roof provides the greatest detachment, the choice to look back down to the private courtyard or out over streets, a collection of other roof terraces, and the tops of trees above other patios.

The ground floor–upper floor relationship helps to determine the degree to which a courtyard looks inward or outward (Figure 2.13). The more shallow the courtyard (the larger the aspect ratio), the more evident is the sky or plants framed against it; the edges of the roof become a frame for a shifting and unpredictable panorama. Deeper courtyards (smaller aspect ratio) emphasize the walls and their openings rather than the sky, and people on the courtyard floor become players on a stage, watched from above. The wide and shallow courtyard will often be a sunny collection of plants and water, while the narrow, deep

FIG. 2.12 TAXCO, MEXICO
Not far above this courtyard's floor, a table in the arcade enjoys both a close overview and a distant vista.

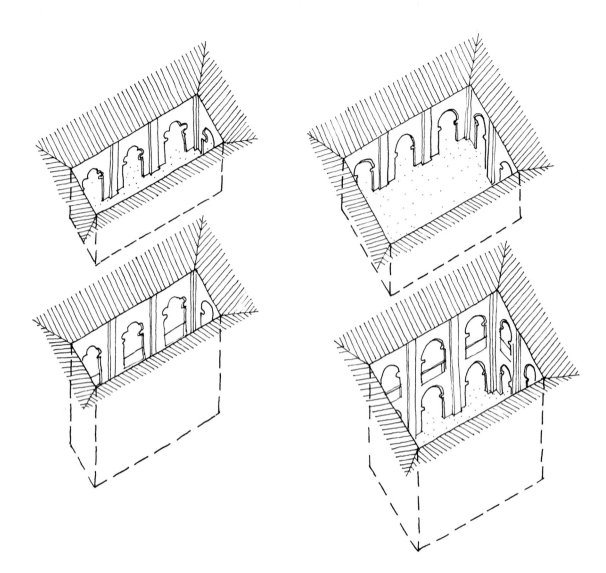

FIG. 2.13
WIDE OR NARROW; SHALLOW OR DEEP?
Four possible combinations that illustrate
the degree of introversion or extroversion
that accompanies courtyard proportions.
(Drawing by Michael Cockram.)

courtyard will be shady and more reverberant with sounds of water and birds. One speaks of sun and sparkle, the other of darkness and "coolth." (Coolth is the opposite of heat, and signifies its absence.)

The sky represents all that lies beyond the enclosure. From it descends sun, wind, rain, and the night. A courtyard without a direct connection to the unpredictable above is little more than another room (albeit strongly lit) within the safety of the building. A permanent courtyard cover may extend the courtyard's usefulness, but it diminishes its significance.

Cycles of Life and Death

Chapter 1 explored the variations of three dimensions: length, width, and height. A fourth dimension is time. Closer to the equator, it is the daily variation of warm day to cool evening that provides the greatest thermal change. Wet seasons and dry seasons strongly impact the courtyard, both its plants and how the courtyard is used. Farther from the equator, seasonal variations are seen in the plants of the courtyard; blooming, fruiting, harvest, and dormancy. Each season has its rituals in a temperate-climate courtyard (Figure 2.14).

Seasons also affect the surrounding building. In many of the two- and three-story Spanish buildings I visited, I heard references to how upstairs rooms were used more heavily in winter (where they had access to sun and whatever heat that rose from the lower floor), while ground floor rooms were used more heavily in summer (taking advantage of the pool of cooler air in the courtyard).

Winter in the courtyard offers the chance to cut back rampant vines, to take down the flowerpots with faded geraniums and replenish their soil. The result is a more barren outdoor space, almost as if to emphasize winter's contrast with the other seasons. It is a time when ceremonial fires are particularly welcome, prolonging light on winter's shorter days, adding welcome heat, drying the floor nearby. North of the equator, for most Hispanics Christmas brings lights and decorations to the cold, dark courtyard; large manger scenes might be arrayed on the floor of the arcade, or even in the courtyard center.

Spring is the time to whitewash the massive walls, then to put the freshly trimmed flowerpots back on the walls and in windows. In Córdoba, early May brings the *Concurso de Patios*, an annual contest (Figure 2.15). The winning courtyards are shown on a map distributed to tourists for the next 12 months.

Summer brings the rewards of plentiful flowers and strong sweet aromas. In the center of a courtyard on a summer night, the heat from the walls is balanced by the cold night sky. It is an experience of radiant heat exchange at its best, reinforced by the starry sky, the sound of trickling water, the scent of jasmine.

Fall is the time of harvest, and the arcades can be filled with food drying in the sun. Potted plants are beginning to fade, fallen leaves are daily more plentiful on the courtyard floor. After months of heat, the courtyard becomes again a cold place by night. The signals are clear—get ready for winter.

The courtyard sees the cycles of generations as well as seasons. It is a place to celebrate the family's rites of passage. The neighbors greet the new baby in the courtyard arcade; children listen to grandparents' stories; the first tree is climbed; the first bicycle wobbles around the arcades. Wedding receptions gather around the well; animals are slaughtered for feasts prepared over open fires; and during wakes, the courtyard falls silent.

Because the Hispanic courtyard can be seen from the street, and figures prominently in special events, and is buffeted by nature, it requires high maintenance. Yet another term for high maintenance is caretaking. Courtyard owners nurture the plants, birds, and animals as a parent would a child. The courtyard's healthy and colorful plants are a source of pride, carefully tended objects viewed from the street, a symbol of good parenting (Figure 2.16). In Córdoba, courtyards entered in the annual *Concurso de Patios* often have hundreds of potted plants, many of which are hung quite high on the walls. Watering, clipping, and placing these plants represents a significant investment in time, labor, and money.

Stephanos Polyzoides, Roger Sherwood and James Tice (1992) observe:

> When people lose their emotional connection to the buildings they occupy, all architecture ends.

Yet, to the Arab especially, the courtyard is more than just an architectural device for obtaining privacy and protection. It is, like the dome, part of a microcosm that parallels the order of the universe itself. In this symbolic pattern, the four sides of the courtyard represent the four columns that carry the dome of the sky. The sky itself roofs the courtyard, and is reflected in the customary fountain in the middle. The fountain, or basin, is in fact an exact projection of a dome on squinches. In plan it is precisely the same, basically a square with, at a lower level, the corners cut off to form an octagon; from each of the new sides thus formed a semicircle is scooped out, so that the whole basin is an inverted model of a dome, just as if a real dome were mirrored in the water.

Hassan Fathy
Architecture for the Poor

Patients, visitors and staff can sit on the patio furniture or pick roses. They can admire the bright flowers and the birds that flit by, or enjoy the fountain with a multi-tiered metal sculpture, stored each winter and re-installed each spring. It has delightful splashing, tinkling sound and reflects the rays of the summer sun.

Nancy Gerlach-Spriggs, Richard Enoch Kaufman, and Sam Bass Warner, Jr.
Restorative Gardens: The Healing Landscape

a

Part 1: Courtyard Characteristics

FIG. 2.14 CÓRDOBA, SPAIN
(a) The "Cat Patio" at the
Palacio de Viana (Courtyard
Museum) is in full flower in May.
(b) In February the plants are
dormant and the sun too low to
warm the floor. (See Figure 1.2 for a
plan of the Palacio de Viana.)

*In summer, a daily nomadism exists when the inhabitants use different levels of
the house and spend most of their day on the first floor, eat in the galleria, take a
nap in the basement and sleep on the roof. In Baghdad, during the winter, the
family lives on the first floor because the basement is too humid and the roof too
cold. The outside gallery is used as a night sleeping area in fall and spring when it
is too warm to sleep inside or too cool to sleep on the roof.*

Fewzi Fardeheb
Passive Solar Cooling Strategies in
Middle Eastern Vernacular Architecture.

(LEFT)
FIG. 2.15 CÓRDOBA, SPAIN
This courtyard has just won first prize in Córdoba's annual Concurso de Patios (Courtyard Competition); chairs will soon accommodate guests at the award ceremony. Calle San Juan Palomares.

(ABOVE)
FIG. 2.16 CÓRDOBA, SPAIN
A tin can tied to the end of a pole provides a simple watering method for potted plants high on courtyard walls. Calle Pintor Bermejo.

CHAPTER 3

Social Roles

Two important features of the patio house are the entryway positioned for visual privacy and the interior hallway that protects the family domain. Entranceways are the thresholds between the private (house and patio) and the public. Activities conducted at the street entranceway include: buying small items from street sellers, social activities, and talking to neighbors. People engaged in these activities block visual contact or verbal communication with the main living spaces where the family daily life occurs.

William J. Siembieda
"Walls and Gates: A Latin Perspective"

Community and Privacy

Writing about the prevalence of courtyard houses in many cultures that are both crowded and hierarchic, Amos Rapoport (1969) observes:

> The principle behind them is the same, and their form remains similar over long periods and large areas. The need is to get away while still in the familiar territory of the family or clan group—and the separation of domains achieves that.

The public domain is the street; the private domain (usually) the courtyard. The semipublic domain includes the front yards of North America, the *zaguánes* of courtyard buildings, and at times the courtyards themselves.

In Islamic cultures there can be a separation of domains within the house, between male and female. Amita Sinha (1989) describes the traditional Muslim houses of Northern India:

> The room fronting the street is made into a *baithak*, meaning a sitting room which is predominantly a male area. It is the room with doors and windows fronting the street. Usually the interior rooms lack windows and ventilators are the preferred openings for light. If they do have windows, they open into the courtyard for privacy. Multiple entrances are preferred…one leading directly into the *baithak* and the other into the *dyodi*, which leads into the courtyard. These entrances can be found side by side. The courtyard may have yet another entrance. Multiple entrances help to segregate paths of men and women, and people outside the kin networks and members of the extended family. They serve as a means to maintain privacy and regulate social interaction.

Where many families share one large courtyard, this outdoor space loses some of its privacy as it becomes an extension of the public street. Yet it still "belongs" to the families that surround it. In their typology of multifamily courtyard buildings built in the first half of the twentieth century in Los Angeles, Stephanos Polyzoides, Roger Sherwood, and James Tice (1992) describe some of these buildings' enduring attractions:

> To this day courts function successfully as dwellings for older people. They combine the advantages of compact, easily maintained living quarters with the provision of communal outdoor places for public contact. The emphasis on the ground plane minimizes stairs and permits an unusual degree of interaction among people of limited mobility.

One great advantage of the typical neighborhood filled with courtyard buildings is that many small shops and services are within a short walk of every home. The upper windows of buildings are filled with flowers that hang down toward the street. (In the lower windows, they are too easily damaged or picked.) The walk through such neighborhoods offers two views: a continual one along the narrow street, and momentary glimpses through a dark *zaguán* into the heart of each courtyard. This is not a subtle change of views; it requires turning the head sharply at the moment of passage. Neither the street view nor the courtyard view is a long-range one, as the narrow street turns frequently (Figure 3.2). All of this helps maintain interest during the walk.

(OPPOSITE)
FIG. 3.1 THE ANDALUSIA COURTS, LOS ANGELES
(*a*) Andalusia Courts is an apartment complex organized around a communal courtyard. (*b*) Plan. (Plan from Polyzoides, Sherwood, and Tice 1992.)

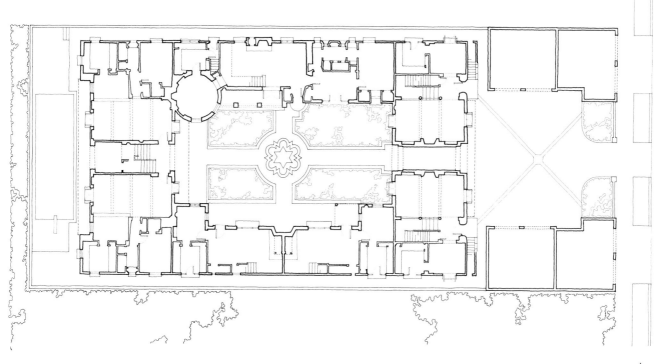

FIG. 3.2 SETENIL, SPAIN
A typically narrow street serves
courtyard houses.

Part 1: Courtyard Characteristics

During siesta, or by night, many of the exterior wooden doors to the *zaguánes* will be closed. If these doors are closed at other times, it is a strong signal that the occupants are not to be disturbed. Windows on the street at ground level also have wooden shutters behind their grilles. These are closed more often than the doors to the *zaguán*; rooms are kept more private than are courtyards.

The *reja* or iron grille gate offers more signals (Figure 3.3). Usually the gate is closed, offering a view to the courtyard but barring passage. At the rare times when gates are left standing open, the message is "everyone's invited." During Córdoba's week-long *Concurso de Patios* the courtyards entered in this contest are required to leave their gates open until midnight.

The door closing the portal is of solid wood and subdivided into three parts to allow for the subtlety of choices of opening positions. It is divided vertically into two sections, one of which is a barn door whose top and bottom open separately. Opening only the small upper section on one side allows visual contact and conversation between street and courtyard, but prevents animals and children from running in and out. When one whole side is open people can easily pass through but donkeys cannot barge in. With both sides open a donkey and its load can enter with ease.

Catherine Bicknell
"The Courtyard Houses of Langatha"

FIG. 3.3 CARMONA, SPAIN
At the interior end of the *zaguán*, an open gate invites entry without knocking.

One role of the Hispanic courtyard is to serve as a kind of show window from the street: the "tease," a narrow view for the public into the heart of a private space. This sharply differs from the Middle Eastern indirect approach to the courtyard, which forecloses any view from street. In Islam, privacy is to be strictly maintained for women. Where the courtyard is the women's domain, it must always be kept from the public eye.

Because it is so easily isolated from the street, and so self-contained the courtyard is by nature an introverted space. When its owners fail to care for it, the courtyard's state of neglect can escape public notice for a long time. Since the facade on the street is usually quite modest—a trait inherited from the Moors—the neglected state of the building and garden within is easily hidden. This is quite unlike the North American garden-around-the-building model, where the condition of one's landscape is always evident. As a courtyard descends into disrepair, there are dire consequences for the surrounding spaces, whose outward view consists entirely of this courtyard. Thus the depressed state of the courtyard building's owners is likely to be especially severe, and to appear inescapable.

The center of the Hispanic courtyard, publicly visible from the *zaguán* during the day, contrasts with the more private arcades around the edge. Again, contrast serves to intensify, here lending a heightened sense of concealment to those within the arcades. Many activities occur here, where they can enjoy the view of the more public courtyard center without being seen from the street (Figure 3.4).

Circulation

But the arcades are really only semiprivate. The courtyard is so frequently the center of orientation within a building that it naturally assumes a primary role in building circulation. In smaller courtyard buildings, it is common to have no other hallways except the *zaguán* to, and the arcades around, the courtyard. Often the stair also sits within the courtyard, and its landing can become a balcony or a stage, depending on the occasion (Figure 3.5).

The courtyard is also responsible for bringing daylight and air to all the spaces around it. Along with the passage of air inevitably comes the passage of sound. Acoustically, a courtyard building has a very hard time concealing secrets between its rooms. The massive walls help isolate sounds, but windows and doors quickly degrade sound isolation. Again, trickling water (Figure 3.6) and birdsong can serve as masking sounds that might allow whispers to remain local. Music is more controllable, though, and can drown out almost anything as it pervades everything.

Degrees of Formality

Where only one courtyard serves a building, it is expected to serve the more formal showcase role as well as to accommodate informal activities in and around it. Buildings with two courtyards are quite common. The one accessed more directly from the street serves as a kind of parlor, a rather formal courtyard where plants are grown for their aesthetic, rather than nutritious, value. The second courtyard, often closer to the kitchen and laundry,

The inward-lookingness of the courtyard house, with no view to the outside world, may have stimulated the concern for privacy to excessive levels. There was a sense of shame in self-exposure. Just as the house was always screened so women were always veiled in public, often wearing a poshiya, a thin black net across the face—in addition to the all-enveloping black abiya. Like the women the house was a private preserve and as such protected.

John Warren and Ihsan Fethi
Traditional Houses in Baghdad

(OPPOSITE)
FIG. 3.4 COLIMA, MEXICO.
The arcade provides a sun-and-shade meeting place for grandmother and grandchildren. Calle Zaragosa.

They retraced their steps along the arcaded passageway, but this time Florentino Ariza knew that there was someone else in the house, because the brightness in the patio was filled with the voice of a woman repeating a reading lesson. As he passed the sewing room, he saw through the window an older woman and a young girl sitting very close together on two chairs and following the reading in the book that the woman held open on her lap.

Gabriel García Márquez;
Love in the Time of Cholera

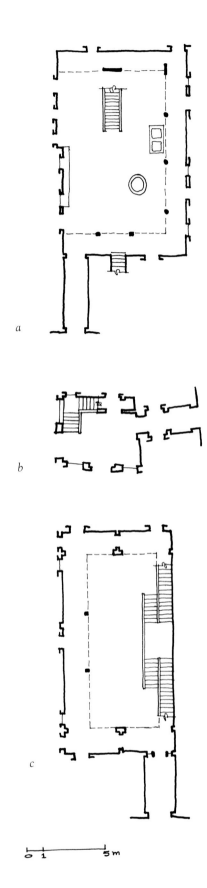

a

b

c

o 1   ⌐5 m

a

b

c

           Part 1: Courtyard Characteristics

(OPPOSITE)

FIG. 3.5 EXPOSED STAIRS
Sometimes a stair is exposed within the courtyard instead of enclosed in or behind an arcade (for stairs within arcades, see Figure 1.12). (a) Rarely is the stair so prominent as in this centered example at Los Amigos de los Patios Cordobeses, Calle San Basilio, Córdoba, Spain. The very strong diagonal dominates the courtyard, with no landing to break the upward sweep of the stairs. (b) A modest residential stair turns the corner and continues its climb along a second side; Calle Zarco, Córdoba, Spain. (c) A large landing could serve as a stage for the courtyard in the Hotel Principal, Oaxaca, Mexico.

FIG. 3.6 OAXACA, MEXICO
Trickling water from a central fountain provides a constant sound within a smaller courtyard of the Hotel Camino Real.

serves as the equivalent of the family room, where children can play more freely, food can grow, and laundry and food can dry in the sun (Figure 3.7).

This informal, working courtyard is fairly often connected to the formal one by an indirect path, keeping this back garden somewhat concealed. Its visual appearance just isn't reliably presentable for guests.

Another reason for multiple courtyards: self-shading. For buildings of the same height, one larger courtyard will admit more sun (and therefore overheat more readily) than will several smaller ones. Again, the aspect ratio (Chapter 1) indicates the degree of exposure both to sun by day and cool sky by night.

The service building was located here, with its enormous kitchen and wood-burning stoves, a butchering shop, and a great bread oven. At the rear was a courtyard, always flooded with dirty wash water, where several families of slaves lived together, and beyond that were the stables, a goat pen, the pigsty, the garden, and the beehives, where everything needed for the good life was raised and grown.

Gabriel García Márquez
Of Love and Other Demons

Most rooms are multipurpose and are not habitually used for a specific activity such as sleeping or dining. Instead the courtyard dwelling allows rooms for specific members of the household, and the family member uses this room for a number of functions: eating, sleeping and entertaining close friends.

Craig Hinrichs
"The Courtyard Housing
Form as Traditional Dwelling"

FIG. 3.7 SALTA, ARGENTINA
Two courtyards serve this home.
(*a*) The first courtyard, seen from the *zaguán*, is filled with ornamental and fragrant plants. (*b*) Behind the first, formal courtyard, the "working" courtyard provides space for household chores, and contains plants that provide food.

Common Activities In and Around Courtyards

Almost any activity can be carried on at least temporarily in a courtyard. The most common usages of courtyards and arcades are as extensions of living, dining , and kitchen activities. Everyday repetitious acts benefit from a change of scene. The things most frequently done here tend to be those done in groups. Often the rooms are too small and dark for several people to work comfortably, especially when compared to the arcades and the open space of the courtyard. After a long time focusing on a close-up task, it is a relief to raise one's eyes and look toward the courtyard's central fountain. Also there is the lure of the unpredictable; the gust of breeze, a cloud over the sun, a spatter of rain, a flock of birds in the tree.

Where the climate is mild, workplaces can occupy the arcades. Here are two examples of such open-air offices from Colima, Mexico (Figure 3.8). White-collar desk jobs can become tedious and repetitive; the unpredictability of the courtyard environment can become a welcome contrast.

Within the safety of the courtyard is a playground of great variety. The typical courtyard floor offers both hard and soft surfaces; one serves toys with wheels, the other for digging, forming earth or sand, channeling water. Children learn here to care for pets, feed the fish in the pond, and observe birds building nests in the vines (Figure 3.9). The courtyard offers children enough contact with nature to be entertaining, yet rarely so much as to be threatening.

FIG. 3.8 COLIMA, MEXICO
The arcades are shelter enough for these office workplaces. (*a*) During the siesta, these desks at the State Health Agency stand empty in the shade. (*b*) A newspaper office opens completely to its courtyard.

FIG. 3.9 COURTYARD CAPTIVES
This courtyard fish pond boasts a turtle as well. Although turtles wander, they usually are safely confined within a courtyard's enclosing arcades.

At times, the bedroom moves to the arcades, the courtyard itself, or the roof terrace. This is common during the siesta, but also happens when the nights are hot, and the exposure to breeze and the cold sky are a quick way to comfort. The hammock in the arcade, or hung from a courtyard tree, is a familiar symbol (Figure 3.10). The courtyard, much less private than the bedroom, is a riskier place for the bedroom activities of sleep or love. Perhaps with the risk comes heightened excitement?

The courtyard may serve as a bathroom; more often for cleansing, more rarely for elimination of wastes. What is more brisk than a shower outdoors? The breeze is particularly bracing to wet skin, and the sun's warmth intense. Perhaps because the courtyard represents the penetration of nature into the building, it may occasionally be used for "recycling," and expected to deal with human waste. This is more likely due to some combination of convenience, urgency, and inebriation. Ultimately, the aroma of plants cannot overcome the scent of too much human waste. Fertilizer straight from the human body is likely too strong for most courtyard plants.

Because access to the courtyard is controlled, and its floor is at least in part soft and malleable, this place can become a private vault. Life in the courtyard is only temporarily disturbed by digging a hole. After burying something, plants or paving stones can quickly be moved to cover and conceal disturbed earth.

As for security in the courtyard, access from the street is controlled easily enough, but access from above is almost as uncontrolled as nature. This is one reason to keep a dog in the courtyard (or on a roof terrace). Sometimes the opening to the sky is filtered, rarely by ornamental ironwork, more often by netting that is fine enough to almost disappear (Figure 3.11). A chicken-wire cover discourages both burglars and bats, the latter reason most commonly given for such a horizontal fence.

Institutional Courtyards

At least as old as monastic courtyards filled with beds of medicinal herb, larger courtyards shared by multiple (nonfamily) users are found throughout the world. The government buildings of Hispanic cultures are often organized about one or more courtyards. One enters a high-ceilinged *zaguán*, often furnished with uniformed armed guards. This leads directly to a large formal courtyard, usually two stories, around which are arrayed the various offices that interact most frequently with the public. A grand staircase is often prominently displayed behind one of the arcades. These government courtyards seem underpopulated with plants; trees and vines are rare, shrubs are tightly contained. Potted plants are small in size and number.

The major differences between the modern and historic courtyards. . . . derive from their use and symbolism. Contemporary business courtyards, intended for relaxation or recreation for workers who commute, are not a part of their domestic life and thus lack the richness of continuous use and individual expression. Whereas historic courtyards embodied a single religious, cultural, or moral perspective shared by the family or community enjoying them, modern courtyards generally do not. Instead, they are planned by the corporation's designers to complement the corporate image.

Nancy Gerlach-Spriggs, Richard Enoch Kaufman, and Sam Bass Warner, Jr.
Restorative Gardens: the Healing Landscape

School courtyards are also typically rather barren of plants, but between classes they fill with students and ring with voices. Given the periodic surge of trampling feet and plucking fingers, perhaps the absence of plants isn't so mysterious. When dense plants are provided, a fence can be employed to keep the people from damaging them, as in the *Rectorado* at the University of Córdoba, Argentina (Figure 3.12). The formality and control of the classroom contrasts with the informality and spontaneity of the courtyard and its arcades, which become a welcoming social center once every hour.

FIG. 3.12 Córdoba, Argentina
(*a*) Students might fill the arcades between classes, but the fence keeps them from trampling the dense plants in this university courtyard.
(*b*) Nearby, a high school's arcades are a pleasant place for less formal studies.

a

Part 1: Courtyard Characteristics

b

FIG. 3.13 WAUSAU, WISCONSIN Hospital is designed (by Skidmore, Owings and Merrill) around several courtyards. Indoor atria gardens and the large surrounding park are contrasting landscapes.

(a) Courtyard outside the children's therapy department. (Photo courtesy of Wausau Hospital, Wausau, Wisconsin.)

(b) Plan. (Based on *Restorative Gardens: the Healing Landscape* by Nancy Gerlach-Spriggs, Richard Enoch Kaufman, and Sam Bass Warner, Jr. © 1998, Yale University Press, New Haven, Conn.)

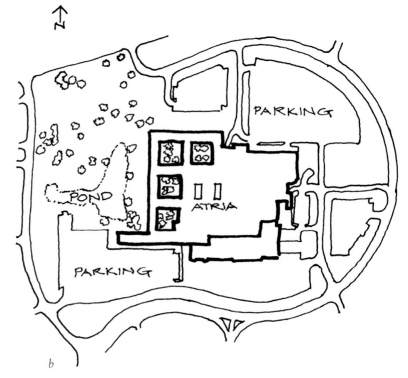

Hospital courtyards might seem the logical heirs to the monastic tradition of growing medicinal plants, but today's hospitals (in Hispanic and most other cultures) are often too concerned with sanitation to tolerate outdoor environments in the midst of patient care. Even at the Wausau (Wisconsin) Hospital, where courtyards are designed to encourage patients to go outdoors, bird feeders in the courtyard outside the children's therapy department were initially controversial because of concerns they could attract muskrats and rats (Figure 3.13). The older courtyard buildings of Spain and Mexico that serve as clinics and doctor's offices take full advantage of their florid and quiet arcades and courtyards as ideal visiting places. Again, the contrast, this time between the controlled and sanitized hospital room and the relaxed courtyard, serves to relieve anxiety and stress.

Office buildings take advantage of the courtyard's ability to deliver daylight to office windows, and a courtyard's value as a place to take a break. The Alquist state office building in San Jose, California, is organized around several courtyards. Overhead are moveable screens, called *toldos* in Spain and Mexico, that modify the sunlight and add to the sense of enclosure (Figure 3.14). For much more about *toldos*, see Chapters 4, 5, 8, 9, 10, and 12.

The courtyards at Wausau Hospital were not built to define or enhance the image of the hospital. They do not make a corporate statement of power but provide a practical solution to a straightforward problem, adapting and reworking the courtyard concept for a cold-weather climate. They provide a close view of nature, richer, denser, and more colorful than that of the park. They also afford an equally or even more important advantage that perhaps was not intended or expected. They allow the actual physical experience of being out of doors. Patients, families, and staff enjoy some of the domestic aspects of historic courtyards: walking, sitting, eating, and socializing. And certain therapies are administered there, especially to adult patients on the rehabilitation unit and to children. To be out of doors in a hospital setting adds a rare dimension of normalcy and makes patients feel less vulnerable. The hospital reeks of limitation: the garden can work to ease that.

Nancy Gerlach-Spriggs, Richard Enoch Kaufman, and Sam Bass Warner, Jr.
Restorative Gardens: The Healing Landscape

FIG. 3.14 SAN JOSE, CALIFORNIA
Courtyard in the Alquist state office building, graced by a *toldo* overhead, provides a place for a break, away from the noise of downtown.

Museums utilize courtyards despite a different threat: too much daylight, with consequent ultraviolet damage to their collections. The arcades of museums are semisheltered places to exhibit artifacts and sculpture, in a light that changes with the position, color, and intensity of the sun (Figure 3.15). Again, the contrast relieves "museumitis," the sudden feeling of too much enclosure and control that prematurely drives patrons away. A few minutes' immersion in the arcades, perhaps with a dip of the hand into the central fountain, and one is ready to re-engage the interior and its riches.

FIG. 3.15 CÓRDOBA, SPAIN
Two courtyards of the Museo Arqueológico. In the foreground (entry courtyard), a large lily pond reflects what is to come. The loggia between courtyards houses some more climate-resistant artifacts from Córdoba's many excavations. The floor of the distant courtyard is white marble, diffusing daylight to the ceilings of the surrounding arcades (see an example in Figure 12.11). That more formal courtyard has almost no vegetation.

The National Museum of Anthropology in Mexico City is organized around a huge courtyard (Figure 3.16). Between each section of this museum is a dividing wall, so that patrons must exit to the courtyard between each era displayed. No arcades here; it's full immersion in the environment. The breath of courtyard air, the long vistas, the bright daylight act as does a taste of sherbet (albeit strong sherbet!) between courses of a gourmet meal.

FIG. 3.16 MEXICO CITY
The courtyard at the center of the famous National Museum of Anthropology. At one end, falling water maintains a cooling sound and fine spray. At the other, still water and papyrus are serene in the sun. I wonder — could the white marble floor at the sculpture (foreground) be deliberate? It can be a blinding contrast to the shadowy interior.

CHAPTER 4

The splendor of the night was responsible for the rest. The scent of jasmine rose from the illu-

minated patio, the air seemed like diamonds, and there were more stars than ever in the sky.

"Like Andalusia in April," he had once said, remembering Columbus. A crosswind swept away

the noises and smells, and all that remained was the thunder of waves against the walls.

Gabriel García Márquez
The General in His Labyrinth

Plants, The Spirit of the Courtyard

The courtyard, with its distinct boundaries, limited access to other landscapes, and manicured plants, is one of the most controlled forms of landscape. It is also a landscape most intimately related to buildings. Close contact between people and plants brings both opportunities and threats. For all their rewards, some plants trigger allergies, are poisonous, or are otherwise dangerous. In Appendix C, a list of common courtyard plants details some of the good and bad of plant selection.

Plants are important to courtyard cooling, directly as they provide shade, indirectly as they transpire (providing modest evaporative cooling) and as the sounds and sights of breezes moving leaves reinforces an impression of coolth. In a study of ten Seville courtyards, Perez-de-Lama and Cabeza (1998) found that "whenever there is vegetation and/or deep shading provided by architectural elements such as porticoes, there is a better cooling performance."

Organic vs. Geometric

There are many contributors to the visual appeal of the courtyard; the geometric ones include the rhythm of dark arches in a white wall, the way the sky is framed by the roof edges, the rising diagonal of a stair, the contrast of the red tile roof and white walls, the pattern of the black and white pebbles of the floor, the intricate designs of tiled walls, the richly ornate iron gates and window grilles. The richness of the organic elements is of another kind.

Plants stand in organic and dynamic contrast to the geometric, static architecture of the courtyard, in a complementary relationship that often brings out the best in each. Courtyards are a landscape with sharply defined edges. In this highly structured geometric order, plants provide organic relief. They are almost subversive in their willful asymmetry, sprawling, hanging, and swaying. Even the most elegant and graceful arch has a fixed, hard edge. A vine softens this edge, changes with the seasons, grows over the years. The hard, geometric order of the courtyard is still there, but partly masked by the softer, subtly changing organic order that moves over it. This softening of hard edges and surfaces also changes the acoustics in courtyards, making them less reverberant. Plants also reduce glare, partly by shading (thus lowering the overall level of daylight) and partly by softening the contrast between bright blue sky and starkly white walls.

This organic/geometric interplay is beautifully evident in courtyard ponds, often highly geometric in form, whose water lilies, ferns, and reeds respond more to sun and seasons than to geometry (Figure 4.1). With the pond comes fish, turtles, perhaps frogs. Pond dwellers are the ultimate captives of courtyard life, dependent upon this microclimate for their existence. These captives in turn captivate; few children, or even adults, can resist watching fish appear and disappear among water lilies.

Sensuality

Plants appeal to all the senses. They delight the eye, in one direction glinting darkly in the sun, in another glowing as sun is filtered through leaves and blossoms. The glowing is made even stronger by the background of dark arches beyond; whenever you are looking toward the sun in a courtyard, the opposite wall will be in shadow. This shadow provides the perfect foil for leaves back-lit by the sun (Figure 4.2). Plants provide a richer variety of color, shape, and texture than almost any tile work that the architecture may offer.

The nose responds to their distinct aromas, as to jasmine on a warm evening. The surfaces of a just-watered courtyard recall the aroma of the refreshing rain. Soft on the courtyard floor, a fragrant ground cover sends up powerful signals that, while walking, you have crushed some leaves. Brushing against fragrant Common Myrtle releases another aroma. A courtyard will be filled for several hours with the aroma of freshly picked lemons.

FIG. 4.2 CUERNAVACA, MEXICO
The sun provides backlit leaves to contrast with shaded arcades.

Courtyard plants provide a rich variety of tastes. Fruits, berries, nuts, and vegetables are cultivated in the controlled micro-climates of courtyards, kept from the climate's extremes, and safe from thieving hands.

A sense of touch can be as subtle as a change in radiant heat felt when passing from sun to a plant's shade. When within reach, plants invite exploration of their varying textures of rough or smooth leaves. The act of harvesting flowers or food is a most satisfying reward for caretaking, which itself involves touching the plants during trimming back, repotting, and fertilizing. Children play among plants, often assigning them imaginary roles in some story; beneath a large shrub or behind a vine, a child-scale space can be inhabited. Plants are cool to the touch, and strands of bougainvillea reinforce an impression of cooling as they sway in the slightest breeze. In a slightly stronger breeze, leaves will rustle and turn.

The ears receive perhaps the most powerful indicator of cooling. The sound of running water reverberates in the hard-surfaced rectangular courtyard. A breeze ruffles leaves, adding another acoustic signal of cooling. Plants bring birds attracted by their berries and the insects they harbor, adding to the collection of desirable sounds.

Ritual/Habitual

Plants in courtyards resemble animals in captivity in that they experience daily interaction with people. The habitual watering pays multiple dividends; evaporative cooling is enhanced (more water soaks into porous surfaces than is used by the plants themselves), shading increases with plant growth, pleasure is taken in sights and aromas of blossoms, food is produced.

Ritual involves those moments of dividend: cutting the blossoms to brighten a room or delight a friend, harvesting the fruit, showing a child the flower on the point of opening. Ritual also involves times of particular caretaking effort; taking down the flowerpots, trimming the plants, repotting with renewed soil, rehanging the pots. By marking the passage of seasons, by their change through growth and decay, plants keep us oriented to the stages of our lives.

Potted Plants

Toward one end of the courtyard plant spectrum are potted plants, moveable as seasons and activities change (Figure 4.3). They might be considered the equivalent of a family pet: to be given food and water regularly (pots hold little soil, so fertilizer and water needs are frequent), and displayed in key positions when at their best appearance. Sometimes they are arranged to direct traffic, subtly blocking a path to some more private place. Potted plants are often given as gifts, and these can take on a shrine-like quality if the giver and occasion are particularly memorable.

The potted plant illustrates that organic-geometric contrast, the fixed versus the changing, the lifeless containing the living. Sometimes, like a cute puppy that grows into a large unruly dog, the potted plant will outgrow this root-limiting environment. It then needs a permanent rooted place in (or out of) the courtyard.

Rooted Shrubs and Vines

If potted plants are "pets," are rooted shrubs and vines "drapes and wallpaper?" Because they can grow so large, rooted plants can eventually become the dominant element in a courtyard. Rooted plants are there for life, and eventually take on an aged quality as do the courtyard walls and floor. Prized roses are given permanent positions of honor. An ornamental shrub at the courtyard center can blaze spectacularly with color, arresting the view from the street with its beauty. (Also, rooted shrubs can become large enough to fill the view from the street through the *zaguán*, thus preserving the privacy of arcades beyond.)

Vines can be trimmed and shaped to reinforce the lines of arches, as their trunks twine beside and around columns. Deciduous vines can provide more shade in hot weather, and less when their leaves fall. They are living awnings, transforming a wall from a tracery of bare branches against a massive wall in winter to a thick tapestry of leaves and flowers in summer.

FIG. 4.3
Courtyard plants range in size from *(a, previous page)* those confined to small pots in Calle Encarnación, Córdoba; *(b)* vines that soften the colonnade at the Museo Rufino Tamayo, Oaxaca; and *(c)* trees that form a sub-ceiling under the sky, at Calle San Juan Palomares, Córdoba.

In hot, humid Fort Worth, Texas, architect Louis I. Kahn designed the Kimbell Art Museum as a series of adjacent barrel vaults brightened by continuous skylights along the apex of each vault. One of these vaults is interrupted by a small, vine-shaded courtyard (Figure 4.4). Situated near the middle of the building, it is a refuge from the tightly controlled museum environment.

Sometimes vines are seen as harbors for mosquitoes or other undesirable insects, unwanted birds, or even for rats. This may explain why so many courtyards contain many potted plants, but few rooted ones.

FIG. 4.4 FORT WORTH, TEXAS
A small courtyard rests below the tracery of a vine at the Kimbell Art Museum, designed by Louis Kahn. (Photo courtesy of Mark E. Palmer.)

Trees

At the other end of the spectrum from potted plants, trees provide a canopy replacing the sky (Figure 4.5). Trees can create a smaller enclosure within the otherwise open courtyard, or fill the opening entirely. As a shading strategy, trees offer the advantage (over the *toldo*) of allowing wind to pass through their canopy. Their lower leaves stay cooler in the shade, thus radiating little heat to the courtyard below. Tree leaves intercept some of the dust that would otherwise collect on courtyard furniture and floor. Trees encourage birds (for better or worse), and provide hanging places for hammocks. They can provide fruit, and celebrate seasonal change.

Then why doesn't every courtyard have at least one tree? Trees keep in the heat by night, unlike the *toldo*, which can be swept away to expose the courtyard to the cold night sky. Trees litter the courtyard floor, and not all the birds they attract are welcome. Falling fruit can break or dislodge roof tiles and injure pets or people. Too much shade can result in an uncomfortably cold, damp courtyard in colder weather. With lightning or wind, a falling tree or limbs can cause substantial damage to the building around the courtyard.

With the courtyard's plants, we see again that mixture of roles: social, aesthetic, and technical. Plants provide opportunities for play, for display, and for harvest; their surfaces and volumes intermingle light, color, and aroma; they can be significant sources of shade and evaporation for summer cooling.

The view of the courtyards from the second-story [hospital] rooms—both the near view of the treetops and the extended view of the canopy of trees outside their windows . . .—is beguiling. This microcosm is an ecosystem unto itself for patients, a natural, ordered world in which they have responsibility. They have the opportunity to lose themselves in the view of the canopy of trees outside their window as in another world—reminiscent of a treehouse or the way one imagines the top layer of a rainforest.

Nancy Gerlach-Spriggs, Richard Enoch Kaufman, and Sam Bass Warner, Jr.
Restorative Gardens: The Healing Landscape

FIG. 4.5 TUCUMÁN, ARGENTINA
Trees form a canopy for the courtyard of the Casa Histórica. (Photo by Edward Allen.)

CHAPTER 5

Perhaps the most satisfying architectural response to the continuously dry tropics is

the Mediterranean residence centered on a courtyard. With a meager but well-

developed water supply, the courtyards feature fountains, ponds, and growing

plants for both evaporative cooling and for aesthetic enhancement. Individual

homes are connected by narrow streets and shared walls. By day, one or two

narrow, tunnel-like entrances from the street provide ventilation through cool ports.

But it is the fine-tuning of the courtyard environment—its optimization of wall

heat resistance, ventilation rate and evaporation rate—that is most satisfying.

William Lowry and Porter Lowry
Fundamentals of Biometeorology

Courtyards, Climate, and Comfort

Why do these Hispanic (and several other) cultures nearer the equator wrap their buildings around an exterior space, while so many cultures farther from the equator wrap exterior space around their buildings? One answer is related to climate. When the climate is very cold, the fire and hearth are at the center of a building (Figure 5.1). When the climate is very hot (and dry), a shaded fountain is at the center.

Degrees of Control

The continuum of spaces, ranging in order from least to most environmentally controlled, is *open countryside, street, courtyard, arcade, room* (Figure 5.2). The contrast between less and more comfortable spaces within this continuum greatly increases satisfaction with the latter, most private and personal. The most dramatic thermal contrast is often between the street and the courtyard, and it is reinforced by the change from public to private, from barren to florid, noisy to quiet, hard to soft.

Those of us who expect a constant indoor climate may be surprised to find that dwellers in courtyard buildings often choose the less-controlled arcade for activities, rather than the most-controlled room. Simply put, the arcades are usually more interesting places to be.

What is thermal comfort in traditional hot-climate courtyard buildings? First, it depends greatly upon the thermal mass of the building for the amount that the temperature fluctuates and by how many degrees, and at what hours it reaches highs and lows. Second, it depends on the personal involvement of the building's occupants, whose actions are often called thermal sailing. This includes watering

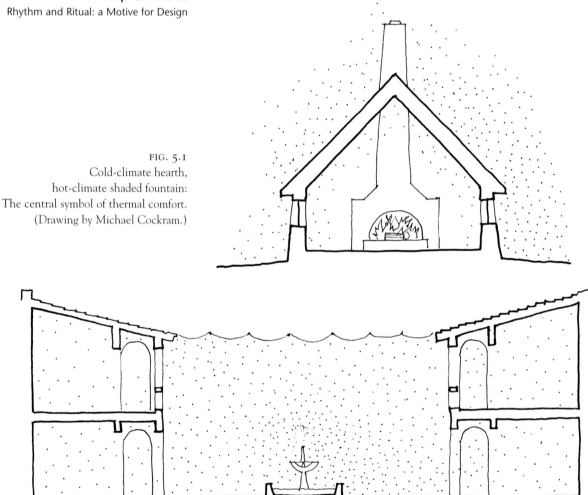

FIG. 5.1
Cold-climate hearth,
hot-climate shaded fountain:
The central symbol of thermal comfort.
(Drawing by Michael Cockram.)

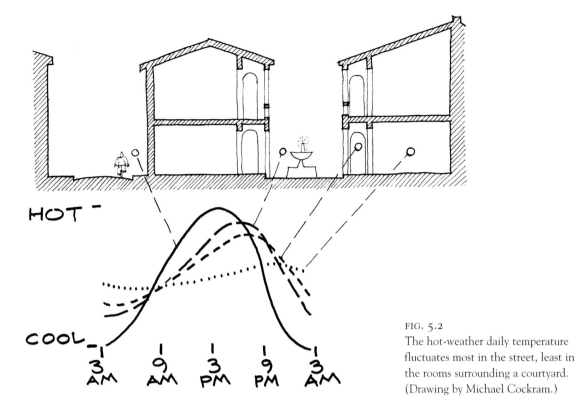

HOT

COOL

3 AM 9 AM 3 PM 9 PM 3 AM

FIG. 5.2
The hot-weather daily temperature fluctuates most in the street, least in the rooms surrounding a courtyard. (Drawing by Michael Cockram.)

the courtyard, opening and closing shading devices and windows, and adjusting one's own clothing and activity level. And third, it depends on accepting less thermal control than would be possible with today's air conditioning equipment.

Taming the Climate

Courtyards represent an attempt to bring the forces of nature under partial control. This is somewhat like trying to regularly feed wild animals; one can never be sure when or how much interaction will result. Expectations of thermal comfort in and around the courtyard might be described as "unpredictable to an acceptable degree."

As pockets of space that are open to the sky, courtyards intensify some aspects of the climate, such as daylight, and dilute others, such as the wind. The horizontal aperture through which nature enters has several characteristics, some of which were shown in Figures 1.6 and 1.7. In winter when the sun is low in the sky, the result is mostly shade on floor and walls, with only the equator-facing wall receiving much direct sun.

The horizontal aperture provides extensive exposure to the sky, which is very cold on clear nights. A horizontal aperture thus emphasizes cold in a cold season, with long nights.

It also emphasizes heat in the hot season, because the sun, now high in the sky, can readily penetrate a horizontal opening. Now the floor and several walls are sunny, with only the polar-facing wall remaining a reliably shaded surface. In the tropics, building shadows provide no escape from the sun directly overhead around noon. This heat emphasis is partially offset at night, when clear skies are coldest.

Thus a courtyard does not guarantee thermal comfort in the surrounding building. In a study of older courtyard housing and newer row housing in Baghdad, Hanna and Simpson (1996) found the newer row houses maintained a lower temperature in July and August. The roofs were uninsulated in both housing types; in the courtyard houses, the density of the neighborhood was greater, and the walls were twice as thick. These authors identified access to ventilation as the important variable; see Chapter 10 for a detailed study of ventilation of the mass by night.

It seems that for courtyard comfort, the best climates are those with hot, dry days and cool clear nights to radiate heat away to the sky; or those with cool but sunny days at lower latitudes where sun penetration is both easy and welcome. It seems that for courtyard comfort, the worst climates are hot and humid, where little wind is available to relieve stuffiness; or cold and cloudy ones at higher latitudes, where little winter sun can penetrate to provide warmth.

Even in one of the "best" climates, that of Andalucía in southern Spain, there remains the problem of choice of courtyard depth. A deeper courtyard will stay cooler in summer, but exclude sun for warmth in winter. It seems that deeper courtyards are generally favored in such climates, perhaps because heating is easier to achieve than is cooling. The inhabitant of a cold-winter courtyard building can burn a variety of fuels (wood, kerosene) in simple heating devices, can wear warmer clothes, can eat hot foods, and can increase activity to cope with the cold. In contrast, the inhabitant of a hot-summer courtyard building has fewer low-technology options; sit near a block of ice, turn on a fan (requiring electricity), drink cold liquids. Fewer clothes, or decreased activity, are rarely options that help much (or are realistic). The architecture is therefore arranged to make spaces cooler in the summer, rather than warmer in the winter.

Strategies for Winter Warmth

In cold weather, a common design strategy is to "huddle," that is, minimize exposure to cold air. Courtyard buildings (as traditionally built in hot dry climates) expose only the street facade, the four walls facing the courtyard, and the roof. Compared to the building surrounded by open space, this design strategy works well to conserve heat.

But a second design strategy is to admit winter sun. Here the courtyard building faces the problem of self-shading: the south (or equatorial) side of the courtyard casts an unwelcome winter shadow on the north (or polar) courtyard wall. In Chapter 1 the "solar shadow index" (and Socrates' advice about lower south walls) explored this dilemma.

In winter, the room facing south into the courtyard will receive warm sun around noon when the sun is strongest; the room facing east into the courtyard will receive warm sun in the morning, and the room facing west, in the evening. This suggests certain functions may be optimum for certain sides.

Because the arcades are so heavily used in so many buildings, they are sometimes enclosed in cold weather. Two buildings with "thermal switches" show how they can transform the arcades. The residence in Colima, at the edge of the tropics, has permanently glazed openings on two sides, each of which can be opened or closed (Figure 5.3). The glazed shorter arcade faces southwest; the glazed longer arcade faces southeast. (Shown also in Figure 3.4.) The shorter arcade facing northeast is always open to the courtyard, with doors on its rear wall to a dining room. The longer side facing northwest is a blank (party) wall.

A social club in Córdoba, Spain (Figure 5.4), much further north and colder in winter, places removable leaded glass fillers behind the arches of its four identical arcades during the winter. During the hottest months, a *toldo* is used to cover the courtyard, partly or wholly.

FIG. 5.3 COLIMA, MEXICO
Variations on arcade openings to a courtyard on Calle Zaragosa.
(*a*) Plan. The arches in the glazed arcades have both fixed glass and a set of doors.
(*b*) Looking east into the courtyard. The dining room is off the arcade to the right.

FIG. 5.4 CÓRDOBA, SPAIN
The arcades around Círculo del
Amistad courtyard experience seasonal
change. (a) In the warmer months, the
arcades are open to the courtyard. (b)
For a few colder months, leaded glass
walls are placed in the arches' openings.

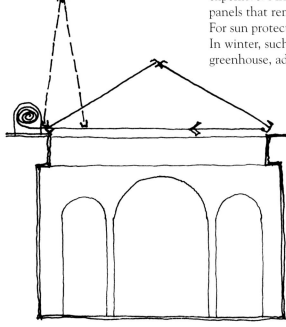

When a courtyard must serve some commercial function, rain or shine, a moveable cover is possible. Moveable skylight technology is now widely available, if expensive. An older example, from a restaurant in Córdoba, uses folding glass panels that remain open at the ends (so blowing rain could still be a problem). For sun protection, a *toldo* is used below the glass (or instead of it) (Figure 5.5). In winter, such a moveable glass cover might be kept closed to act as a kind of greenhouse, admitting and retaining solar heat.

FIG. 5.5 CÓRDOBA, SPAIN
A moveable transparent cover protects the diners in the courtyard of El Churasco Restaurant. (*a*) A motorized winch pulls on the far side of the hinged roof, drawing it up and open. (*b*) During rainy or cold weather, the roof is closed. When the sun is too hot, the *toldo* is drawn shut, whether or not the cover above is open.

If you see a courtyard and you're an architect, your instinct is to put a roof on it.

Simon Allford, architect
The Architect's Journal, 4 November 1999

The most drastic step is to cover the courtyard permanently with some rain-shedding device. This is more than cosmetic surgery, because it fundamentally changes this space's relationship with the climate. Simply put, it is no longer a courtyard; the wild animal is now preserved in a glass case. Glass covers hold heat for winter warmth, but also for summer discomfort. The best such examples preserve the color of daylight and allow both sun and shadow (Figure 5.6). The worst examples turn everything green or some other monochrome.

Avoiding Heat Gain

Shading, or otherwise avoiding heat gain, is the first rule of thermal comfort in hot-climate courtyard buildings. While the courtyard is by definition open to the sky, there are reasons in addition to the hot sun for at least temporarily filtering this aperture, including dusty wind, and bats or other intruders from above.

A wide-mesh screen, of chicken-wire, for example, serves to discourage intruders. For one courtyard in Colima, it also becomes a trellis for vines (Figure 5.7). The vines filter sun and diminish both daylight and wind. But when wind passes through them, they sway and reinforce the impression of air motion.

A restaurant's courtyard in Oaxaca is covered with a lavender-flowering vine, attracting bumblebees and small birds (Figure 5.8). It rests just far enough above the tables to allow people to walk comfortably below. The upper leaves absorb the sun, shading the lower leaves, thus keeping them cooler just above one's

FIG. 5.6 SEVILLE, SPAIN
A few courtyards have been covered permanently with a transparent roof. This one, shaded by *velas* (sails) above, keeps rain out of the stair and courtyard of the residence of painter Santiago del Campo. Jaime Lopez de Asiain, architect.

Part 1: Courtyard Characteristics

The courtyard houses of the south are mostly two- or three-story houses with high gables and a relatively narrow courtyard called the "light-well." This can be attributed to the hotter and rainier climate of the south. The taller the house, the smaller the light-well appears, thus providing effectively better shelter from sun and rain. The hall and the courtyard can be interlinked by means of opening up the door panels so that both ventilation and lighting are facilitated.

David Lung
Chinese Traditional Vernacular Architecture

FIG. 5.7 COLIMA, MEXICO
Vines grow up the walls and out over the courtyard, supported on a "chicken wire" netting designed to discourage bats. Calle 27 de Septiembre.

head. (This vine, common in Oaxaca, had many names; my favorite was *rompe platos*, because, legend has it, if you pick one of the blossoms instead of letting it fall, you'll break a plate. Botanist Tom Ogren suggests it may be *thunbergia grandiflora*.)

Shading cloth is a narrow-mesh material gaining wide usage, available in varying degrees of sun blockage (90% is quite common). It still allows a small percentage of direct sun through, so there are still patterns of sun and shadow below it. The amount of light and heat is greatly reduced, yet the view through it surprisingly clear. A restaurant at the edge of the tropics in Salta, Argentina benefits from the sparkle of direct sun, but gets little of its heat (Figure 5.9).

FIG. 5.8 OAXACA, MEXICO
The courtyard of the Restaurant El Gecko, rests in the shade below a thick vine of lavender flowers.

FIG. 5.9 SALTA, ARGENTINA
At the Restaurant Santana, contemporary shading cover of "greenhouse cloth" keeps most of the sun's heat out while allowing the visual contrast of sun and shade.

FIG. 5.10 VARIATIONS ON THE *TOLDO*
The *toldo* is the moveable fabric cover over hot-climate
courtyards. (*a*) A translucent white *toldo* is arrayed in strips
at Oaxaca's Museum of Graphic Arts. (*b*) An opaque *toldo*
casts a very dark shade. (*c*) A translucent blue *toldo* is left
open at one end, allowing a contrast between the patch of sun
and the cool-colored shade. Calle Fernando Colón, Córdoba.

Is the shade from a *toldo* preferable to shading by plants? In its open position, a *toldo* is folded against one wall. Like a large tree, the toldo casts shade over the whole courtyard; unlike a tree, it is swept away in the early evening to facilitate both ventilation and cold-sky radiation, all night long. The *toldo* changes the microclimate, providing even more control of this highly managed landscape. With its daytime shade, it favors the more delicate ferns and vines.

A key characteristic of the *toldo* is its degree of translucence (Figure 5.10). The more translucent this cover, the more diffused light is cast over the entire courtyard, rather than the unshaded contrast of bright sunlight and deep shadow. This diffused light is influenced by the color of the *toldo*. Physiologically, the translucent *toldo* favors plant growth and provides evenly distributed daylight to the arcades. Psychologically, an orange or yellow *toldo* connotes heat while flattering the human complexion; a blue or green *toldo* connotes coolth while rendering human complexions cadaverous. The most neutral *toldo* is white. From a maintenance viewpoint, the translucent *toldo* will show the silhouette of dirt and debris on its surface. Patterns of daylight distribution through a translucent versus an opaque *toldo* can be seen in Figure 10.4.

An opaque *toldo* casts a deep shade, leaving a ring of daylight at its edges, and a grid of small elliptical sunspots across the courtyard. This is due to the grid of grommets, provided so that the horizontal *toldo* will not collect water and collapse in a rainstorm. Besides discouraging plant growth, the opaque *toldo* absorbs sunlight, becoming a huge radiant heater. The closer this hot surface is to the floor, the greater the daytime discomfort. Yet the opaque *toldo* is fairly common, probably because it doesn't show accumulated dirt and debris as does the translucent one.

As typically applied, both the translucent and opaque *toldo* nearly fill the sky opening, all but eliminating the possibility of ventilation while they are closed. Another impact is increased reverberation; any toldo will be more reflective of courtyard sounds than is the open sky. For more details about the impact of *toldos*, see Chapters 8, 9, 10, and 12.

More Strategies for Summer Comfort

The combinations of air temperature and relative humidity that are considered to be within the "comfort zone" are shown in Figure 5.11. This range is specific to the United States; far hotter temperatures are still considered comfortable in the hotter seasons in both Spain and Mexico.

Cooling strategies are more numerous for hot-dry climates than for hot-humid ones. These include evaporation, radiation, and convection. Evaporation cools both building and human skin surfaces quickly, and the drier the air, the faster the evaporation. Dry climates have much less water vapor in the air, so radiant losses to the cold sky are much greater. And dry climates enjoy much cooler air by night, providing a diurnal convection "heat sink" that humid climates lack.

Wind

Wind is almost always a friend in a hot humid climate (see Figure 5.11a). It is sometimes helpful in hot dry and temperate climates, especially for night ventilation when outdoor temperatures are lower. Wind moves primarily horizon-

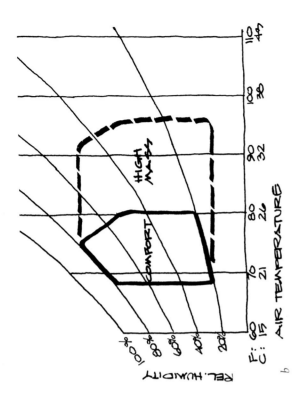

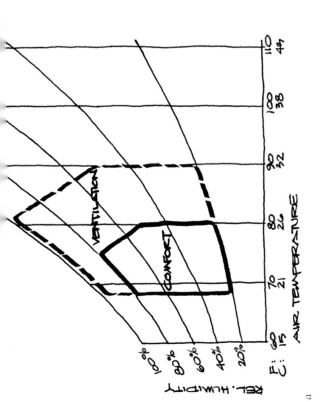

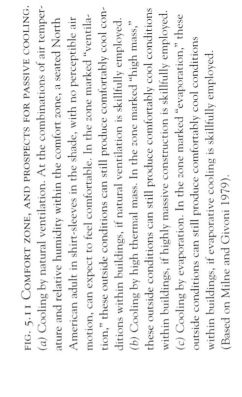

FIG. 5.11 COMFORT ZONE, AND PROSPECTS FOR PASSIVE COOLING. (a) Cooling by natural ventilation. At the combinations of air temperature and relative humidity within the comfort zone, a seated North American adult in shirt-sleeves in the shade, with no perceptible air motion, can expect to feel comfortable. In the zone marked "ventilation," these outside conditions can still produce comfortably cool conditions within buildings, if natural ventilation is skillfully employed. (b) Cooling by high thermal mass. In the zone marked "high mass," these outside conditions can still produce comfortably cool conditions within buildings, if highly massive construction is skillfully employed. (c) Cooling by evaporation. In the zone marked "evaporation," these outside conditions can still produce comfortably cool conditions within buildings, if evaporative cooling is skillfully employed. (Based on Milne and Givoni 1979).

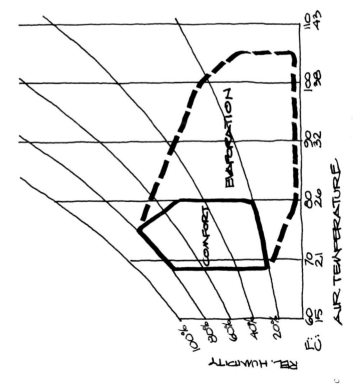

tally, and thus easily skips over the horizontal opening to a courtyard. If wind is to be encouraged, several strategies are available. One is to use the *zaguán* as a tunnel for wind; similarly, open windows on both sides of the rooms that separate the street from the courtyard can help. But narrow streets and limited openings to streets inhibit wind near the ground level. Wind openings admit dust and noise as well.

Another wind-catching strategy, advocated by Baruch Givoni (1998), is to raise the height of the courtyard wall downwind (assuming that a site has a prevalent wind direction). As wind moves across the lower roofs and the courtyard opening, it then strikes this higher wall. Most of the wind will move up and over, but a down draft at the wall can be enhanced if there is an outlet at the bottom— that is, if some wind can continue below the roof as well as over it (Figure 5.12).

A third wind-catching strategy was tested by Gideon Golany (1990) in his study of Chinese pit-type courtyard houses and cave dwellings (Figure 5.13). In this humid summer environment, air motion proved crucial to comfort. As Golany describes it,

FIG. 5.12
One strategy to encourage wind to scour a courtyard is to place one high wall downwind, with a *zaguán* below that wall to allow some wind to pass through to the street beyond.

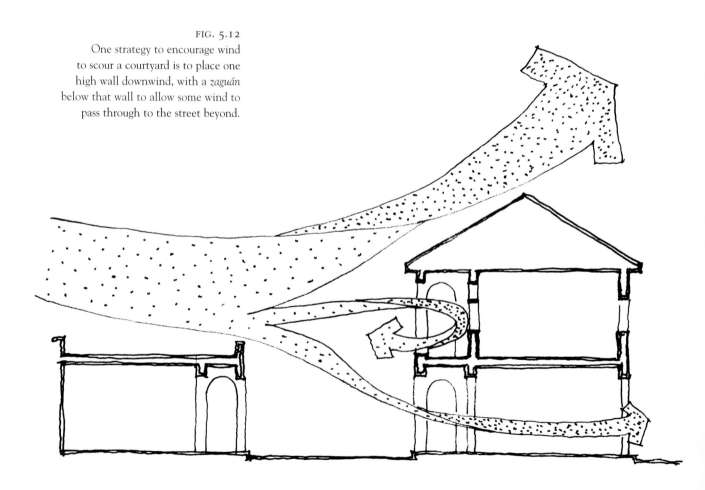

The proposed ventilation system would take in air through a chimney to be constructed above the courtyard level. The warm air coming into the above-ground opening of the chimney and directed by self-rotating wind catchers will be cooled through the long, dark passage, both factors forcing it to flow downward. Also, due to the heated air rising in the courtyard, air will be sucked out of the cave rooms through the windows, and be replaced by new air sucked down the chimney, thus accelerating the rise of the hot air in the courtyard and establishing effective air circulation within the dwelling.

If there is no wind, there will be no wind-induced air motion. Air motion can then be induced by the "stack effect," where cool air falls and hot air rises, although this effect is usually weaker than wind. A tall chimney would then move air in the reverse direction from the above example, with cool air at the courtyard floor flowing into the rooms, replacing hot air that flows up through the chimney. However, this only works when the air outside the top of the chimney is *cooler* than the air leaving the interior.

Hassan Fathy describes how two courtyards of unequal size, separated by a loggia (or *takhtabush*), might induce this rather weak air motion. More sun penetrates the larger courtyard's opening, creating a hot air space. As this hot air rises out the opening, cooler air must flow into the smaller courtyard. This air is likely drawn either into the smaller courtyard's roof opening, or into rooms through open windows at the street. In either case, this "new" air is cooled as it passes through the shaded smaller courtyard or cool room, and for those seated in the loggia between courtyards, a perceptible (if gentle) breeze of cooled air is available for increased comfort.

FIG. 5.13
Using a "wind catcher" to direct outdoor air to the rear of a room in a courtyard (or cave) dwelling. Plan and cross section of Wang Xiang Suo family cave dwelling in Dian Po Village, Mazhuang County, near Taiyuan City, Shanxi province, where research was conducted by Gideon Golany. (Reprinted by permission from Golany 1990.)

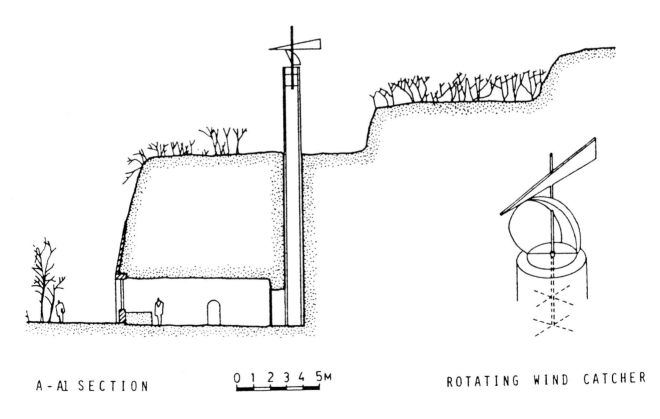

A - A1 SECTION

0 1 2 3 4 5 M

ROTATING WIND CATCHER

Thermal Mass

"Thermal mass" is a term for the thermal conductivity and capacity of materials. Materials with high thermal mass function best as heat regulators in expanses with a large surface area and ample depth. They act as thermal flywheels, slow to increase in temperature as air temperatures rise, and slow to cool as air temperatures plunge.

High thermal mass is the most obvious characteristic of traditional courtyard buildings, and its primary cooling effect—delaying the arrival of the afternoon heat—is aided by shading. In hot-dry climates, high thermal mass can be cooled by radiation to the night sky, by evaporation, and by ventilation at night (see Figure 5.11b).

Thermal mass provides a surface that, when at a temperature below that of the air, is perceptibly cool to anyone with bare skin nearby. In addition, because this massive material is highly conductive, it *feels* cool to the touch even when at or slightly above air temperature. Our fingers sense conductivity more than temperature in such a case. Of course this works against thermal mass for comfort in winter, unless the mass has sat in the sun for awhile.

The courtyard floor plays an important cooling role, because it looks straight up to the cold night sky. The more shallow the courtyard (the higher the aspect ratio), the more the floor "sees" of the sky rather than the walls, and so the more radiant heat loss by night. However, this advantage is easily removed with only gentle air motion, which can scour cool air from the floor of a shallow courtyard.

Evaporative Cooling

Evaporative cooling works in a hot-dry climate by accepting a higher humidity in exchange for lowered air temperature; see Figure 5.11c. As a mist is added to hot dry air, its temperature falls while its relative humidity rises.

The courtyard floor is a promising surface for evaporative cooling because it is a natural collecting place for water, it is in contact with the earth (an especially useful trait when a cistern sits below the courtyard), and unlike walls, it can be built of absorptive materials without threat to a building's structural stability. Working against evaporation from the floor is the lack of air motion—the least wind velocity occurs at the greatest courtyard depth—and a tendency for the coolest air to pool at the floor. Since the capacity of air to absorb moisture rises with increased temperature (as shown throughout Figure 5.11), evaporation will most rapidly occur in the hottest air, not at the courtyard floor. Nevertheless, if this surface is damp, in dry air it will contribute to evaporative heat exchange.

Some courtyards utilize white marble floors, perhaps because they contrast so beautifully with dark green leaves and vivid blossoms, or because the floor seems lighter and cleaner with the white glossy surface, or because marble connotes wealth. These marble floors remain damp for only a short time, thus curtailing evaporative cooling. The majority of courtyard floors utilize some combination of exposed earth, dark porous brick, pebbles set in mortar, and unglazed tile. All these hold moisture and thus increase the time over which evaporative cooling can occur.

In two identical courtyard buildings, bioclimatic thermal conditions (dry bulb temperature, humidity, mean radiant temperature, and air speed) were monitored inside the ground-level corridor of a north-facing arcade looking onto the courtyard. This study was conducted in mid-June, under clear skies, by Amr Bagneid (1989). The courtyards were rather large (200 m²) and shallow (aspect ratio 4.08). The floor of one was dry concrete; the other floor was mostly a water pool with two large water sprays (fountains). His measurements for one day are shown in Figure 5.14. The Predicted Mean Vote (PMV) thermal comfort index developed by P. O. Fanger was used to estimate the combined effect of the measured variables on a seated quiet person (PMV, where neutral = zero). This shows the advantage of evaporation at the courtyard floor. In this 24-hour period both courtyards were much too hot for comfort (PMV above 2) at midday. The dry courtyard experienced about 11 hours of PMV = 2 or less; at coolest, PMV = 0.8 (still slightly warm). The fountain courtyard experienced about 16 hours of PMV = 2 or less; at coolest, PMV = -1.4 (slightly cool).

For a closer look at the role of the courtyard floor in evaporative cooling, see Chapter 9. There, two identically sized courtyards have white marble floors; a slightly larger one has pebbles in absorbent mortar. There are other differences that affect cooling performance, including shading. But all three are in the same neighborhood and were monitored on the same series of days.

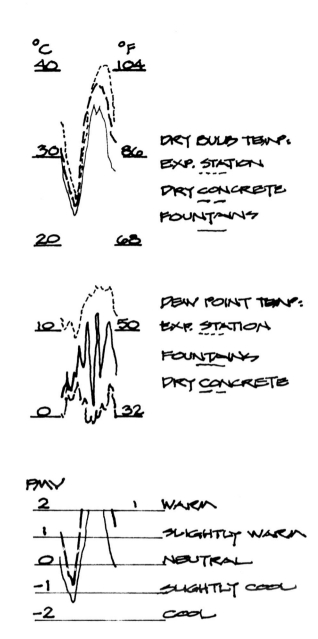

FIG. 5.14

Comparing a dry, concrete-floor courtyard with one of equal size that is evaporatively cooled by fountains. This is a 24-hour period (midnight to midnight) of a sunny June 19 in Phoenix, Arizona. The temperatures at an adjacent experimental weather station are included for contrast. Note the large temperature difference between dry bulb and dew point; the greater this difference, the greater the potential for evaporative cooling. Note also that the fountain courtyard has a longer time during which at least some degree of comfort is likely (PMV = 2 or less). (Based on Bagneid 1989.)

CHAPTER 6

The courtyard . . . is usually rectangular in shape, though its size and shape change as the house grows and the building takes place from the outside in. The first step in building a house is enclosing the land with a boundary wall. Thus a courtyard is born and a house grows by adding rooms to the four sides as the household increases in size. Similarly, fission in the household structure (i.e. breakup of the joint family into several nuclear families) results in the courtyard being divided by walls.

Amita Sinha
"Traditional Rural Settlements and Dwellings in Northern India"

Courtyards and Change

Although many architectural historians emphasize the unchanging monuments of our past, most buildings change with time, and many change radically. New owners change colors, textures, appliances; new functions may change spaces completely, recombining them, sweeping away or adding walls, opening or closing skylights.

The family home, in the very center of the historic district, was an old mint, denatured by a Florentine architect who came through here like an ill wind blowing renovation and converted many seventeenth-century relics into Venetian basilicas. It had six bedrooms and two large, well-ventilated dining and reception rooms, but that was not enough space for guests from the city, not to mention the very select few from out of town. The patio was like an abbey cloister, with a stone fountain murmuring in the center and pots of heliotrope that perfumed the house at dusk, but the space among the arcades was inadequate for so many grand family names.

Gabriel García Márquez
Love in the Time of Cholera

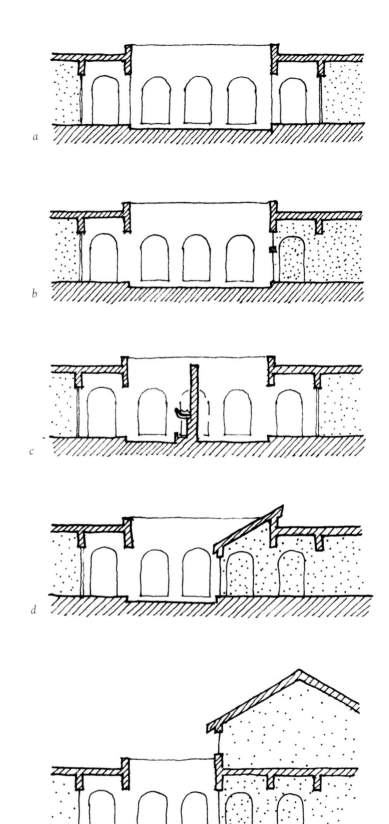

FIG. 6.1
Courtyards are compromised by building expansion in several ways. (*a*) Original form of courtyard. (*b*) Fill in an arcade. (*c*) Divide the courtyard. (*d*) Encroach on the courtyard's open space. (*e*) Add another floor. (Drawing by Michael Cockram.)

In the North American culture that surrounds a building with exterior space, there are many opportunities for building expansion. But in courtyard buildings, consider these limited opportunities for expansion (Figure 6.1):

- Fill in one or more arcades
- Divide the courtyard between two owners
- Encroach on the courtyard with a new arcade (or enclosed space)
- Add another floor

Fill in One or More Arcades

When the arcade is eliminated as a "buffer zone," rooms are exposed to more daylight, as well as the heat or cold of the open courtyard. (Figure 6.2) Where possible, the front of the arcade is enclosed and former wall at the rear of the arcade is removed to enlarge the room adjacent to it. If that approach proves structurally unsound, enlarged openings in the rear wall might allow the room to strongly relate to the newly enclosed arcade. Sometimes the newly filled arcade becomes a separate room; a long thin one perhaps, but at least a new addition. Then, the "old" room behind it likely changes to a function satisfied with little or no daylight. Ghosts abound, of former arcades that are now mostly solid walls, or an open arcade now glazed.

FIG. 6.2 CÓRDOBA, SPAIN The windows are part of an arch infill; (a) a formerly "open" facade is now "closed," and (b) those seated at the tables look directly out to the courtyard. Calle Osio.

Divide the Courtyard

Many older courtyards in Spain present one entirely solid wall. This is often the result of a family splitting its rather large courtyard residence when two of the children become adults, begin their families, and wish to stay in their home. The solid wall becomes a foil for an array of potted plants or a climbing vine. The aspect ratio of the two new courtyards is but half that of the former, larger courtyard. Any object in the center of the former courtyard is either cut in half (as a fountain's basin might be) or removed (as a large tree).

In turn, either of the new half-courtyards might later be similarly divided, and thus one large courtyard could eventually become four smaller ones, each with two adjacent solid walls (Figure 6.3).

Encroach on the Courtyard

With either increasing pressure for space or a change in function, a building might expand to fill the space available. When a courtyard is seen more as a convenience than a necessity, its open space will be sacrificed, piece by piece, for building expansion.

Consider an older residence without indoor plumbing (Figure 6.4). When urban water and sewer services become available, how will the pipes be installed, and which room will be given over to the toilet, lavatory, and tub? Trenches for water and sewer lines are easily dug

FIG. 6.3 CÓRDOBA, SPAIN
A courtyard has been divided to form three smaller ones. (a) From the roof terrace, a dividing wall and one courtyard's *toldo* are evident. (b) The same courtyard with *toldo*, from below. Calle Antonio Castillo.

Part 1: Courtyard Characteristics

through the *zaguán*, and a corner of the courtyard is tempting as the location of a new bathroom, where construction needn't disrupt any existing room's use. The well in the courtyard is supplanted by pipes and fixtures within the courtyard's space.

Sometimes, after an arcade has been filled in, the desire may arise for a new arcade to serve this enlarged interior space. The courtyard's open area is then diminished as the new arcade is constructed.

FIG. 6.4 CÓRDOBA, SPAIN
An old courtyard has a newer addition: a bathroom. The exposed soil stack might be an abstract tree, flanked by the many potted plants. In the center background, higher apartment buildings encroach on the privacy of this old courtyard. Calle Martin de Roa.

Add Another Floor

Floor additions were more common in the past, when building regulations were lax or nonexistent. The added structural load of a new top floor may seem readily accommodated when the existing walls are of great thickness, but the seismic problems that accompany added weight with height are potentially catastrophic.

When new floors are added, the aspect ratio plunges. Consider a "typical" 50 m² courtyard floor. When one story surrounds this courtyard, its wall height probably averages about 4 m.

The aspect ratio is then $50/(4)^2 = 3.13$.

A second floor, same height, produces $50/(8)^2 = 0.78$.

Add a third floor, same height, and $50/(12)^2 = 0.35$.

The floor area remains constant while the aspect ratio has diminished to 1/9 of the original.

FIG. 6.5 SEVILLE, SPAIN
Many small rooftop additions complicate the scene from Giralda Tower.

For structural reasons, new additions on a roof tend to be open and of light-weight construction, covering less than half the roof area (Figure 6.5). The remaining roof, when flat, offers many potential uses such as hanging clothes to dry, raising pigeons, or playing kickball.

Change the Function

Functional change can be happier for the courtyard than the previous forms of encroachment, because a mature patio can be so attractively adapted to so many uses, often with only modest changes (Figure 6.6).

(OPPOSITE)
FIG. 6.6 OLD COURTYARDS WITH NEW OCCUPANTS.
(a) A restaurant makes beautiful use of a former residence's courtyard and arcades in Colima, Mexico. (b) A hotel nearly fills its small courtyard with a pool, Oaxaca, Mexico. (c) A gift shop in a former residence uses its courtyard as just another display space in Córdoba, Spain.

A residence with a rather large courtyard and surrounding arcades can easily become a retail store, a small hotel, an office for a professional firm, a social club, or a restaurant (although the commercial kitchen creates problems elsewhere in the building). With more extensive alteration, courtyards have accommodated chairs and a stage, a basketball hoop, a sculpture garden, even a swimming pool. A convent became a first-class hotel in one picturesque example of adaptation to new uses; Oaxaca's present-day Hotel Camino Real is shown in Figures 1.8 and 3.6. Chapter 11 traces the fate of courtyards overtaken by change in the span of only fourteen years; they range from demolition to improvement.

PART TWO

Some Particular Courtyards

The following five chapters describe in detail a few of the 43 courtyards that I measured, beginning with 30 in Mexico and adding 13 in Andalucía. Beyond their initial attractiveness, these particular courtyards drew me back so many times that I took their dimensions as well as photographs. Later, I measured many for their thermal performance.

Some were unusually beautiful; some were unusually cool in hot summer; some were highly accessible and heavily used (hotels, civic buildings). Some home owners were especially kind and tolerant of a curious foreigner. Some (in Córdoba) were on the tourist map of courtyards from previous years' *Concurso de Patios* (courtyard competition, with monetary prizes), whose owners expect and usually welcome visitors. A very few owners (the wealthier ones) were initially suspicious, but eventually cooperative.

Are these 43 courtyards "representative"? From the several hundred courtyards I have seen and photographed in Mexico, Spain, Peru, and Argentina, I consider these a reasonably typical sample. From very small to very large, shallow to deep, bare to florid, very poor to very wealthy occupants, single-family residence to government functions, these courtyards show a very wide range of possibilities.

CHAPTER 7

The colonial style of the Spanish patio house, an ancient layout designed to meet living conditions,

came into being between 1895 and 1930, when groups of immigrants were desirous of preserving

their architectural tradition. Inside the towns the inner courts are small, shaded by high walls and deep

eaves. In general the inner courts of rural houses serve to admit more sunshine into the house. The

relationship of the inner court to the house is therefore governed by the surrounding housing.

Werner Blaser
Atrium: Five Thousand Years of Open Courtyards

Courtyards Observed: Mexico and Andalucía

For a six-month sabbatical leave in the early eighties, I chose to live in Colima, Mexico, because its December-January weather closely matched that of the summer (July–August) in my home of Eugene, Oregon. I was particularly interested in passive cooling strategies, and I reasoned that whatever succeeded in Colima in December might also be successful (technically, at least) in Oregon's summer.

The passive cooling strategy I encountered was beautiful and ubiquitous: courtyards.

There were of course some problems in this juxtaposition of an American in Mexico, not least being that to the Colimense, what I considered "hot" weather was quite cool. Unlike me, they were not trying to avoid heat in December. I was walking on the shady side of the street; they were seeking the sunny side. I was in shorts and sandals, they were wearing light sweaters. When I might sweat, they might shiver.

If I sought a direct transfer of cooling strategy, then sun position was a problem: solar altitudes in Colima (19° north latitude) in December were, at midday, closer to those of September in Eugene (44° north latitude) than to our hotter months of July–August. Therefore sun penetration into the December courtyard in Colima was somewhat less than it would be into a Eugene courtyard in July.

I observed and photographed well over a hundred courtyards, but ultimately took physical measurements of 30. All 30 of these courtyards are within a few blocks of Colima's main plaza. They include official, commercial, institutional and residential usages. They are one or two stories in height. They serve a very wide range of socio-economic groups.

FIG. 7.1

(a) A survey of courtyards in Colima, Mexico resulted in these categories of plantings and courtyard depth. (b) Map of the center of Colima, with locations of the courtyards in the survey ("D2" denotes cell category in the matrix). Note the diagonal, rather than cardinal, orientation of the streets. Around the margin are a grid of typical block sizes and street widths in the United States, for contrast.

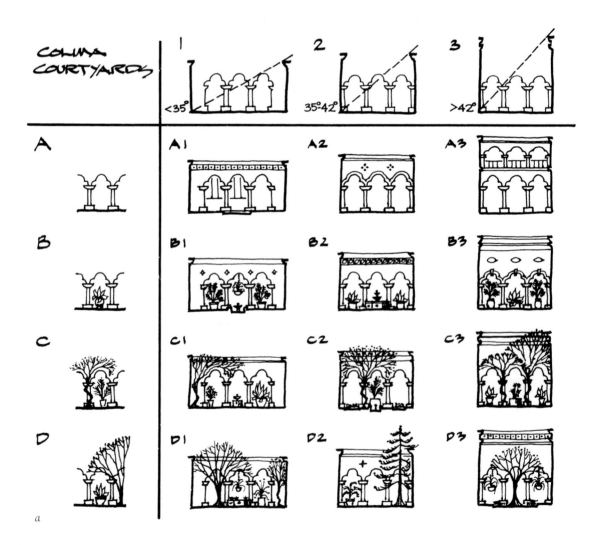

The matrix in Figure 7.1 is based on my first impressions, and contains those aspects which seemed to me most crucial: vegetation and depth. When I later measured these courtyards I was sometimes surprised by a dark courtyard proving to be rather shallow (high aspect ratio), or a light courtyard proving to be deep. Wall and floor color influenced these impressions, but plants were far more often a determinant of a feeling of depth; barren courtyards with less shadow always seemed more shallow.

After this Mexico experience, I wondered about the influence of the earlier courtyards of Spain. With a faculty grant from the University of Oregon, then a sabbatical leave and a Graham Foundation grant, I explored towns in Andalucía, settling on Córdoba as an especially promising collection of accessible courtyards, thanks to their promotion of the annual *Concurso de Patios*. Again, I observed and photographed a large number of patios, and then added 13 measured Spanish patios to the collection.

The physical characteristics of the 43 measured Mexican and Andalusian courtyards are listed in Table 7.1.

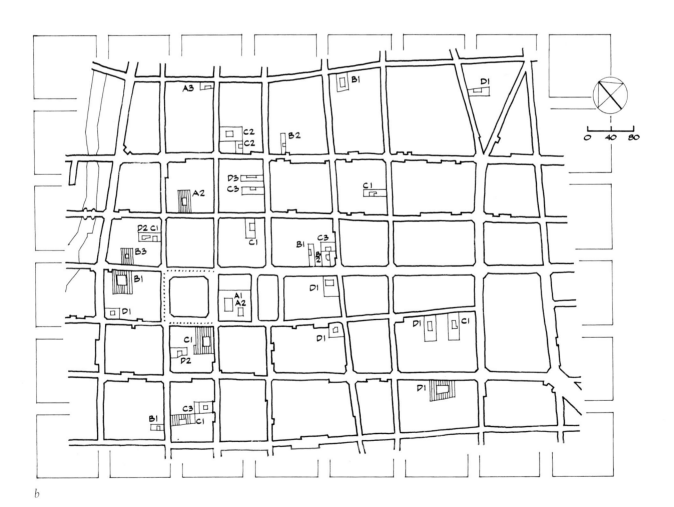

b

TABLE 7.1 SOME HISPANIC COURTYARDS (IN ORDER OF ASPECT RATIO)
PART ONE: COLIMA, MEXICO

	Location	Floor Area (m²)	Width N to S[a] (m)	Wall Height, S side (m)	Aver. Wall Height (m)	Solar Shadow Index[b]	Aspect Ratio[c]	Floor Surface	Shading; Vegetation	Water	Function
1*	Morelos #178[d]	247	12–14	4.75	4.75	0.37	10.95	large gray stones	huge tamarind tree at center	washing sink at NE corner	'81:Single room occupancy; '96: demolished
2	Hidalgo #188	96	12	3	3.4	0.25	8.30	grass	none; several large shrubs	ctrl. fountain, standing water	'81: doctor's office '96: hotel
3*	Presidencia Municipal	296	17.3	6	6	0.35	8.22	red tile	none; pots	ctrl. fountain, standing water	city hall
4	Hidalgo #174	112	14	4.75	4.75	0.34	4.96	light gray pavers	one tall tree, several shrubs	dry fountain at center	clinic
5	Allende #116	119	13.2	5	5	0.38	4.76	red tile	none; many small pots	ctrl. fountain, standing water	residence
6 *	Degollado #133	92	8	4.5	4.5	0.56	4.54	grass	none; vines at south wall; shrubs	ctrl. fountain, moving water	residence
7	Carranza #27 (rear)	95	4–6.5	4.25	5	0.21	3.8	concrete pavers, small stones	huge mango tree, pots	none	multifamily residence
8	Madero #94[d]	108	9	5.5	5.5	0.61	3.57	concrete paver paths, soil	none; very large plants	ctrl. fountain, standing water	'81: abandoned residence '96: bank
9	Obregon #69	28	4.3	2.8	2.8	0.65	3.57	light gray concrete, soil	none; large shrub, pots	ctrl. fountain, standing water	residence
10	Medina #138[d]	72	5.5	4.5	4.5	0.82	3.56	small concrete pavers	large bougainvillea	ctrl. fountain, standing water	residence
11*	Hotel Casino[d]/ Museo	192	15.5	7.5	7.5	0.48	3.41	light gray concrete tiles	extensive bougainvillea	ctrl. fountain, standing water	'81: hotel '96: museum
12	Degollado #148	24.5	7	2.7	2.7	0.39	3.36	dark gray concrete	none; many pots, hanging	ctrl. fountain, standing water	residence
13*	16 de Septiembre #90	42	7	4	3.7	0.57	3.07	red tile, soil	huge mango tree in center, pots	none	residence
14	Ocampo at Hidalgo[d]	68	7.5	5	5	0.67	2.72	concrete pavers	large magnolia tree, vines, pots	none	'81: restaurant '96: office
15*	Zaragosa #38	83	11	5.5	5.6	0.5	2.65	light red pavers	none; extensive vines	ctrl. fountain, standing water	residence
16	Palacio de Gobierno	320	20	11	11	0.55	2.64	checkered white, red tiles	none; very few pots	none	state capitol
17	Constitucion #116[d]	86	7.4	5.8	5.8	0.78	2.56	red tile	four pine trees, pots	sunken pond with papyrus	'81: residence '96: art gallery
18	Carranza #27 (front)	51	8.5	4	4.75	0.47	2.26	light gray concrete, soil	none; many small plants	none	multifamily residence
19	Madero #93	48	8.3	7	5.5	0.84	1.59	light gray concrete	awning on s, w sides; many pots	ctrl. fountain, standing water	retail
20	Guerrero #79	20	5	3.7	3.7	0.74	1.46	red concrete	none; few pots	none	residence
21	Guerrero #35[d]	36	6.5	5	5	0.77	1.44	concrete and soil	small tree, many plants, roses	none	'81: residence '96: gallery office
22	Madero #85[d]	32	8	4.75	4.75	0.59	1.42	red tile	none; few pots	none	'81: residence '96: demolished
23	Barreda #85[d]	35	2.8	6	5	2.14	1.40	concrete	tall catalpa tree	none	'81: residence '96: retail and residence
24	Galindo #3[e]	25	2.7–3	4	4.7	1.4	1.13	light gray tile	none; pots	none (dry fountain, 1981)	'81: recreation center '96: clinic

	Location	Floor Area (m²)	Width N to S[a] (m)	Wall Height, S side (m)	Aver. Wall Height (m)	Solar Shadow Index[b]	Aspect Ratio[c]	Floor Surface	Shading; Vegetation	Water	Function
25*	5 de Mayo #36	78	12	9	9	0.75	0.96	checkered white, light green tiles	none whatever	none	'81 government office '96: abandoned
26*	27 de Septiembre #27	43	5.6	9	6.9	0.62	0.90	grass and soil	vines above on screen; shrubs	none	residence
27	Degollado #93[d]	35	6–8	5	6.25	0.71	0.90	light gray concrete	citrus tree, hanging vines	open tank at north side	'81: office '96: abandoned
28	Reforma #124[d]	42	7	7.5	7.5	1.07	0.75	smooth gray small stones	none; many pots	ctrl. fountain, standing water	'81: residence '96: abandoned
29	Barreda #77	20	3	7.5	6.6	2.5	0.46	concrete and soil	none; some vines	none	residence
30*	Tesorería[e] Quintero #93	32	5.5	9	9	0.61	0.40	gray pebbles	none; pots on upper corridor	ctrl. fountain, standing water	'81: hotel '96: city offices

Part Two: Andalucía[f], Spain

	Location	Floor Area (m²)	Width N to S[a] (m)	Wall Height, S side (m)	Aver. Wall Height (m)	Solar Shadow Index[b]	Aspect Ratio[c]	Floor Surface	Shading; Vegetation	Water	Function
31*	San Basilio #50	78.5	10	6	5.6	0.6	2.50	gray stones	none; vines, many pots	functioning deep well	meetings and conferences
32*	Anqueda #3	64.2	6.4	11.5	6.26	1.80	1.64	concrete; black & white tile	jasmine arbor ¹/₂; many pots	functioning deep well	residence
33*	Osio #4 (rear)	56	7	6.5	7.23	0.93	1.07	pebbles	opaque *toldo* ¹/₂; pots lemon trees, vines	raised pond, SE corner; deep well	restaurant
34*	San Basilio #14	35.6	5	6	6	1.2	0.99	concrete	none; many pots	none	workshop and residence
35*	Zarco #13	15.0	3.15	4.67	4.57	1.48	0.72	black & white pebbles	none; many pots	shallow bowl for turtles	residence
36*	Encarnación #12 (front)	24.5	5.1	6.2	6.2	1.22	0.64	white marble	none; many pots	ctr. fountain, standing water	retail, workshop and residence
37*	San Basilio #17	22.5	2.85	8.8	6.07	3.09	0.61	red tile	opaque *toldo*, many pots	small well E end, fountain SE crnr.	residence
38*	Osio #4 (front)	25.5	4.4	6.5	6.5	1.48	0.60	white marble	opaque *toldo*; vines, pots	none	rooming house
39*	Casa Alta, Bornos (Cádiz)	47	5.6–6	9	8.6	1.55	0.58	red brick	translucent *toldo*, small tree, vines, pots	fountain in corner, adjacent flooded patio	residence
40*	Arenillas #28	20.6	3.88	6	6	1.55	0.57	gray stones	none; vines, many pots	none	residence
41*	Armas #14	30.4	7	10.6	7.6	1.51	0.53	black & white tile	opaque *toldo*; many pots	none	residence
42*	Herrero #6 Hotel Marisa	19.4	4.5	8	7.2	1.78	0.37	black & white pebbles	none; many pots	raised pond, E arcade	retail and hotel
43*	Las Casas de la Judería, Sevilla	40.8	5.5	15	13.6	2.73	0.22	red and beige tiles	translucent *toldo*; pots	ctr. fountain, running water	hotel

* Sites where temperature measurements were taken.

[a] For diagonal orientations, N side = NW side; and S side = SE side.

[b] Solar shadow index = $\dfrac{\text{height of S wall}}{\text{width N-S of floor}}$

[c] Aspect Ratio = $\dfrac{\text{floor area}}{(\text{average wall height})^2}$ (Note: actual opening to sky is usually less than floor area, due to roof overhangs.)

[d] As encountered in 1981, altered since.

[e] As encountered in 1996, after alteration.

[f] In Córdoba unless otherwise noted.

The aspect ratio (see Figure 1.9*a*) is the overall indicator of exposure to the weather: sky, daylight, sun, and wind. Figure 7.2 graphs these 43 courtyards for their relationship between courtyard floor area and aspect ratio. In general, the smaller the courtyard's floor area, the lower the aspect ratio. The courtyards of Colima averaged a much higher aspect ratio (more sky exposure) than those of Córdoba, largely due to a prevalence of one-story buildings in Colima, while all courtyards in Córdoba had more than one story on at least one side.

FIG. 7.2
Forty-three courtyards in Mexico and Spain, comparing their floor area (shown on logarithmic scale) to their aspect ratio (as defined in Chapter 1). Each courtyard's number refers to its description in Table 7.1.

Why this greater depth of Andalusian courtyards? In Córdoba, they are concentrated in the *Casco Histórico*, a densely settled area whose buildings are hundreds of years old. Córdoba was a walled city when these buildings were born. Many have grown an additional floor (or two) over their life span. Notice that most of these courtyard floor areas (in both countries) are in the range of 20 m^2 to 80 m^2. The Mexican courtyards in this range have an average aspect ratio of about 1.5. The Andalusian courtyards in this range average about 0.8.

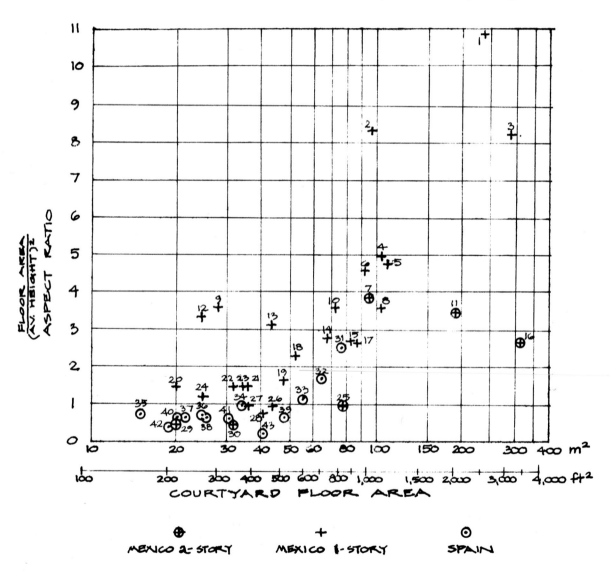

Part II: Some Particular Courtyards

Daylight

Daylight is one consequence of aspect ratio. Building interiors are usually evaluated for daylighting by their interior daylight factor (DF), where

$$DF = \frac{\text{daylight on an interior horizontal plane}}{\text{daylight on an exterior horizontal plane}}$$

Chapter 12 will show target DF for design (Table 12.1), and a graph that relates DF to aspect ratio in atrium buildings (Figure 12.11). For now, consider that a DF between 2 percent and 4 percent is adequate for most daytime tasks in residences and offices. Courtyards with light-colored walls and arches all around can expect these approximate DF in the surrounding arcades:

Aspect ratio	DF, adjacent arcades
5	4.0 percent
4	3.8 percent
3	3.5 percent
2	3.0 percent
1	2.1 percent

The rooms behind these arcades would have, of course, considerably lower DF, being farther from the courtyard. Arcades are often favored over such rooms as work spaces with adequate daylight and more contact with the weather (Figure 7.3; see also Figure 3.4).

Sun and Shade

Direct sun not only influences the DF, it provides almost all the heat gain in a courtyard. The higher the sun and hotter the weather, the more that shade should be valued. This raises questions about some of the differences between Mexican and Spanish courtyards. In summer, the Colima courtyards (at 19° north latitude) experience sun directly overhead for several hours a day, and they have higher aspect ratios (greater exposure). In Córdoba (37° north latitude), the sun is high in the summer, but *never* directly overhead. Also, they have lower aspect ratios (less exposure).

Why then are *toldos* widely used in farther-north Spain, but rarely used in Mexico? And why are relatively few courtyards in Colima (only 5 of 30) shaded by large spreading trees? Are these Mexicans, dwelling at the edge of the tropics, simply more tolerant of sun? By contrast, of the 13 courtyards in Andalucía, 6 had *toldos*, one a large pergola of jasmine, and one a grove of citrus trees alongside a *toldo*.

FIG. 7.3 OAXACA, MEXICO
The arcades around a courtyard, with ample daylight, are the preferred location for weavers at the Instituto Cultural. Colors of yarn can be compared in either the yellow-rich direct sunlight, or the blue-rich shade.

I believe that the prevalence of *toldos* in Andalucía, and their absence in Colima, has a little to do with latitude, something to do with density (one vs. two or more stories), and much to do with humidity.

Summer in Colima is hot and humid; wind is helpful for comfort, and nearly every office has a ceiling fan to provide air motion. *Toldos* discourage air flow because they block almost the whole courtyard opening, and might thus be seen as disadvantageous, despite their obvious shade. Also, a *toldo* becomes a large radiator as it intercepts the sun; in the predominantly one-story courtyards of Colima, it might be uncomfortably close overhead.

Summer in Córdoba is hot and dry; wind may carry a cargo of gritty dust. At night, air temperatures are cool and the sky is cold; by the summer dawn a courtyard is far colder in Córdoba than in Colima. A *toldo* closed just after dawn can be seen as helping to hold in coolth as it shuts out the rising sun. In the deeper Córdoba courtyards, the *toldo* floats high, and its radiant heat is thus less perceptible on the courtyard floor.

Winter Sun

In winter, direct sun is the courtyard's friend. Although aspect ratio is an indicator of sun penetration, the solar shadow index (SSI, see Figure 1.9b) is more precise, as it compares north-south floor width to the south wall's (shadow-casting) height. Figure 7.4 graphs the relationship between courtyard floor area and SSI in these 43 courtyards. In general, the smaller the courtyard's floor area, the higher the solar shadow index. Note the striking difference between Colima (whose "winter" is nearly identical to the summer of the Pacific Northwest) and Córdoba (whose winter is indeed wet and cold).

In Chapter 12, Table 12.3 shows, for a given latitude, the maximum SSI that would yield winter sun access. For now, consider that at Córdoba's 37° north latitude, for four hours of midday sun:

- Maximum SSI = 0.32 (none of these Córdoba courtyards qualify) for sun on north wall and at least 1/3 the courtyard floor.

- Maximum SSI = 0.49 (none of these Córdoba courtyards qualify) for sun on north wall only.

In the following chapters, sun-path sky charts are provided for several courtyards in Córdoba, showing exactly in which hours of which months sun can arrive at the northernmost corner of the courtyard. For all of them, direct sun is a summer, but not a winter, visitor to the courtyard floor. Ironically, of Colima's 40 courtyards, in a winter climate that suggests cooling rather than solar heating, the relationship between SSI, latitude, and courtyards is:

- Maximum SSI = 0.62 (17 of these Colima courtyards qualify) for sun on north wall and at least 1/3 of the floor:

- Maximum SSI = 0.93 (26 of these Colima courtyards qualify) for sun on north wall only.

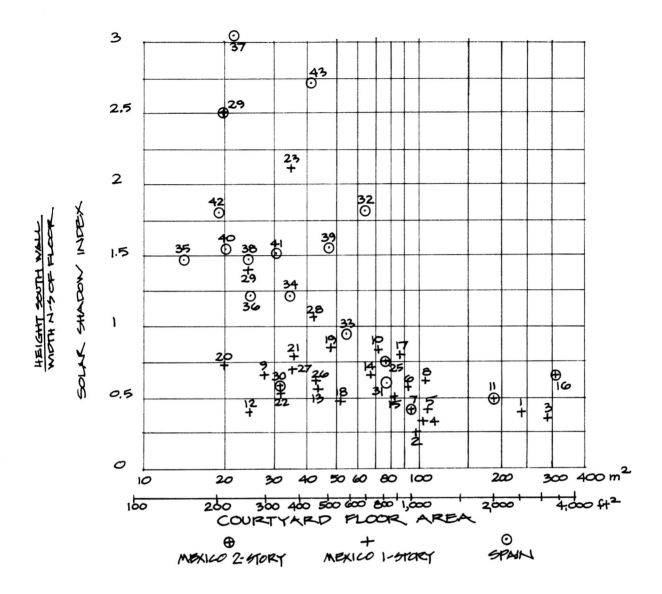

Function

How are these 43 courtyards used? Slightly more than half belong to residences. (Table 7.1) About one-quarter of the courtyard buildings appear to have originally been residences but now serve another function. This leaves about one-quarter that were built to serve some function other than residence.

In the following chapters, particular combinations of courtyards will illustrate the importance of the aspect ratio, shading, evaporation, "thermal sailing," and adaptability of courtyards and their surrounding buildings to the many changes forced on them as cities grow and neighborhoods change.

FIG. 7.4

Forty-three courtyards in Mexico and Spain, comparing their floor area (shown on logarithmic scale) to their solar shadow index or SSI (as defined in Chapter 1). Each courtyard's number refers to its description in Table 7.1.

CHAPTER **8**

In the dense pattern of urban settlement a courtyard enhances the quality of life. It provides an open-air room of an intimate character and serves as the nucleus of the house; in summer it is an extra room to live in, in winter it is a link between man and nature, bringing the changing seasons into the heart of the house. Those living there are protected from noise, overlooking and wind.

Werner Blaser
Atrium: Five Thousand Years of Open Courtyards

Variations in Proportions

Compared to a deep courtyard, a shallow courtyard admits more sun in both summer and winter, admits more wind, and radiates more easily to a cold night sky. Without intervention by either plants or inhabitants, the shallow courtyard in a hot dry climate will be harder to cool on a summer day, but probably warmer on a winter day. As urban density increases, buildings grow higher, and so the depth of typical courtyards increases. These trends are complementary, because with increasing density the urban heat makes summer cooling more of an issue, while diminishing the need for winter heat. But the floor of a deep courtyard will still be cold on a sunny winter day, while comfortably cool on a summer day. The deeper courtyard will also be darker, with varying cultural significance. To the northern temperate-climate dweller, dim daylight is often a sign of deprivation of the sun's warmth. To the hot dry climate-dweller, dim daylight more often signifies welcome coolth.

Three Andalusian Courtyards

These residential courtyards of varying depth experienced quite different temperatures on a series of hot August days, as shown in Figure 8.1. Temperatures, light level and relative humidity were recorded with "Hobo" data loggers made by the Onset Computer Corporation. The three homes are within 1,200 meters of one another in the old *Casco Histórico* of Córdoba. Only the deepest courtyard was shaded by a *toldo*. The *toldo* depressed this courtyard's midday temperature even further.

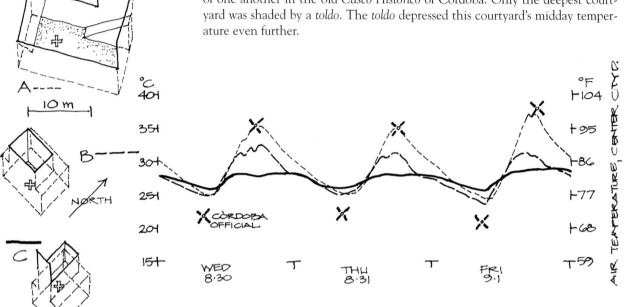

FIG. 8.1 SHALLOW, DEEP, AND DEEPER COURTYARDS Graph shows the daily temperature range of three courtyards during Córdoba's hot weather (August–September). Courtyard A is the most shallow, with highest temperatures nearly identical to those at Córdoba's airport. Courtyard B is considerably deeper; its highest temperatures are almost within the comfort zone even in this hot weather. Courtyard C is deepest, and in addition shaded by a *toldo*.

These three courtyards are shown in Figures 8.2 through 8.9. Courtyard A, #32 in Table 7.1, is the most shallow (aspect ratio 1.64), and sits near the northeast edge of Córdoba's *Casco Histórico* on Calle Anqueda. Courtyard B, #40 in Table 7.1, is considerably deeper (aspect ratio 0.57), and is near the eastern edge of the *Casco Histórico* on Calle Arenillas. Courtyard C, #41 in Table 7.1, is a bit deeper (aspect ratio 0.53), but more long and narrow, and was shaded each day by a *toldo*. It is closer to the center of the *Casco Histórico*, near the Corredera, on Calle Armas. These were monitored simultaneously to allow a direct comparison in early September 1995.

Courtyard A in Figures 8.1 and 8.2 is wide and shallow. Perhaps because the sky exposure was excessive, a trellis of wisteria and jasmine sits along one side of the space. There is a second story along two sides (northeast and northwest). A central well, about 6 meters deep, is used extensively for watering the many plants (Figure 8.3). Two stairs climb along the northwest side: one to the second story rooms, the other to a small roof terrace with clotheslines. There is a distinct separation between the rooms and the courtyard, with little evidence of activity in what limited arcade exists (along the southeast side). The rooms behind this small arcade are used for storage, including paintings by an artist who maintains a studio in the front room off the *zaguán*. The floor of the courtyard, once exposed pebbles, is now covered with a thin layer of smooth concrete. Observing the elderly women who live here walking with canes, perhaps this was done to make the floor less dangerous.

FIG. 8.2 COURTYARD A
The shallow (aspect ratio 1.64) courtyard,
on Calle Anqueda, with a working well,
and a pergola covered in jasmine.
Looking north toward *zaguán*.

FIG. 8.3 COURTYARD A
Looking down toward the well at watering time. Shallow wells (this one about
6 meters deep) serve as sources of
irrigation in this section of Córdoba.
(Plan, Figure 8.8.)

FIG. 8.4 COURTYARD B
The deeper (aspect ratio 0.57) courtyard,
on Calle Arenillas, seen from the inner
arch of the *zaguán*. (Plan, Figure 8.8.)

The temperature measurements were taken at the neck of the statue that sits beside the well; the sensors were usually shaded by the statue. This statue, flanked by lilies, fills the narrow view from the street through the *zaguán*.

Courtyard B in Figures 8.1 and 8.4 is slightly elongated east-west, and two stories all around. The *zaguán* leads to the west arcade of the courtyard, a rather unusual less-direct entry. There are arcades on the east, north, and west sides. There is no well in this courtyard. The stair sits within the building, entered abruptly from the courtyard through an opening in the south wall. The north arcade is a pleasant extension of the living room; the other two arcades (east and west) have no doors or windows to any rooms behind them.

Part II: Some Particular Courtyards

The temperatures were taken on a small palm tree in the center of the court-yard that shaded the sensors.

The residents of this courtyard home work about 50 meters away in a very small neighborhood grocery store (Figure 8.5). During the day they return often along the very narrow street to enjoy their courtyard.

FIG. 8.5
The owners of courtyard B, in their small neighborhood store within 50 meters of their home.

Courtyard C in Figures 8.1 and 8.6 is elongated north-south, with two stories on three sides and three stories on the south. Access to the sun is therefore very restricted, even without using the *toldo*. There is no well in this courtyard. The second floor overhangs the ground floor on the longer (east and west) sides. The stair climbs behind the north side. All four second-floor sides have wood-frame openable windows with small panes (Figure 8.7), an unusual and appealing feature. This courtyard is the house's center of activity; a small dog is the guardian, a sewing machine sits below the east overhang, and a grandson's motorcycle is sometimes parked alongside it.

The temperatures were taken on a small palm tree near the middle of the court-yard but toward the east, the sensors shaded by the depth of the courtyard.

FIG. 8.6 COURTYARD C
The deepest (aspect ratio 0.53)
courtyard, on Calle Armas. When
the opaque *toldo* is closed, very little
daylight is available to the spaces around
the courtyard. (Plan, Figure 8.8.)

How influential is the aspect ratio on a courtyard's temperatures? Comparing these three courtyards in Figure 8.1, it is evident that the temperature at the statue in the center of shallow courtyard A almost matched the official Córdoba outdoor daily high temperatures both in quantity and time of arrival. Here, the aspect ratio of 1.64 yielded little modification of daily highs; however, the daily lows were several Celsius degrees above the Córboba official lows, and they arrived a bit later in the courtyard than at the official (airport) station.

Courtyards B and C have almost identical aspect ratios (0.57 and 0.53), but very different maximum temperatures; minimum temperatures were somewhat more similar. This can be attributed partly to their quite different orientations, as we saw in the elongated courtyard study in Figure 1.6. In this case, the east-west

Part II: Some Particular Courtyards

elongated courtyard resembles B, and the north-south elongated courtyard (resembling C) has an added advantage of a third floor "penthouse" on its south side, shading the courtyard even more. The *toldo* in C further reduces the daily maximum.

For these three courtyards then, aspect ratio alone would be an inadequate predictor of center courtyard temperatures.

Temperatures were also recorded in a room adjacent to each courtyard (Figure 8.8). Over this stretch of hot weather, the storeroom adjacent to courtyard A experienced the greatest temperature variation, from 26°–31° C (78°–87° F). This is due partly to the shallow adjacent courtyard, but even more to the roof directly overhead. The other two courtyards' adjacent rooms were protected by an upper story. Yet the temperature difference between these three rooms was slight; at the most, when Córdoba was officially 38° C (101° F), the difference between the rooms adjacent to courtyards A and C was only about 4 C° (about 7 F°). Given the differences at the courtyard centers, and the one- vs. two-story conditions, this difference is surprisingly small. At night, these rooms' temperatures were almost identical.

FIG. 8.7 COURTYARD C
The glazed windows all around the upper floor are quite unusual, and this horizontal band probably makes this courtyard seem less deep. These windows simplify watering of the many adjacent potted plants.

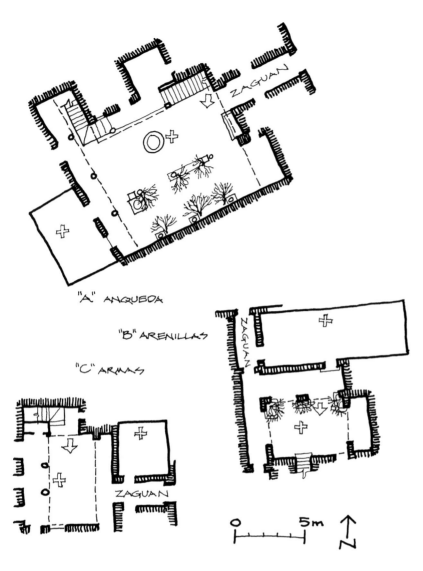

"A" ANQUEDA

"B" ARENILLAS

"C" ARMAS

ZAGUAN

0   5m

N

FIG. 8.8 PLANS OF THE THREE CÓRDOBA COURTYARDS
Temperatures were monitored in a room adjacent to each courtyard (marked by cross). (Temperatures at courtyard center, also marked by a cross, were shown in Figure 8.1.) The greatest variation (as shown in the graph), adjacent to courtyard A, is due in part to a roof directly overhead. Rooms adjacent to courtyards B and C, both sheltered by rooms above, maintained a range between 26° and 30° C (78° and 86° F) while Cordoba's official range was between 21° and 38° C (69° and 101° F).

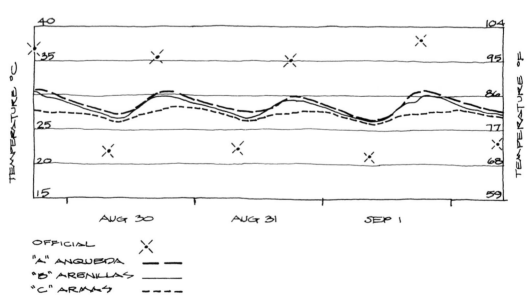

OFFICIAL   X
"A" ANQUEDA   — —
"B" ARENILLAS   ——
"C" ARMAS   ----

In Córdoba's Winter

In Figure 8.9, ground-floor access to direct sun at eye level in each courtyard's northernmost corner is shown for hours of the day, by month. In these sun-path sky charts, the total annual hours of solar access in Courtyard A is about 780; Courtyard B about 580; and Courtyard C about 300. But this is sun from cool March through warm September; the dearth of sun in cold winter is evident.

Courtyard A could expect winter sun to enter easily over the single-story southeast and southwest sides. However, a higher building farther southeast compromises this solar access; as a result it has a high solar shadow index (SSI) of 1.8, indicating deep and prolonged winter shadows. This courtyard does get a few hours of afternoon sun in February and October. The sunniest corner of this courtyard is at the point where one enters the courtyard from the *zaguán*. Thus the view from the street is marked by a sharp contrast between the shadows of the *zaguán* and the sun backlighting the flowers clustered around the well. This provides a most appealing glimpse. But there is no arcade to take advantage of winter sun; instead a stair with flowerpots inherits this winter warmth.

Courtyard B has a lower SSI of 1.55, indicating more winter sun than the previous courtyard with SSI of 1.8. But instead it gets fewer total hours of winter sun. In this case, the aspect ratio was a somewhat better measure of winter sun exposure, because the high walls on all four sides cut off early and late sun in winter. This courtyard is elongated east-west, so that the entire north side (facing south) gets the best sun, not just one corner. The living room sits north of this sunniest of arcades, and is strongly connected to it, so that people are invited out into the sun while sheltered from cold sky exposure. The *zaguán* opens into this arcade at its corner with the west arcade. The rooms above this sunny arcade, of course, have even better access to winter sun.

Courtyard C is the real paradox: an even lower SSI of 0.51, yet the fewest annual hours of sun. The misleadingly low SSI is due to this courtyard's elongation north-south; even though the south wall is very high, the north-south floor dimension is very large. It does get sun a few days earlier than courtyard B in March, and a few days later in September, but for only about one hour around noon. On a February day, I found the two elderly women residents wrapped in blankets while watching TV in a dark room off the courtyard's southwest corner.

These three courtyards show the difficulty of relying on a convenient single-number factor (SSI) to evaluate winter sun exposure. The more complicated but far more revealing sun-path sky chart tells a richer, truer story. These courtyards also show the inherent conflict between density of settlement and access to winter sun.

FIG. 8.9 Sun-path sky charts for the three Córdoba courtyards The measurements were taken at seated eye level (about one meter above floor) in each courtyard's northernmost corner (shown by the arrow on the plans in Figure 8.8). Note the absence of winter sun, even in the most shallow courtyard.

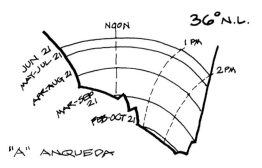

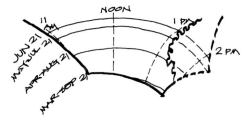

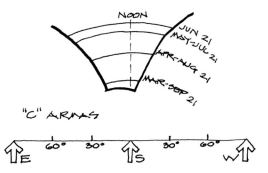

FIG. 8.10 COLIMA'S PRESIDENCIA
MUNICIPAL (CITY HALL).
(a) Looking toward the street; *zaguán*
is at left edge of the photo. (b) One of
four very similar arcades surrounding this
wide and shallow courtyard. The *zaguán*
arch is seen at center left.

Two Colima Courtyards

And now, moving from Spain to Mexico, an extreme contrast in proportion. Just one block from the central plaza, and facing one another across Colima's main east-west street, two civic buildings have very different courtyards. The Presidencia Municipal (City Hall) is a one-story building with a wide and sunny courtyard; see #3 in Table 7.1. With a high aspect ratio of 8.22 and a floor area of 296 m², this courtyard is indeed exceptionally shallow, as seen in Figure 8.10. In contrast, the Tesorería (Figure 8.11) is a remodeled two-story hotel, with the deepest of my observed Colima courtyards; see #30 in Table 7.1. With a low aspect ratio of 0.40 and floor area of only 32 m², it resembles a typical courtyard of Córdoba more than one of Colima. Both courtyards have a central fountain, and plants only in pots.

FIG. 8.11 COLIMA'S TESORERÍA
The building was formerly a hotel for the indigent elderly (as can be seen in Figure 11.8). (a) The small, deep courtyard with its new octagonal fountain. (b) Citizens wait in line (lower left) while two University of Colima architecture students take vertical measurements.

Looking first at winter in Colima, Figure 8.12 compares the "official" early January temperatures with those at the center of the City Hall's wide patio (the sensor was tied within a rosebush next to the fountain) and those near the floor of the shaded patio of the Tesorería (sensor was tied to a rubber plant). The sheltered deep patio maintains temperatures in the comfort zone, while the exposed sunny patio swings from chilly (down to the official low, about 15° C [59° F]) to very hot (just above 35° C [95° F]). This is well above the official high, because the rosebush and its sensor were in direct sun.

The winter sun is much higher in the Colima sky than in Córdoba. In summer, it passes directly overhead. The sun-path sky charts are plotted for these two courtyards, as seen from a seated position in the northernmost corner of each courtyard (Figure 8.13). The sun paths for May–July 21 and June 21 are omitted, as they pass overhead and to the north at this latitude, and thus are not accommodated by this solar format.

What about comfort in the offices surrounding these courtyards? During these January days, the ground-floor offices facing onto these two patios maintained a very even, comfortable temperature range of 23°–25° C (73°–77° F; see Figure 8.14). Both offices are entered directly from an arcade, and neither has any other exterior opening. An upper-floor office in the Tesorería is entered indirectly from the arcade, and the occupant leaves a window (facing west over rooftops) open 24 hours a day (Figure 8.14). This office experienced a range of 19°–25° C (66°–77° F), somewhat chilly in mid-morning, but otherwise within the comfort zone, and more than amply supplied with outdoor air!

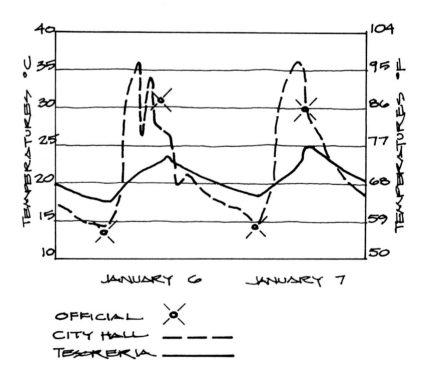

FIG. 8.12 EARLY JANUARY TEMPERATURES IN THESE COLIMA COURTYARDS
Official temperatures are from the University of Colima, about 1 km distant. The exposed sensor in the City Hall's wide courtyard reached the official lows, and (in full sun) exceeded the official highs. The sensor in the deep Tesorería courtyard stayed within the comfort zone.

Part II: Some Particular Courtyards

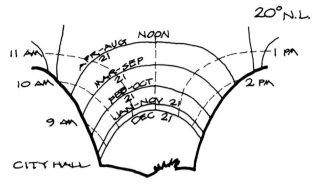

FIG. 8.13 SUN-PATH SKY CHARTS FOR THE COLIMA COURTYARDS
Measurements taken from the northern corners, at seated eye level. At this tropical location (20° north latitude), the summer sun passes overhead and north of the observer, so June 21 and May–July 21 lines are not shown. The full exposure (large aspect ratio) of the City Hall courtyard is very evident in this chart.

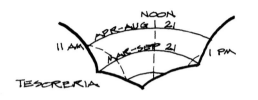

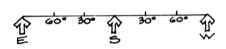

b

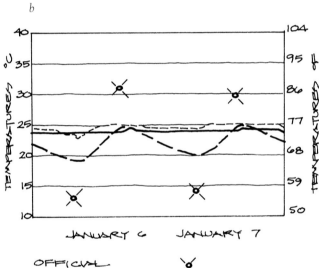

OFFICIAL ⊗
CITY HALL OFFICE – – – –
TESORERIA 1ST FL OFF. ———
TESORERIA 2ND FL OFF. — — —

FIG. 8.14 PLAN OF THE COLIMA COURTYARDS AND ADJACENT OFFICES
(*a*) Crosses indicate temperature measuring sensor locations. (*b*) Early January temperatures in three Colima offices, all adjacent to the arcade on the northwest side of either the City Hall or Tesorería courtyards. The offices on the ground floor, with openings only to the arcade, range from 22° to 25° C (72° to 77° F), with the ground-floor office in the Tesorería maintaining slightly lower temperatures. The upstairs office, with a window kept open, ranged from 19° to 25° C (66° to 77°F).

a

FIG. 8.15 THE THREE COLIMA OFFICES

(a) The upper-floor office in the Tesorería. The secretary points to the location of the sensor, in the bookcase. The large open window was never closed during my periods of observation. (b) The ground-floor office in the Tesorería. Note the portable fan and the high ceiling. (c) The office in the City Hall. Note the ceiling fan. Doorway to arcade on the left faces southeast, with plentiful sun at time of this photograph. Yet this office maintained slightly lower June temperatures than the more interior ground-floor office in the Tesorería. (d) Early June temperatures in the offices. The offices on the ground floor, with openings only to the arcade, range from 28° to 32° C (82° to 90° F). The upstairs office, with a window kept open, ranged from 27° to 33° C (81° to 91°F).

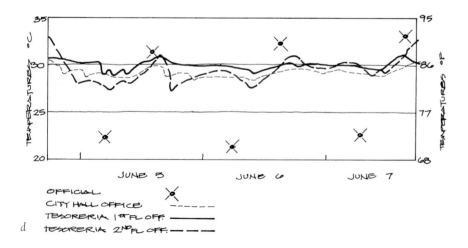

Colima in Summer

Early June in Colima is hotter and more humid than in January. Figure 8.15 shows that the same ground-floor offices maintained an early June range of 28°–31° C (82°–88° F), comfortable if fans provide air motion (both offices had fans; indeed most offices in Colima had them). The upper-floor office, still with its window open much of the time, swung from 27° by night to 33° C in late afternoon (81°–91° F). In North America, this late afternoon heat would arrive about as we were leaving for the day; in Colima, it arrives as one returns from siesta. But the open window provides air motion (given at least some breeze) as well as outdoor air, along with that heat.

Despite these near-comfortable conditions, an occasional air conditioner can be found. My June visit was enlivened by watching workers respond to a problem created by a small air conditioner that serves a ground-floor office on the west arcade of the Tesorería. This air conditioning unit sits in a small opening above the office door (Figure 8.16). On humid days, it removes enough moisture (condensed from the air it cools) to produce a small stream of water, directed down the wall by a small copper pipe, then allowed to trickle across the arcade floor toward the fountain.

Was this a problem? For a city concerned with lawsuits from people slipping on the wet floor, yes. After all, this is the tax office—not likely to improve the mood of its visitors. For many days each month, a long line waits in these shaded arcades. (The air conditioner makes the arcade hotter, as it pumps the heat from the enclosed office, adding the heat of its fan and compressor—another argument for passive cooling strategies.)

The solution: remove a rather wide strip of arcade floor tile and slab, continue the copper drainpipe below the arcade floor out to flow over the recessed courtyard floor to the fountain, and patch the arcade floor back again. Not pretty, but dry.

FIG. 8.16

A simple unit air conditioner sits in its opening above an office door in a lower-floor arcade of the Tesorería. Note the excavation in the arcade floor, soon to receive a pipe to carry condensate from this air conditioner safely below the arcade floor.

CHAPTER 9

The Arab wants to secure his house against the desert on the outside, opening parts of the inside of the house to the sky, such as courtyards which give relief to the inner rooms. This courtyard space gives the inhabitants a sense of ease and calm, and the feeling that they have their own piece of sky to use and protect them. The calmness provided by this courtyard is a fact that can be felt by anyone entering an Arab house. To an Arab this courtyard is more than an architectural element, because in his subconscious it is a global symbol springing from his innermost emotions. Its four corners carry the sky which covers the courtyard. That is why he symbolizes it as a fountain in the middle of the courtyard, shaped like the drafted cross-section of a dome.

Hassan Fathy
"What Is a City?" (In Fathy and Steele 1988)

Variations in Shading

These three Andalusian courtyards were chosen because two of them were so similar in all respects except for the *toldo*. The third, somewhat larger courtyard is shaded half by a *toldo* and half by citrus trees. The three courtyards are within 50 meters of each other, shown in Figure 9.1. There are also differences in the way water is used, and differing opportunities for cross ventilation. In Table 7.1, these are courtyards #33, 36, and 38. These were monitored simultaneously to allow a direct comparison in late August 1995.

FIG. 9.1
Plan of a neighborhood near the famous mosque of Córdoba, whose Court of the Orange Trees begins in the lower left corner. Three courtyards, Encarnación #12, and two at Osio #4, were monitored simultaneously so as to compare their relative success in maintaining cool microclimates. Note the huge variety of courtyard sizes and orientations; some are little more than light wells. (From the *Plano del Casco Histórico*, Geréncia Urbanismo de Córdoba.)

Encarnación #12

This courtyard (# 36 in Table 7.1), shown in Figure 9.2, is two stories deep, with an aspect ratio of 0.64. Its function is almost entirely decorative, although it provides passage for a small number of people living behind it, and brings light and air to the leather workroom on its southwest side. The busy retail leather shop on the opposite (northeast) side is air-conditioned and visually closed off from the courtyard; it is entered from the *zaguán*, so the many shoppers upon entering get a glimpse, but usually not a walk, through this courtyard. The *zaguán* opens onto an extremely narrow one-lane street (the rearview mirrors of passing cars are a distinct danger to anyone on the narrow sidewalk). A corner of Córdoba's huge mosque is a few steps away.

There is an open passageway, more or less aligned with the *zaguán*, leading from the front courtyard to a rear courtyard of similar design; an interior stair to the second floor begins off this passage, but is not visible from either courtyard. The front courtyard has a few large potted plants, but no significant shading. There is a small fountain in the center with standing water, but I never in many visits saw water flowing, so evaporation is limited. The floor is white marble, again limiting evaporation.

Temperatures representing the center of this courtyard were taken at the statue in the shallow niche near the southwest corner, rather than on the central fountain (Figure 9.3), because the water in this fountain posed too great a threat to the sensors.

FIG. 9.2
Courtyard at Calle Encarnación #12, serving a leather retail store and workroom, and residences. The front courtyard, as seen from the *zaguán*, looking northwest to the rear courtyard.

FIG. 9.3
Axonometric section through the *zaguán*
at Encarnación #12 front courtyard.
Points A and B are locations of temperature sensors. (Reprinted with permission
from Reynolds and Lowry 1996.)

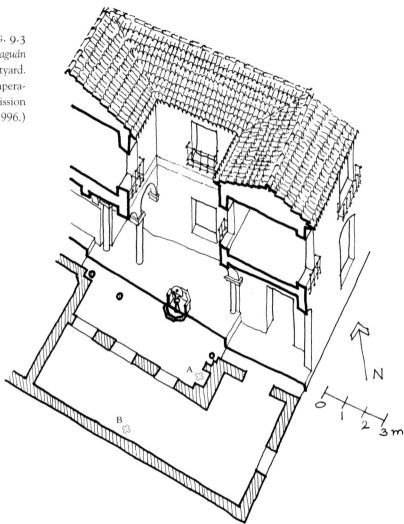

Osio #4, Front and Rear

The two courtyards at Osio #4 are in the same building, and shown in Figure
9.4. The front courtyard (Figure 9.4a, Figure 9.5) is quite similar in size (aspect
ratio 0.60), appearance, and limited function to Encarnación #12, except for
several key differences:

- there is an opaque dark-green *toldo*,

- there is no standing water,

- there are a few narrow-canopy trees that stop short of the *toldo*, and

- the *zaguán* opens to a long-range view down a very narrow street toward the
  Guadalquivir River (neighborhood map, Figure 9.1).

Instead of a fountain at the center, there is a small potted palm. Temperatures
were taken within this central small tree's foliage (Figure 9.5). As at
Encarnación #12, the floor is white marble. Two rooms open onto the courtyard,
both rented as bedrooms by students. The arcade on the northwest side (from
which the photo in Figure 9.5 was taken) separates the two courtyards, and contains a small table that seems rarely used.

Fig. 9.4
Courtyards at Calle Osio #4, the Taberna Santa Clara (Restaurant). (*a*) View from the *zaguán*, looking through both courtyards. Ropes for the front courtyard's *toldo* are tied to the gate. (*b*) The rear courtyard, looking back toward the *zaguán*. Here also, *toldo* ropes are visible.

Fig. 9.5
The front courtyard at Osio #4. The small palm in the center contains the sensors. The exterior wooden door at the street is closed, so the *zaguán* is dark.

Also as at Encarnación #12, an interior stair to the second floor begins off this arcade, at the point where it connects the two courtyards. The rear courtyard is extensively used as restaurant seating space. All customers of the restaurant, however, enter through an interior passage rather than through this arcade.

The rear courtyard, seen in Figures 9.4(b), 9.6, and 9.7, is larger in floor area than the front courtyard, and has a third story along two of its sides. It has a much higher aspect ratio of 1.07, thus is more exposed to the sky. There is a dark-green opaque *toldo* over about half of the opening above the second story; the other half of the opening is shaded by citrus (orange and lemon) trees that rise to the level of the *toldo* (Figure 9.7). Because the *toldo* does not cover the entire courtyard, there is increased opportunity for ventilation; wind along the Calle Osio can thus enter through the *zaguán*, pass through the first *toldo*-covered courtyard and arcade, and exit up through the citrus trees.

FIG. 9.6
The rear courtyard at Osio #4. The *toldo* is folded in the open position against the upper wall. A porous clay water jug, kept cool by evaporation, hangs above the well. The chair in the northern corner was the place from which this courtyard's sun-path sky chart (Figure 9.12) was plotted. (See also Figure 6.2.)

FIG. 9.7
View over rooftops at the Osio rear courtyard, showing the *toldo* (folded open) to the right, citrus trees to the left. The tower at Córdoba's mosque rises beyond at left.

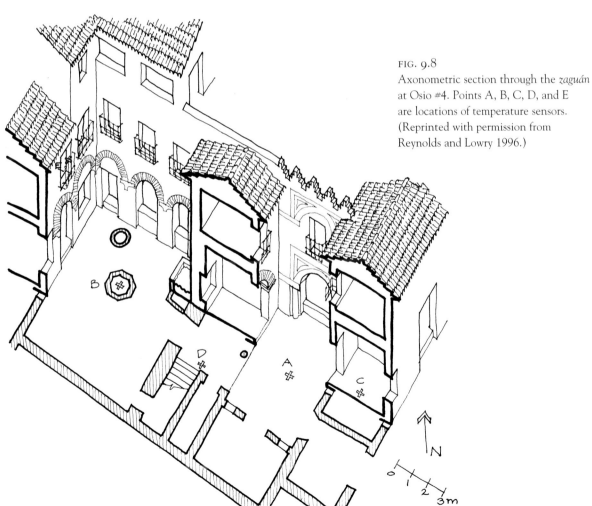

FIG. 9.8
Axonometric section through the *zaguán* at Osio #4. Points A, B, C, D, and E are locations of temperature sensors. (Reprinted with permission from Reynolds and Lowry 1996.)

Unlike the previous two courtyards, this one is periodically filled with people who remain for some time; there are eight tables with chairs where lunch and dinner is served, causing temporary heat gain within the courtyard. There is a dry fountain basin with a small potted fig tree in the center (seen in Figure 6.2). Center-of-courtyard temperatures were taken within this tree's foliage. There is an 18-meter deep, narrow well (without water) near the north corner (Figure 9.6). A raised pond of concrete in the east corner is home to a small school of goldfish; a thin stream of water runs constantly into this pond, and consequently the pond constantly seeps out onto a short stretch of the uneven pebble floor, increasing evaporation. Temperatures in both courtyards were taken at the points shown in Figure 9.8.

The *toldos* in both these courtyards are operated daily by the landlord and restaurant chef, Giovanni Miceli Baglioletti, a Sicilian transplanted to Córdoba. The ropes for the toldos are fairly prominent in the photographs. Giovanni makes a lovely ritual of these openings and closings, pulling on the ropes with great sweeping tugs, then elaborately knotting the gathered ropes before hanging them on either the gates or hooks, or tying them around a column. I sense the *toldos* are his personal friends, even though a few years ago he fell from the rear courtyard's roof while tending to that courtyard's *toldo*. A table broke his fall (and a few ribs), a better alternative perhaps than falling to that pebbly floor.

Comparing the Three Courtyards

The air temperatures at or near the center of these three courtyards over a period of several August days are shown in Figure 9.9. For Encarnación #12, the sensor was just behind a stone statue in a shallow niche in the southwest wall, at about standing eye level (point A in Figure 9.3); no sun reached this section of the courtyard. For the courtyards at Osio #4, the sensors were tied to the branches of the small trees at the center, at about chest height for an adult (points A and B in Figure 9.8).

The sensor in (unshaded) Encarnación #12 was the warmest of the three. I attribute this to several factors, including the absence of a *toldo*, less regular use of water for the plants, less sky exposure for the sensor, and proximity to the statue's thermal mass. It is also evident to what degree these courtyards maintained average temperatures below the average official high temperatures (taken at the airport), and maintained low temperatures above the official lows.

To better understand how thermally comfortable these three courtyards are, Figure 9.10 shows the range of air temperatures with relative humidities for the very hot day of Sunday, August 27, 1995; the official Córdoba temperatures were a high of 39.4°C (103°F), and low of 19.6°C (67.3°F). The limited water in Encarnación #12 clearly led to drier, hotter conditions here than in the other two courtyards. The larger, rear courtyard of Osio #4 maintained cooler, moister conditions—despite its considerably higher aspect ratio. For this we can thank the *toldo*, full-grown citrus trees, presence of running water, and more absorbent floor.

Appendix A uses this rear courtyard to explore the relative influences of evaporation and transpiration.

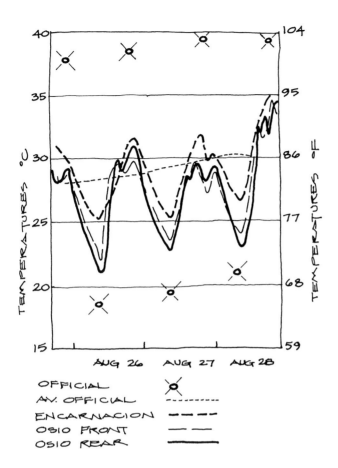

Fig. 9.9
Air temperatures in three courtyards.
The sensor in Encarnación #12 (point A in
Figure 9.3) was just behind a stone statue in a
southwest wall niche, about three meters from
the courtyard center. In both Osio front
(point A, Figure 9.8) and Osio rear (point B,
Figure 9.8), the sensors were tied to the
branches of the small potted trees in the center of each courtyard. Official (airport) maxima and minima are shown as points at the
time of their occurrence; the average of these
official temperatures is shown as a dotted line.

FIG. 9.10
Ranges of air temperature and relative humidity
in the three courtyards on a hot day. (Courtyard
#3: Encarnación; Courtyard #2: Osio front;
Courtyard #1: Osio rear.) The sensors were in
the locations described in Figure 9.8. The day is
Sunday August 27, 1995; the official Córdoba
temperatures were a high of 39.4°C (103°F) and
low of 19.6°C (67.3°F). The average official
temperature was 29.5°C (85.1 °F), shown (coincident with the official mean relative humidity)
as a circled point on the graph. (Graph is based
on Milne and Givoni 1979. See Figure 5.11 for
details. Reprinted with permission from
Reynolds and Lowry 1996.)

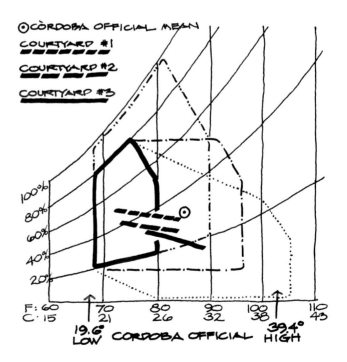

Spaces Around the Courtyards

The highest air temperature of any ground-floor space adjacent to these three courtyards was, for about one hour, 30°C = 86°F. This occurred in the leather workroom (point B in Figure 9.3), adjacent to the warmest courtyard. The sensor was on a head-high shelf; the room contained fluorescent lights that were constantly on, and it was used for moderate manual labor. Here the workers wore no shirts.

The coolest room was the unoccupied ground-floor bedroom (point C in Figure 9.8; its blue door is behind the column in Figure 9.5) off the Osio #4 front courtyard. This room stayed below 27°C (80 °F) for most of this time period. Figure 9.11 compares this bedroom's temperatures with those near the bottom of the stair between the front and rear courtyards (point D in Figure 9.8), and with those just outside an upstairs window (point E in Figure 9.8; the sensor, tied to the railing, is visible at the upper center of Figure 6.2) at the northwest side of the rear courtyard. Even though thoroughly shaded by citrus tree leaves, as well as the dark-green opaque (but therefore quite warm) *toldo*, the upstairs window sensor maintained much higher daytime temperatures than any ground floor location in all three courtyards. This recalls another strategy for coping with hot dry climates: seasonal migration (see Chapter 2). If it's too hot upstairs, move downstairs.

In Tunisia, for example, the traditional two-story house encloses a central courtyard with colonnades along all sides. In the summer when the sun is high, the colonnade creates a deep shade. The family spends the day in the interior rooms of the first floor where the thermal mass of the building best protects them from the sun's heat. At night they move out onto the open roof, which quickly loses its heat to the clear night sky. In the wintertime the pattern is reversed. The family members spend their days on the roof and the upper loggia where the winter sun can still reach to warm them. At night they retreat to the rooms of the upper story, whose walls have retained some of the heat from the day's sun, where they can take advantage of any heat rising from below.

Lisa Heschong
Thermal Delight in Architecture

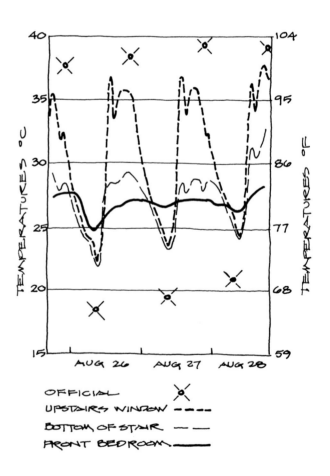

FIG. 9.11
Air temperatures around, between, and above the two Osio #4 courtyards. Compare the stable temperatures in the ground-floor front bedroom (point C, Figure 9.8) off the Osio front courtyard, with the varying temperatures near the bottom of stair (point D, Figure 9.8) between the two courtyards, and the widely varying temperatures at the Osio rear courtyard's south-facing second floor window (point E, Figure 9.8), even though shaded by citrus trees and the *toldo*. Official (airport) maxima and minima are shown as points at the time of their occurrence.

Winter and Summer Contrasts

What about these courtyards in winter? Is the coolest summer courtyard necessarily the coldest and least sunny one in winter? Figure 9.12 compares the "skyline" as seen from a seated position in the north (most sunny) corner of each of these three courtyards. These skyline configurations show that neither Encarnación #12 (SSI = 1.22) nor Osio #4 front (SSI = 1.48) receives any direct sun from October to February. Their ground-floor rooms can expect no solar heating in winter. Osio #4 rear, while it is slightly cooler in summer, has a skyline that permits entry of some direct sun even in early December (SSI = 0.93). With deciduous trees in this courtyard (rather than the citrus trees that are there now) the result might be that, of these three courtyards, the coolest in summer would have the most sun in winter. It promises the best performance in both seasons.

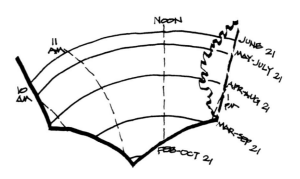

I had the opportunity to more closely observe this rear courtyard in winter. I lived for one week in early February in a room on the upper floor, looking southeast into the lemon trees. The window was very small, while the ceiling, walls, and floor were of massive construction. Even with its upper-floor thermal advantage, I found the room very cold. When I dared occupy it for anything other than sleep, I tried to warm it with a small portable electric resistance heater provided by the owner. It was quite overpowered by the unrelentingly cold surface temperatures. The coping strategies that worked were hot showers, warm food, and heavy blankets.

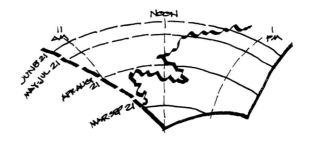

FIG. 9.12
Sun-path sky charts for the three courtyards. Córdoba is near 36° north latitude. The skyline is charted from a seated position (about one meter above floor) in the north corner of each courtyard. The lines that show the apparent path of the sun, when solid, indicate that the sun can be seen from the north corner; when dashed, the sun is filtered through vegetation (potted plants, vines, or trees). (Reprinted with permission from Reynolds and Lowry 1996.)

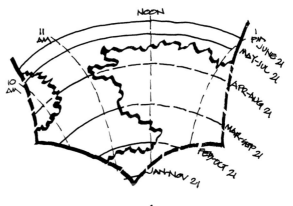

CHAPTER 10

The face of all the world is changed in rhythm. We may stand and watch as natural alterna-tions of time and the seasons transform a scene, or we may join directly in the repeated actions of people as they respond to the changes around them. In either case, whether we stand and watch, or ourselves move with the ebb and flow, there is an impression of recur-ring boundaries in space. We traditionally adjust our dwellings to nature's rhythms in ways that change our understanding of space.

Ralph L. Knowles and Karen M. Kensek
"Interstitium: A Zoning Strategy for Seasonally Adaptive Architecture"

Thermal Sailing

This chapter looks at combined shading, watering, and night ventilation in one Andalusian courtyard building. The cycles of temperature and relative humidity at the center of this courtyard floor reveal a pattern of "thermal sailing," where skillful manipulations of shading, evaporative cooling, radiation, and night ventilation result in indoor comfort, despite the very high outdoor daily temperatures.

A thermally massive, ancient courtyard house called the Casa Alta in Bornos (Cádiz) Spain was monitored for 25 days in summer 1995 (Figure 10.1). Data for light, relative humidity and air temperature were recorded near the floor's center in the 3-story-deep courtyard. Temperatures were also recorded in one ground-floor and one second-floor room adjacent to the courtyard, and on the roof terrace. Architect Victor Carrasco, the owner, kept a daily record of his actions of shading (with a *toldo*), watering the courtyard's absorbent floor, and opening windows for night ventilation.

This chapter is based on a study by Carrasco and Reynolds (1996).

FIG. 10.1
(a) The courtyard of the Casa Alta in Bornos (Cádiz) Spain.
(b) Looking out over the walled garden in the rear.

Casa Alta began centuries ago as part of the Islamic fortifications of this small town southeast of Seville. The courtyard has both a direct (Hispanic) and an indirect (Islamic) entrance from the street (Figure 10.2). Architect Victor Carrasco found the building in ruins, and his restoration included three outdoor spaces. The main courtyard (# 39 in Table 7.1) has an absorbent brick floor, a small fountain in one corner, and a small tree in the center, as well as abundant vines. This tree is planted directly over the ancient opening to an underground cistern. The courtyard has a white translucent *toldo*, an aspect ratio of 0.58, and an SSI of 1.55 (very little winter sun at noon).

The second, smaller courtyard is adjacent, with an open window between the two courtyards. This smaller one has in its center a moon lemon tree, notable

for simultaneously bearing buds, blossoms, and fruit. The tree is surrounded by a shallow pool into which ripe lemons fall, harmlessly. Some evaporation from this surface helps cool the area during hot dry summer days.

The third open space is a large walled garden, several meters lower than the courtyards. It is separated from them by a salon and its terrace. The garden features plants chosen for their fragrance, and has a long narrow lap pool along the north side.

The building around the main courtyard has 80-cm-thick walls made of irregular boulders compacted with Roman cement (tapial). The interior and exterior wall surfaces are built up of hundreds of layers of whitewash, which interferes somewhat with thermal storage and transfer.

Architect Victor Carrasco explains:

> From the beginning of the design, I worked with all three heat sinks in a local, traditional manner. The Sky: by using a toldo that shades the house during the day but cools it at night by allowing heat to be radiated to outer space. The Air: with high ceilings, cross-ventilation at night, pools and fountains, plants and trees, and evaporative cooling practices; the entire building is kept tightly shut during the day and completely open at night. Also, the house is very open both horizontally and vertically to allow even minute temperature differentials within the house to create small air movements that will extend the upper edge of the comfort zone. The Earth: very thick walls, and partially bermed rooms. In the lower living room, a partially buried room overlooking the garden, it can be 25°–26° C in the afternoon when the outside (pergola) temperature is 38°–40°C.
>
> Various devices help in keeping the temperatures within the comfort zone, such as whitewashing for maximum insulation and reflection of heat, vine-covered pergolas and awnings as shading devices Also, the sound of trickling water echoing through the house from the fountains and pools in the garden and patios is a great psychological help in fighting heat. There are two pools and three fountains in the house. The only concession to active systems is a very low-tech method for heating the pool to extend the swimming season to May and October: a little pump and a few hundred yards of black pipe on the roof. (Carrasco and Reynolds 1996.)

The monitoring was accomplished with six Onset data loggers with four sensors that measured air temperature, one for relative humidity, one for daylight. The time interval between measurements was about 36 minutes, and none of the data gathered was read until after the monitoring period.

In the center of the courtyard, the small tree provided a mounting site (point A, Figure 10.2) for three sensors, one for air temperature, one for relative humidity, and one for light. Temperatures (only) were also measured in a ground-floor room adjacent to the courtyard on the west (point B, Figure 10.2), with windows of translucent glass facing the courtyard. Another sensor was immediately above in the second-floor salon (point C, Figure 10.2). This room has windows facing both the street and the courtyard, of transparent glass, equipped with slatted roller blinds. The final sensor was on the railing of the roof terrace (point D, Figure 10.2) where it was exposed to full sun when the toldo was opened, and shaded when it was closed.

The sensors were installed on July 17, 1995, during a stretch of unusually hot and dry weather. Luckily, southern Spain's highest temperatures of the twentieth century were recorded during the first week of monitoring. Here, we examine the period July 22 through July 28. Figure 10.3 shows the high and low temperatures beginning July 17, recorded at an agricultural research station at Campo de Villamartin, about 8 km (and visible) from Bornos. High and low temperatures in the center of the courtyard are also shown. Note that the courtyard's highs were often equal to those at the weather station, but the courtyard lows were usually not quite as low. A brief period of direct sun on the courtyard sensor may be responsible for the highest readings. (The sun-path sky chart for this courtyard is shown in Figure 12.15, where it is compared to several other Andalusian courtyards.)

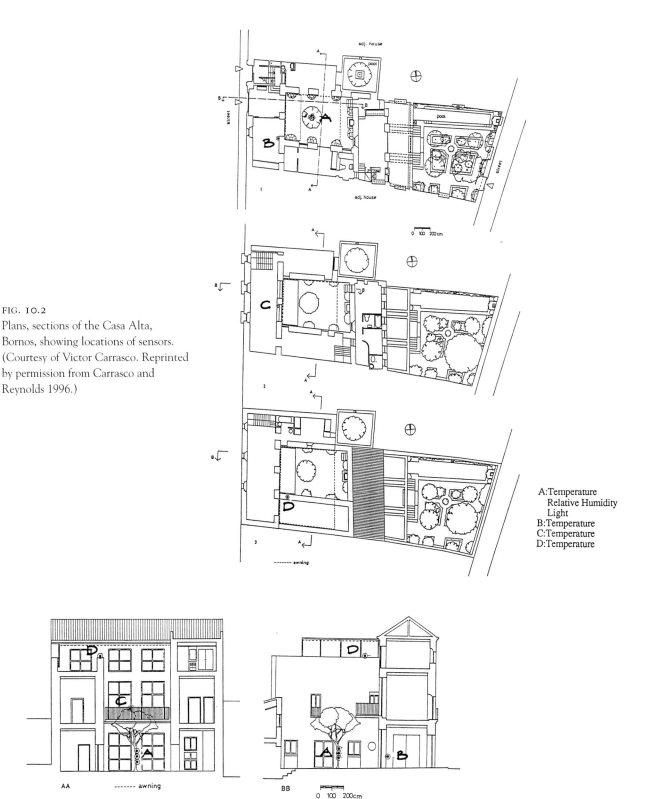

FIG. 10.2

Plans, sections of the Casa Alta,
Bornos, showing locations of sensors.
(Courtesy of Victor Carrasco. Reprinted
by permission from Carrasco and
Reynolds 1996.)

A:Temperature
  Relative Humidity
  Light
B:Temperature
C:Temperature
D:Temperature

SECTIONS

The Casa Alta in Bornos (Cádiz) Spain.

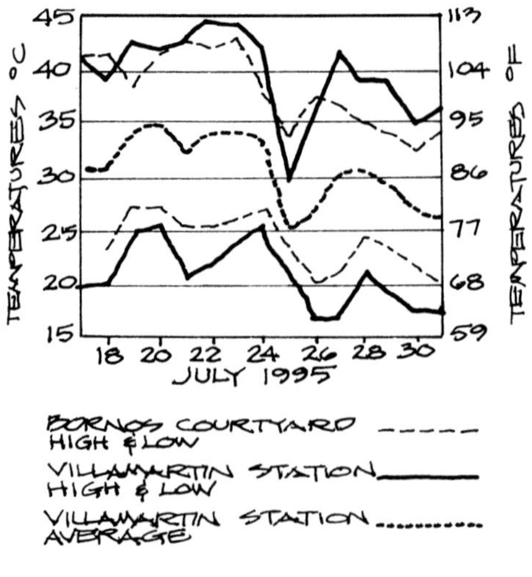

FIG. 10.3
Comparing the temperatures for July 1995 at Campo de Villamartin weather station, and in center of courtyard floor.

Shading

This courtyard relies upon a movable horizontal white translucent canvas cover, or *toldo*, for shading. There are vines along some walls and a small tree in the center of the courtyard, but the *toldo* is the primary shading device. It sits quite high above the courtyard floor, about 2 meters above the third-floor terrace. Thus considerable morning sun can still enter the courtyard below the closed *toldo* (section BB in Figure 10.2). Also, warm air can easily escape below the *toldo*.

In its open position the *toldo* is folded against the south wall. It cannot be safely unfurled in times of high wind, it reduces the solar energy available to plants in the courtyard, it becomes a radiant heater by day and interferes with outgoing radiation by night—but it also shades. Is the *toldo*, then, a net benefit or not? Here, the lower terrace temperatures while shaded indicate a benefit. In addition, Victor Carrasco considers the *toldo* a benefit to courtyard plants, because it provides ample filtered light without the direct heat of the sun on the leaves.

A *toldo*'s translucence was discussed in Chapter 5. The difference in daylight between a translucent and opaque *toldo*, as seen from the center of the courtyard below, is shown in Figure 10.4. This Bornos courtyard (# 39 in Table 7.1) is compared to a somewhat deeper one in Córdoba (#41 in Table 7.1), measured about a month later, with a nearly opaque *toldo*. Thus it is not the quantity of light, but the pattern of its arrival, that matters here. Because the Bornos courtyard's cover is translucent, there is virtually no evident impact on the quantity of daylight when the *toldo* is opened or closed. But the Córdoba courtyard's opaque *toldo* greatly changes the quantity of daylight both when it is closed and opened.

As typically applied, the *toldo* nearly fills the sky opening, interfering with ventilation. In this courtyard, however, the height of the translucent *toldo* allows considerable ventilation, with a vertical opening of about 5 meters above the east wall, and about 2 meters above the south terrace rail (sections AA and BB, Figure 10.2).

Part II: Some Particular Courtyards

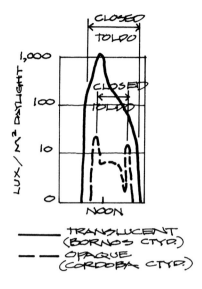

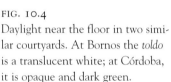

FIG. 10.4
Daylight near the floor in two similar courtyards. At Bornos the *toldo* is a translucent white; at Córdoba, it is opaque and dark green.

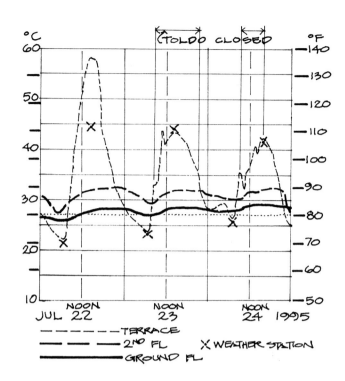

Since any *toldo* will be more reflective of sound than is the open sky, it amplifies the psychological cooling of the sound of trickling water.

Figure 10.5 compares the temperatures of two enclosed and mechanically unconditioned rooms with that of the roof terrace, in the very hot, dry July 22–24 period. Maximum and minimum weather station temperatures are also shown. The ground-floor room nudges the top of the comfort zone (shown as a dotted line at roughly 27°C, 80°F). The second-floor room runs about 3 to 4 C° warmer, but with minimal added air motion (such as from a small fan), comfort is within reach. (The contrast between the second floor room's temperatures and those outside is so great that the room is, in fact, perceived as quite comfortable.) The extreme high temperatures of the roof terrace, particularly on July 22 when the *toldo* was open due to high wind, are in part due to direct sun on the sensor. We are seeing "sol-air," rather than simply air, temperatures. When the toldo is closed, the terrace high temperature is almost identical to that at the weather station. The low temperatures of the terrace and the weather station are consistently almost identical. The impact of the opening and closing of the *toldo* is much more evident in the temperature sensor than it was with the lighting sensor shown in Figure 10.4.

Water

One of the most appealing characteristics of this courtyard building is that there is the sound of running water throughout. Several very small fountains can generate a great deal of sound in a highly reverberant space. A trickling stream of water in the courtyard corner permeates the adjacent spaces (Figure 10.6).

FIG. 10.5
Temperature comparisons, July 22–24, 1995. (Reprinted by permission from Carrasco and Reynolds 1996.)

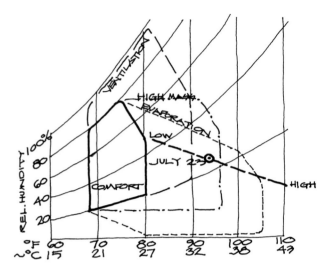

FIG. 10.7
Temperature and relative humidity at
the center of the courtyard floor: July 23, 1995. Circle
indicates the median daily temperature and relative
humidity at Villamartin weather station. The early
morning low is almost within the comfort zone; the
afternoon high very far from it! (Graph is based on
Milne and Givoni 1979; see Figure 5.11 for details.)

FIG. 10.6
In the corner fountain, a very small
stream of water generates a surprisingly
strong sound in the quiet courtyard.
The moon lemon tree is visible through
a window between courtyards.

The courtyard floor is made of absorbent brick set in porous mortar. A layer of
earth is between the brick floor and an ancient cistern. This floor is capable of
absorbing water, splashed on it during watering of the plants in the courtyard.
Water is also deliberately sprayed for cooling, sometimes several times daily.
The porous floor slowly releases the water, providing continuing evaporative
cooling.

The combination of temperature and relative humidity at the center of the
courtyard floor is shown for the low-to-high period of July 23. Figure 10.7 shows
the difficulty of maintaining comfort in extremely high temperatures; July 23
conditions at the courtyard center were above the comfort zone for almost all of
the hours of the day.

(OPPOSITE) FIG. 10.8
In the lower walled garden, a lap pool
offers immediate cooling in hot but
fragrant surroundings. The *toldo* can be
seen above the courtyard in the distance.

Maybe the best way to celebrate water's coolth is just to jump in. In the rear
walled garden, Victor Carrasco has installed a lap pool that starts at the rear garden wall and ends in a small grotto below the mid-level salon (Figure 10.8). A
small bench on either side of this grotto provides a cave-like retreat on the
hottest of days.

Night Ventilation of Thermal Mass

Figure 10.9 again compares the temperatures of the two rooms (salon and ground floor) with those of the roof terrace and the weather station in the cooling-down July 25–28 period. Both rooms show a quick recovery from the record-high temperatures. The ground-floor room continues to maintain a comfortable temperature, now about 2 C° below that of the second-floor salon. For most of the period noon July 25 and noon July 28, the salon was within the comfort zone, whose upper edge (about 27°C) is shown as a dotted line on the chart.

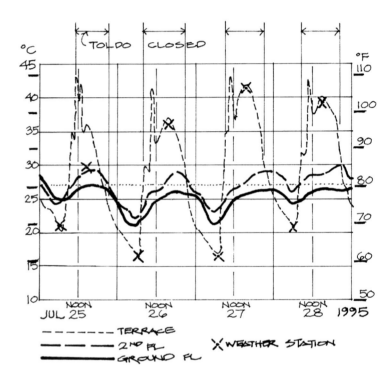

FIG. 10.9
Temperature comparisons, July 25–28, 1995. (Reprinted by permission from Carrasco and Reynolds 1996.)

The impact of night ventilation on the second-floor salon is shown in Figure 10.10. This cooling strategy depends upon someone opening the windows of enclosed rooms in the cool evening and closing them as the next day begins to warm. On July 25 and 26, note that the windows were opened just as the falling outdoor temperatures enabled cooling to begin. But on July 27, the owners drove to Seville for a late dinner, and the windows were left closed until 1:00 AM. The room had less opportunity to cool, and consequently the salon became quite warm the afternoon of July 28.

The role of the inhabitant in the traditional courtyard building thus involves three thermal-sailing activities: operating the *toldo* (or awnings at individual windows), watering the patio plants and surfaces, and opening windows by night and closing them by day.

To some extent, the hotter the exterior, the higher the interior temperature can be while still feeling comfortable. The more often someone passes between inside and outside, the more frequently one is reminded that it is cooler inside. This "relative" comfort can be aided by psychological effects such as the sound and sight of running water or leaves rustling in a breeze. Further, the very actions of thermal sailing reinforce a sense of being in control of one's comfort, with a heightened probability of satisfaction with the results.

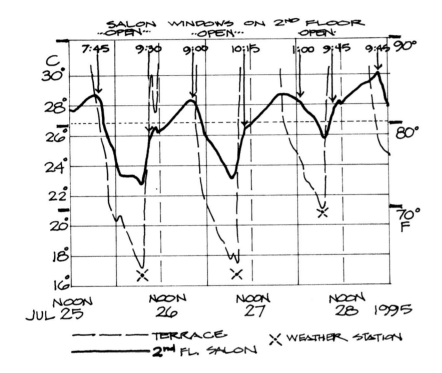

Victor Carrasco's notes:

July 25: *Toldo* drawn (closed) at noon, pulled back at 10 PM;

courtyard watered at 10:10 PM;

two windows left open by guests until 4 PM

July 26: *Toldo* drawn at 7:30 AM; pulled back at 9:45 PM;

courtyard watered at 10:10 PM;

top terrace watered at 10 PM

July 27: *Toldo* drawn at 10 AM; pulled back between 8 and 9 PM;

courtyard watered at 8 PM;

July 28: *Toldo* drawn at 9 AM; pulled back at 8:30 PM;

top terrace watered at 8:35 PM

FIG. 10.10
Temperature comparisons showing the impact of night ventilation, July 25–28, 1995. (Reprinted by permission from Carrasco and Reynolds 1996.)

CHAPTER 11

The former palace of the Marquis de Casalduero, historic residence of the Urbino de la Calle

family, had not escaped the surrounding wreckage. Dr. Juvenal Urbino discovered this with a

broken heart when he entered the house through the gloomy portico and saw the dusty

fountain in the interior garden and the wild brambles in the flower beds where iguana wan-

dered, and he realized that many marble flagstones were missing and others were broken on

the huge stairway with its copper railings that led to the principal rooms.

Gabriel García Márquez
Love in the Time of Cholera

Changes Over Time

Courtyards and their surrounding buildings will generally change over time. This is especially true with heavily used buildings in densely settled neighborhoods, sometimes undergoing a change in socio-economic status. Here are some examples of changes in a span of less than one generation.

Thanks to support from the Graham Foundation for Advanced Studies in the Fine Arts, and another sabbatical leave, I was able to return to Colima, Mexico in early January 1996, after an absence of fourteen years. I returned again in June 1996, for a look at hot and humid conditions.

I measured and photographed thirty courtyards in 1981–82 (listed in Part One of Table 7.1). Of these, two have been demolished, and several others have been covered to various degrees with various structures that block much of the daylight, making gloomy that light that does get through. Others have lost the large trees that gave them special character and protection; still others have had most of the larger plants removed, leaving an empty bowl. One-third of these courtyards still enjoy their collection of plants and activities, and two are now better cared for than before. But the overall score is: declined, 18; sustained or improved, 12.

The change over time falls into these categories (numbers of courtyards in parentheses): demolished (2); completely covered over (2); partially covered (3); open but stripped of major vegetation (6); neglected (5); sustained (10); and improved (2). One courtyard in each category is shown here, with the locations of six remaining shown in Figure 11.1.

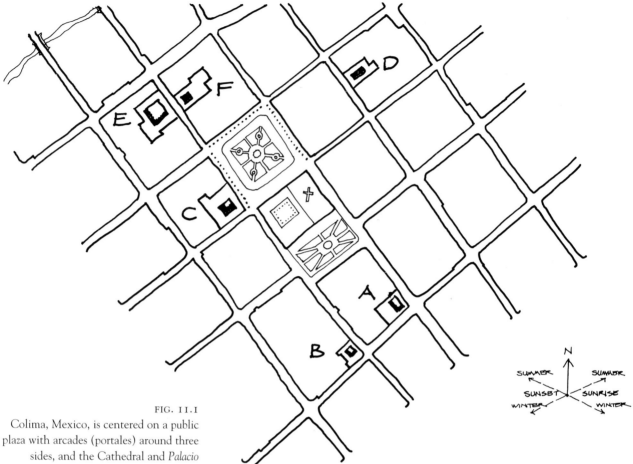

FIG. 11.1

Colima, Mexico, is centered on a public plaza with arcades (portales) around three sides, and the Cathedral and *Palacio Gubierno* (capitol of the state of Colima) on the fourth side. Buildings discussed in this chapter include:

A. Madero 94
B. Ocampo at Hidalgo
C. Portal Morelos
D. Cinco de Mayo 36
E. Presidencia Municipal
F. Tesorería

Demolished or Disappeared

At Morelos 178, four blocks southeast of the central plaza, stood a one-story rooming house for street-cart food vendors, the last such *mesón* in Colima (Figure 11.2; courtyard #1 in Table 7.1). The inhabitants were among Colima's least wealthy. The rooms were tiny and almost lightless; a red tile roof and massive whitewashed walls enclosed them. The *corredor* on each side of the courtyard was supported by crudely painted columns made from tree-trunks. This courtyard had the highest aspect ratio of them all: 10.95. Perhaps in response to such exposure, a huge tamarind tree spread in the courtyard center, casting shade over almost the entire space, and supporting at least one hammock. The courtyard floor was uneven with large rounded stones, and sloped gently away from the street. Piles of coconut husks from one of the street vendors mounted slowly under the tamarind; an open stone sink in one corner served for washing clothes.

This entire rooming house is now a parking lot and conference center for the new Hotel America; the huge tamarind is gone, although small newly planted trees dot the parking lot. There are two quite sanitized new courtyards within the four-story Hotel America. One has a decorative cart filled with flowers; the ghost of a vendor's cart?

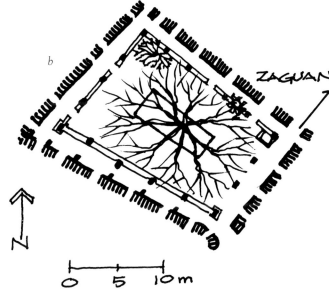

ZAGUAN

N

0   5   10 m

FIG. 11.2
(a) A single-room occupancy for street vendors at Calle Morelos 178, as photographed in 1982.
(b) Plan, in 1982 condition. This building was demolished to make room for a parking lot.

Covered

On the main street, at Calle Madero 94, was the former home of a wealthy family (Figure 11.3; courtyard #8 in Table 7.1). Perhaps because the widening of Calle Madero had eaten half the width of the front rooms and *zaguán* along with its colonial facade, the house had fallen into disuse when I saw it in 1981; all was covered in dust. With an area of 108 m^2 and an aspect ratio of 3.57, the remarkably cool courtyard was filled with mature shrubs and small trees, with a small raised fountain in the center, and a beautiful set of iron gates opened onto the *zaguán*, then to the main street. The family members showed me old photos of garden parties under pergolas, hanging with vines, on the roof.

The building is now a bank. The remodeling removed nearly all traces of past richness, leaving only the columns, arches, and iron gates. Even these gates cannot easily be seen from the street because exterior doors of dark glass obscure the view of the lobby. These beautiful gates appear to have been imported from

FIG. 11.3

(a) A prestigious family had abandoned this old residence on busy Calle Madero, (A on map) but a kind of dusty beauty lingered in 1982. (b) Plan, in 1982; note the absence of front rooms resulting from an earlier widening of Calle Madero. (c) The former courtyard is now the lobby of the Banco Unión, an interior space scarcely aware of the sky.

some other building to impart character to this space. This lobby (former court-yard) is covered by a grid of bubble skylights, now visibly coated with grime because they in turn sit just under a mostly opaque metal roof for sun protec-tion, thus cannot be cleaned from above. This achieves an interior impression both dirty and dark.

The stone columns are now covered with stucco and painted white with accents of teal blue (the bank's official color). This interior reminds me of cake frosting, both in color and nutritional value. The building is fully air conditioned; the machinery inhabits the former garden on the roof. Many more people now use this building than was the case when it was a wealthy family's residence. But the courtyard, tamed and painted, is horribly disfigured.

Partially Covered

This example again demonstrates the axiom "a building expands to fill the space available." Roofs added within the patio are typically of the cheapest construction. The former Leonardo's Restaurant, at the corner of Ocampo and Hidalgo, is now the office of an educational advocacy group (Figure 11.4; courtyard #14 in Table 7.1). The courtyard had a multitrunk, large-leafed mag-nolia tree in one corner that sheltered the courtyard and the roofs around it, so high that it gave the building's silhouette a memorable softness from either street. With an aspect ratio of 2.72 plus this spreading tree, Leonardo's was a refuge from the daytime heat.

No sign of the tree remains. That corner of the courtyard is now covered by an opaque shed roof that has been added to two sides of the courtyard, with glar-ing strips of chartreuse translucent fiberglass. The crude stone fountain in the courtyard's far corner now sits revealed, dry, and empty; Leonardo's had merci-fully nearly covered it with potted plants. This courtyard used to seem wonder-fully cool and refreshing. Now desks and files fill the arcades, with almost no potted plants. It is a depressing setting for educational advocacy.

Open but Stripped

The courtyard of the Hotel Casino (Figure 11.5; courtyard #11 in Table 7.1), in the Portal Morelos on Colima's main plaza, was framed with abundant bougainvillea, and graced by a multitiered fountain in the center. Downstairs, stone columns and arches were softened by the flowering vines. Upstairs, sim-ple columns supported beams in a very open colonnade. The aspect ratio of 3.41 seemed less exposed because of the thickness of the bougainvillea.

The University of Colima bought the building for a museum and gallery, stripped all the bougainvillea, moved the fountain to a small side courtyard where it sits self-consciously large, and made the upper floor's open colon-nade into a wall with punched windows. The formal architecture has improved, as the courtyard facades have been unified with a window above each arch in a two-story field of yellow stucco. But this is architecture at the expense of landscape. Two small trees have been planted in corners and pot-ted palms sit within the arches; but the soul seems to have departed with the bougainvillea and fountain.

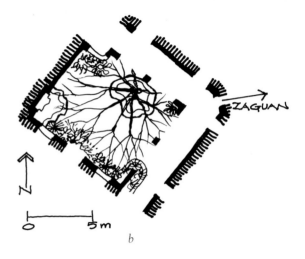

b

FIG. 11.4

(*a*) At Calle Ocampo and Calle Hidalgo, Leonardo's Restaurant (B on map) was organized around a shady courtyard in 1982. (*b*) Plan, in 1982; note the unusual corner entrance to building and courtyard. (*c*) CONAFE (Consejo Nacional de Fomento Educativo), an educational advocacy group, subsequently removed the tree and encroached on the courtyard.

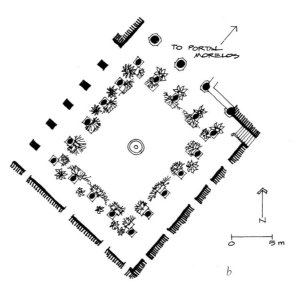

FIG. 11.5

(*a*) At the end of the Portal Morelos nearest the state capitol (C on map), the Hotel Casino featured abundant bougainvillea and a central fountain in 1982.
(*b*) Plan, in 1982 condition. (*c*) By 1996, the building was converted to the Museo Regional de Historia, with a major shift in the ambiance of the courtyard.

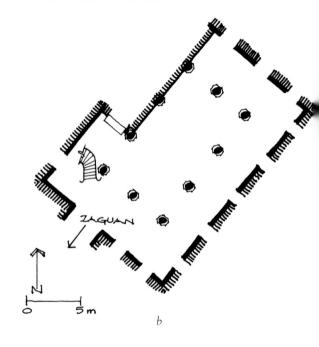

FIG. 11.6
(a) An older structure on Calle Cinco de Mayo
(D on map) served government offices in 1982.
(b) Plan, in 1982. (c) In 1996, abandoned and
for sale, its future looked bleak.

Neglected

One of the most successfully cool courtyards that I measured in 1981 was in a two-story building just north of the central plaza at Cinco de Mayo 36 (Figure 11.6; courtyard #25 in Table 7.1). Its low aspect ratio of 0.96 contributed to this coolth. Surrounded by the offices of the Colima state health department, this was one of only two courtyards that had no plants whatever. It was also rumored to be haunted.

It is now shuttered, with a sign offering sale or rent. The building appears to be in good structural shape, but cheap partitions chop up many of the arcades, and piles of bat dung have formed under each light fixture. A few straggling plants have pushed through the courtyard floor. The owner, hoping to attract a commercial tenant, suggests that cars might be parked in the courtyard. The intricate iron gates would have to be removed for a car to pass the *zaguán*. It may be thus tortured before its impending death.

Sustained

Half a block from the central plaza, the Presidencia Municipal, or City Hall, looks about as it did in 1981 (Figure 11.7; courtyard #3 in Table 7.1). Now rosebushes occupy the pots around the fountain, and there are more dense collections of large potted plants in each corner. None of the offices around this very wide (aspect ratio 8.22), unshaded courtyard are air-conditioned, so each has at least one ceiling fan. There is a hallway toward a rear door that offers a path for breeze from the front entry through to the back of the building. The four arcades are filled with light.

Fig. 11.7
Colima's Presidencia Municipal (City Hall) courtyard (E on map); described in detail in Chapter 8 (Figure 8.10). Only superficial changes were apparent from 1982 to 1996. (For courtyard plan, see Figure 8.14.)

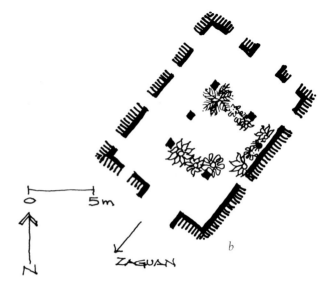

Fig. 11.8 Across the street from City Hall, in 1982 the (*a*) Hotel Regis's deep and shaded courtyard (F on map) was the coolest I encountered. (*b*) Plan, in 1982. (*c*) By 1996 it had gained a fountain, an expanded upper floor, and a new function, the Tesorería of Colima (described in detail in Chapter 8, Figure 8.11).

Improved

A deep and small courtyard with the lowest of the Colima aspect ratios (0.40) belonged to the Hotel Regis (Figure 11.8; courtyard #30 in Table 7.1). Formerly it held a small population of indigent elderly, who sat just inside the arcade, their backs to the rather bare but cool courtyard, looking south through the *zaguán* at the activity on the street.

It now belongs to the city of Colima, and is used as the Tesorería, an annex to the City Hall across the street. It has been expanded upstairs (now two stories all around the courtyard), and quite a few citizens line the arcades in the morning waiting to transact official business. A yellow tile octagonal fountain has been added, and although rather crude and heavy in this small courtyard, it at least provides a central focus where there was none before. A substantial breeze moves through both levels of this courtyard, helped by open hallways leading to another courtyard farther back on the site.

When so few new ones are being built, it is sad to lose courtyards rich with plants and past activity. But the adaptability of the courtyard building form is very evident in these thirty Colima courtyards over fourteen years. Some additional examples: the courtyard in the home of a very wealthy man is now covered with a skylight; his and his neighbor's homes have become the new art gallery of the University of Colima. The neighbor's courtyard has been restored in the process, and kept open to the sky. Another former residence, converted before 1981 to a rather shabby youth recreation center with a barren courtyard (Figure 11.9), has now become a doctor's office with the arcades forming a very pleasant waiting area. Some of Colima's most appealing restaurants are in the arcades and courtyards of former residences, as was shown in Figure 6.6.

FIG. 11.9
(*a*) In 1982, this former residence was a youth social center, barren except for the ping-pong table. (*b*) By 1996, it had become a doctor's office, with the waiting room occupying the arcades. Calle Galindo, Colima, Mexico.

PART THREE

Courtyard Design

Why don't architects design buildings around courtyards any more?

In cultures where courtyards are a tradition, one reason they are vanishing is a growing individualism supplanting the collective societies that valued the courtyard: tribes, families, religious orders, parishes, guilds, and ethnic groups (Perez-de-Lama and Cabeza 1998). Another is the growing dominance of scientific thought, with a concurrent devaluing of the mythical and religious significance of the courtyard.

In North America, residential zoning regulations that prohibit building at the property line are one effective impediment to courtyards. After meeting the required front, side, and rear yard setbacks, and considering the mandated outdoor space they provide, who has space remaining for—or even needs—a courtyard?

In commercial zones where property lines and walls coincide, architects and clients tend to depreciate the commercial value of courtyards. Land values are high, and why dedicate ground-floor space to a place that gets wet in the rain and hot in the sun? If a central space in contact with the sky is built, it is usually covered with glass, air conditioned, and called an atrium.

Then there is the stigma of "nostalgic designing," scorned by critics as merely imitative, a kind of stage-set architecture having nothing to do with contemporary ideas and materials. If a new courtyard has arches in its walls, it risks this dismissive label.

This section on courtyard design is a reminder that these outdoor-but-surrounded places offer not only aesthetic benefits, but social and technical performance benefits as well. It may seem risky to offer nature entry to the heart of a building, but with those risks come the varied benefits that prompted this book. The next chapter reviews the observations of preceding chapters, condensed into 44 design guidelines. The last chapter shows contemporary proposals in which courtyards are integral to the design concept.

We begin with some newer buildings that are organized around this older design feature.

Especially in these days the desire for the atrium as a source of light is interpreted in terms of personal freedom. For example, the word for atrium in Greece (aithrius ouvranós) means 'clear sky.' In small towns and on restricted lots the rational nature of this system, and the maximum use it makes of the available space, is calculated to elicit growing interest. At the same time the arrangement of the plan affords ample scope for ingenuity of design.

Werner Blaser
Atrium: Five Thousand Years of Open Courtyards

Guidelines for Planning and Design

In Colima, Mexico, architect Gabriel de la Mora created a courtyard in the corner of a large garden (Figure 12.1a). A mature *huamúchil* tree stands within this new courtyard, in a green lawn that also surrounds a shallow pond (home to at least a dozen turtles). The architect's office adjoins two sides of the courtyard.

Also in Colima, a new home for a family who formerly lived in a colonial courtyard home in the *centro* (see Figure 11.3, and #8 in Table 7.1) has been organized around a central courtyard (Figure 12.1c). Broad arcades with the most simple arches surround the courtyard, large trees provide shade, and a small fountain flanked by ferns marks the center.

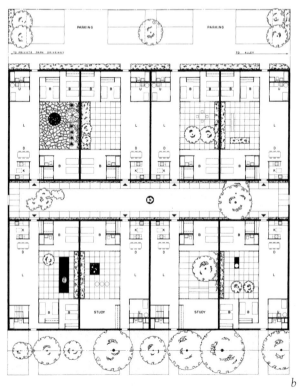

Part III: Courtyard Design

Chicago's humid summers and savage winters did not deter architect Y. C. Wong from his courtyard scheme for eight dwellings (Figure 12.1b). These are located in a downtown residential district (Madison Park), with parking off an alley. Designed in 1961 with one (remote) parking space per dwelling, each courtyard serves its house on three sides. Only two openings, each a door, penetrate each row house's exterior walls. Half these houses place the living room north of the courtyard, where it can receive winter sun.

The courtyard building has a very long history, serving (as we have seen) a very wide variety of purposes. Writing about the early twentieth century multifamily courtyard buildings in Los Angeles, Polyzoides, Sherwood, and Tice (1992) discuss building type:

> Two forms can belong to the same type but can appear and can be construed as different from each other. Therefore, a typological precedent does not necessarily lead to imitation, but can lead to transformation. It does not necessarily bring about sterile repetition of forms, but can reinforce architectural attributes shared by many buildings at an urban scale.

The previous chapters have shown a very wide variety of buildings, all of which are examples of the courtyard type, but are hardly copies of one original model. The following design guidelines for new courtyard buildings are derived from observations in Mexico and Spain.

City and Courtyard

1 **The public plaza can become an example of a courtyard on a grander scale.**

In many cities, arcades on the front facades of buildings only occur around the central plaza (Figure 12.2). Thus the presence of a plaza can be anticipated from some distance, as an open sidewalk becomes an arcade several blocks ahead.

(OPPOSITE)
FIG. 12.1
(*a*) Contemporary courtyard buildings include the office of architect Gabriel de la Mora, Colima, Mexico, designed around a mature *huamúchil* tree.
(*b*) Plan of Chicago townhouses, each organized around a courtyard. (Architect: Y. C. Wong, 1961. From Blaser 1985.)
(*c*) Residence of the Brun family in a newer section of Colima. Small side yards surround this contemporary courtyard residence. (See also Fig. 2.2)

FIG. 12.2
Early morning in the arcades around the Plaza de Armas, Cuzco, Peru. This central square acts as a huge courtyard, symbolizing the civic center.

FIG. 12.3
The Plaza Mayor, Madrid, another
huge civic courtyard, this one entirely
enclosed by buildings, and unmolested
by automobiles.

2 The more unique the value of the plaza, the more unique should be its characteristics.

Surrounding arcades, width of streets and their traffic patterns (or traffic banishment), plants within the plaza, features such as a central bandstand or fountain—all can be varied according to the relative importance of the plaza.

Some plazas are in fact courtyard forms, that is, entirely surrounded by walls (Figure 12.3). In Spain, both Madrid and Salamanca feature a *plaza mayor*, walled plazas accessible by high arched openings for pedestrians on ground level, but continuous surrounding walls and windows with a visible sloped roof above. These large outdoor spaces, safe from cars and bright with umbrella tables, become the center of civic celebrations.

3 A typical zoning regulation for courtyard-type neighborhoods is that 25% of the site must be open to the sky, whether in one large or several smaller courtyards.

For urban planners, these tightly-packed courtyard buildings promise a rather high density compared to the individual house-in-the-garden approach typical of North America. The courtyard building requires much less land per building, because it wraps its rooms around a relatively small outdoor space. This obviously leads to smaller "footprints" than a similar sized building that is surrounded by outdoor space. Yet the building surrounded by open space can reach many floors before the quality of light and access to breeze is seriously compromised on its lower floors. For one- and two-family, or one- to three-story buildings, greater densities are achieved with courtyard buildings. At higher concentrations on smaller sites, courtyards become too deep to serve effectively as a conduit to light and air. The influence of aspect ratio on daylight and on cooling is detailed in later guidelines.

In a world where no nation is wealthy enough to afford waste, the land-use efficiency of the [courtyard] urban residential pattern is worthy of emulation in terms of both land use and energy conservation. Densities of up to 81 per hectare (200 per acre) are quite possible utilizing single story dwellings.

Craig Hinrichs
"The Courtyard Housing Form as Traditional Dwelling"

4 Consider more than one courtyard to serve differing needs.

A large courtyard on a large, multifamily site brings air and light into the surrounding building just as successfully as a similarly proportioned but smaller courtyard, since their aspect ratios would be the same (Figure 12.4). The difference is social; the smaller courtyard is more personal, and within but one family's control. Therefore, where sites allow, several smaller courtyards serving individual families may be preferable to one larger but less private one. Even single-family residences can have more than one courtyard. One courtyard is often the formal, flowering one while the other is more utilitarian.

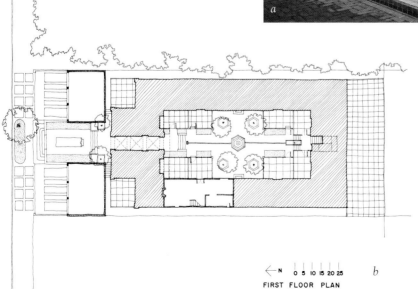

FIG. 12.4
The "Villa d'Este," a Los Angeles apartment complex. (*a*) Central fountain, with a bench against the whitewashed wall. (*b*) Plan. (From Polyzoides, Sherwood, and Tice 1992.)

N 0 5 10 15 20 25

FIRST FLOOR PLAN

b

Cars and Courtyards

5 Resolve the location of parked cars relative to the courtyard as an initial design decision.

FIG. 12.5
The narrower the street, the wider must be the garage door, to accommodate the turning radius of even a small automobile. Calle La Palma, Córdoba, Spain.

The traditional hot-dry climate courtyard-type neighborhood has very narrow streets that encourage shading of buildings by those across the street. This leaves little room for sidewalks or for parked cars. These older traditional buildings rarely provided room for vehicles of any kind with access to the street. With so many neighborhood stores and services within easy walking, who needed vehicles? Sometimes, alleys allowed horses and carriages room to park at the rear. But today's older courtyard neighborhoods are choked with parked cars, and when garages are carved into these buildings, they displace the more formal ground-floor rooms that stood between street and courtyard. Also, some streets are so narrow that the garage doors must be quite wide to provide a proper turning radius, requiring even more space from the building's ground floor (Figure 12.5). A two-car-sized garage is needed to park a single car.

Streets today are made wide by the requirements of traffic, fire-fighting equipment, and (sometimes) daylight and winter solar access. So the street width and orientation are set by considerations independent of climate, and are not usually an issue for the designer of a courtyard building. Thus the most challenging street-related issue may be storing the cars that accompany the courtyard.

6 Consider putting the carport behind or below the courtyard, rather than between courtyard and street.

Single-family residential courtyard buildings today are most likely to be built in a row-house configuration, where zoning allows common side walls. There may be access from a rear alley, but street frontage is common. Space planning suggests that the car should be stored as close to the street (or alley) as possible, so as to consume a minimum of a site. Yet, at minimum, covered (better yet indoor) parking is expected in our society, especially in harsh climates. Most residential neighborhoods mandate some setback from the street; the usual minimum would allow for a parked car in a driveway between the sidewalk and the building's front facade.

When the car enters the site from a rear alley, it does not compete with the more public rooms such as living rooms that expect a close relationship with the front yard and sidewalk. But when the car enters the site from the street, this puts a garage door very close to the sidewalk. Planners decry the "snout houses" that put a wide garage door farthest forward, dominating the street facade of contemporary suburbs. Courtyard houses fall easily into this trap; but several alternatives also develop from the courtyard building type, taking advantage of the *zaguán*.

7 The *zaguán* might serve as a carport.

One alternative is to use the *zaguán* as the carport (Figure 12.6). For a single-car family, this is fairly easy, necessitating a wide enough *zaguán* to allow comfortable passage beside the parked car. For a two-car family, it suggests a long enough *zaguán* to accommodate two car lengths, and the inconvenience of moving one car to allow another's departure. Another variation is a wider *zaguán* to accommodate side-by-side autos. This potentially exposes a great deal more of the courtyard to the sidewalk, with greater loss of privacy.

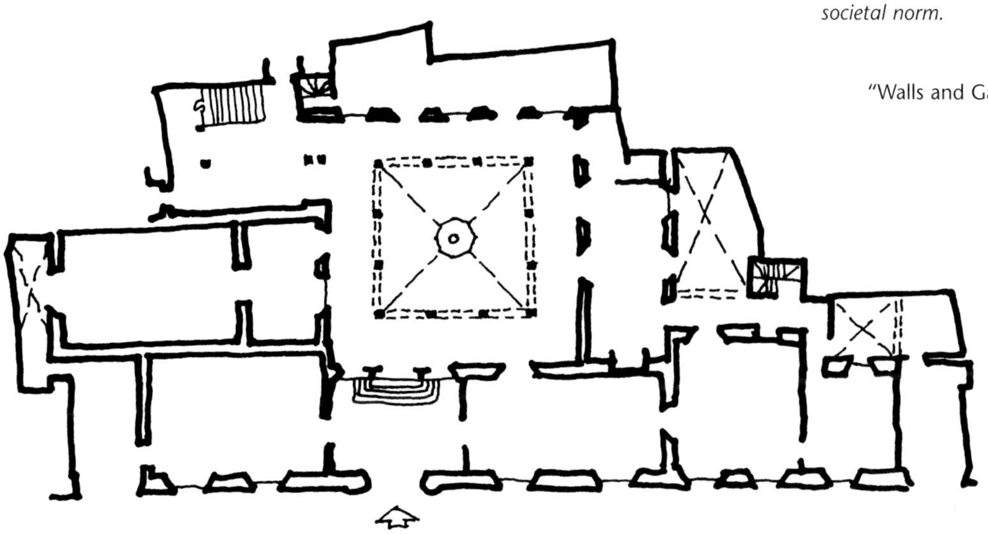

8 The *zaguán* might serve as a ramp.

Another alternative is to combine within the *zaguán* a plunging driveway to a below-grade garage, and steps (or a ramp) up to a courtyard above the garage (Figure 12.7). The garage can be large enough for several cars, and the covering courtyard might be of crude construction, allowing minor water leaks onto the cars below. The ramps might be quite steep, especially if no front yard setback is involved. The raised courtyard might not be handicapped-accessible, and there will be little or no earth below the courtyard to sustain major plants such as vines and trees. But the *zaguán* would not be excessively wide, and car storage would not unduly dominate the facade.

9 The *zaguán* might serve as a driveway.

Perhaps the saddest alternative is to use the *zaguán* as the driveway, and the courtyard as the parking area (Figure 12.8) . Yet cars and other activities can coexist in a courtyard; after all, the car may be away for most of the daytime hours. An alternative is to drive across the courtyard to a garage at the rear of the building. Either of these preserves the *zaguán* as an open passageway to the courtyard, while making a driveway of the courtyard.

In contemporary single family housing, the courtyard has been moved to the front of the house and now serves as the "car courtyard." In older neighborhood houses, entrances have been widened to accommodate the car. The gates and walls now separate the car from the street. The need for functional adaptation has come about in part from the narrowness of the streets. However, the need to protect the car as well as the family has become an accepted societal norm.

William J. Siembieda
"Walls and Gates: A Latin Perspective"

FIG. 12.6
A very wide *zaguán* might be scaled to accommodate a parked automobile, and still allow comfortable passage through to the courtyard. Palacio de Villapanés, Calle Santiago 31, Seville. (Based on Collantes de Terán Delorme and Gómez Estern 1976.)

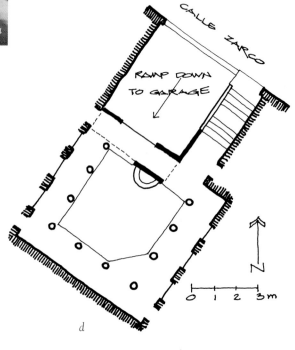

FIG. 12.7 CALLE ZARCO, CÓRDOBA.
A house rebuilt in the mid-1980s resolves the car
and the courtyard. (*a*) The one-lane street makes a
wide garage door necessary. An upward-rolled curb
keeps rainwater from flowing down the ramp.
(*b*) The very wide *zaguán* contains stairs up to the
courtyard, and a steep ramp down to the garage
below. (*c*) The courtyard over the garage, looking
toward the *zaguán*. (*d*) Plan (scale is approximate).

Courtyards and Neighborhoods

10 Keep the building in touch with life on the street.

The streets suffer when courtyard owners become discouraged about dirt and vandalism outside. Dogs litter sidewalks and stain walls; walls on narrow streets are scratched by bumpers, rearview mirrors, or other appendages on trucks and cars; dirty water from the street, and graffiti, splash across whitewashed walls. This may result in all attention turning inward, lavishing on the courtyard that share of the care that formerly went to washing off sidewalks, whitewashing exterior walls, watering and tending plants at windows. It is true that, by contrast, the less pleasant the street, the more spectacular will appear even an ordinary courtyard. Unfortunately, this can lead to a downward cycle for the streetscape.

11 Within the *zaguán,* solid doors and iron grille *rejas* are "switches" that give occupants a degree of control over privacy.

(Examples: Figures 2.6, 3.3, 9.4 and 9.5, 11.6, 12.7, 12.17)

The closer the facade to the street, the more urgent the need for switches, which in closed position should be capable of blocking sound and sight. In Chapter 3 ("Community and Privacy") the exterior wooden doors to the *zaguánes,* if closed, were cited as strong signals that the occupants are not to be disturbed. But when only the *reja* or iron grille gate is closed, it provides a view to the courtyard while barring passage. And, when these gates are left standing open, the message is "everyone's invited."

FIG. 12.8
Parked cars leave little room for any other activity in this courtyard in Carmona, Spain.

12 Where the facade can or must be set back from the street, a privacy screen can be developed within this setback.

Such a screen might include shade trees for the street and ramps down to parking or up to a courtyard. The indoor spaces at ground level that open onto the front yard/sidewalk are usually the most public spaces of the building; they are often living rooms or home offices in residences. These spaces can greatly enliven the sidewalk, especially when they can display some degree of their function to the passerby. Again, switches on all openings are crucial when the public realm passes so close to the private one.

13 The *zaguán* can be the public eye on the courtyard—and vice versa.

(Examples: Figures 1.2, 3.3, 9.2, 9.4)

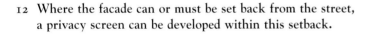

For a great number of Hispanic courtyards, the *zaguán* provides a controlled visual corridor into (usually) the center of a courtyard. This important transition space also connects the courtyard to a view of life on the street. The *zaguán* may well be as important as the fence in North American suburbia—"good *zaguánes* build good neighbors?"

Courtyards and Their Buildings

14 Make the courtyard floor initially as large as possible.

(Examples: Figures 6.1, 6.3, 11.4)

Both Chapters 6 and 11 discussed the changes over time that shape courtyard buildings. Perhaps the most obvious lesson is that a courtyard will likely be encroached on over the life of the building. Therefore, the designer might anticipate these future encroachments by "oversizing" the courtyard.

This might translate as "one large courtyard is better than two smaller ones," yet the designer needs to remember that a front "formal" courtyard is often followed by a back "working" courtyard; see Chapter 3 on degrees of formality.

15 A shallow courtyard can have deeper arcades and rooms;

16 A deeper courtyard should have shallower arcades and rooms.

If the form of the courtyard can be entirely independent of the size and shape of the site, the designer's first task is to determine its proportions: length, width, and height. This choice of deeper or more shallow is fundamental, affecting the courtyard's social role (introverted or extroverted), technical performance (deeper means cooler and darker), and aesthetics (sunny or shady).

The choice of deep or shallow proportions also affects the arcades and rooms around the courtyard. The less daylight at the courtyard floor, the less penetration of daylight is possible within these adjacent spaces.

17 The rooms that face the courtyard ideally are wider along the courtyard than they are deep.

A typical proportion is three times as wide as the depth (Figure 12.9). In this arrangement, daylight from the courtyard can fill the room more evenly. Obviously, this limits the number of such "ideal" rooms that can face the courtyard.

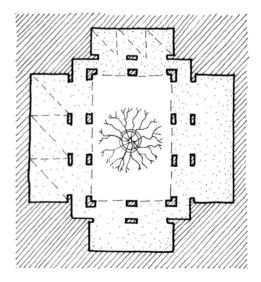

FIG. 12.9
For even distribution of daylight, preferred proportions of a room adjacent to a courtyard are 3:1, length along courtyard to depth to rear wall. (Drawing by Michael Cockram.)

Courtyards, Daylight, and Aspect Ratio

Some rough daylighting guidelines for courtyard proportions are based on the daylight factor (defined in Chapter 7; the ratio between the daylight available at some point within a room, and the daylight available outdoors at the same moment). Because daylight coincides with the sun's heat, rooms in colder climates benefit from higher daylight factors, while rooms in hotter climates are often content with lower daylight factors. Recommended DF for specified tasks are shown in Table 12.1.

TABLE 12.1. RECOMMENDED DAYLIGHT FACTORS (DF)

| | DF | |
Task	Ample winter daylight (nearer equator)	Scarce winter daylight (nearer pole)
Ordinary seeing tasks, such as reading, filing, and easy office work	1.5%	2.5%
Moderately difficult tasks, such as prolonged reading, stenographic work, normal machine tool work	2.5%	4.0%
Difficult, prolonged tasks, such as drafting, proofreading poor copy, fine machine work, and fine inspection	4.0%	8.0%

Source: Millet and Bedrick (1980).

18 **The higher the top of the window above the floor, the deeper the daylight penetration into a room.**

19 **The larger the window relative to the floor area, the higher the daylight factor (DF).**

The diagram in Figure 12.10 is based on the assumption that, at a distance into a room that exceeds 2.5 times the height (H) of the daylight opening, there will be so little daylight *relative to the daylight just inside the opening* that electric lights will probably be routinely used. In courtyard buildings with arcades, this 2.5H distance must be measured from the face of the arcade at the courtyard edge. Clearly, the arcade intercepts daylight that would otherwise serve the room beyond.

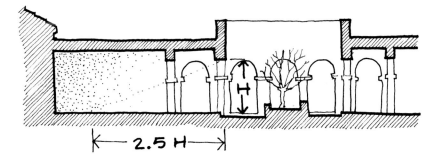

FIG. 12.10
Daylight penetration from windows or doors usually appears adequate in a zone that extends to a maximum distance of 2.5H from the opening, where H is the opening's height above the floor. For the floor area <u>within</u> this zone,

$$DF_{av} = \frac{(0.2)\ window\ area}{floor\ area}$$

$$DF_{min} = \frac{(0.1)\ window\ area}{floor\ area}$$

(Based on Stein and Reynolds 2000; drawing by Michael Cockram.)

FIG. 12.11

Daylighting and the aspect ratio. *(a)* Daylight factor (DF) estimates for spaces adjacent to courtyards. For each range (top floor, middle floor, bottom floor), the upper boundary curve "no windows" assumes a light-colored wall (70 percent reflectance) across the courtyard, while the lower boundary curve "50 percent windows" assumes a light colored wall with openings in half its area (40 percent average reflectance), across the courtyard. *(b)* Daylight factor (DF) estimates for courtyard floors. Plant growth demands sufficient daylight; under overcast skies, up to 40 percent DF is needed, while under clear skies, a considerably lower DF is adequate. (Reprinted by permission from Brown and DeKay 2001.)

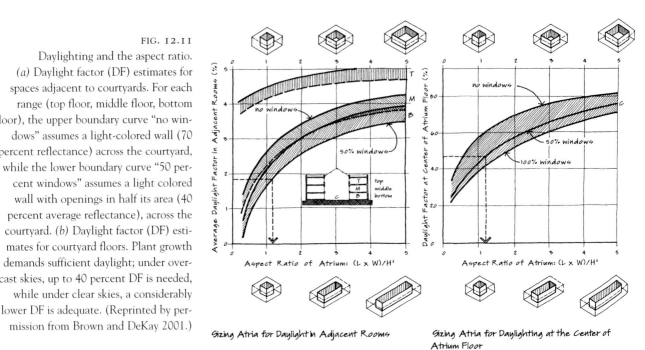

Sizing Atria for Daylight in Adjacent Rooms

Sizing Atria for Daylighting at the Center of Atrium Floor

20 Aspect ratio influences the available DF.

Figure 12.11 charts the relationship between buildings with a square, white-walled "atrium" of given aspect ratios, and the expected DF in surrounding rooms. Note that three floor-level positions are listed: top floor, middle floor, and bottom floor. For each position, there is a range from most light (0 percent windows) and least light (50 percent windows); these refer to the *opposite walls* of the atrium that act as light reflectors toward the windows being evaluated. A light-colored wall without windows reflects more daylight, since any openings in such a wall will be darker in color, especially if they are arches with walls in shadow behind them.

Using this graph requires some additional judgment. Figure 12.11 assumes the contemporary office building atrium, with continuous horizontal strip windows that begin at the ceiling and take up 50 percent of the wall area. The typical arcade, however, reaches toward but rarely touches the ceiling, and then only at the center of the arch. On the other hand, the arches typically constitute well over 50 percent of their wall area.

I believe that this graph predicts the DF in the arcades rather well. But for spaces beyond the arcades, even using the "bottom floor" position might overpredict the DF available.

FIG. 12.12

(a) Daylight reflected from a white marble floor illuminates the detail around the arches in the Patio de las Doncellas (Courtyard of the Maidens), Reales Alcazares, Seville. *(b)* Strong reflections from the white marble floor at Córdoba's Museo Arqueológico are filtered by a dark wooden *mashrabiya*. *(c)* This same reflected daylight illuminates objects from below. (This building is also shown in Figure 3.15.)

Apply this graph to the room facing the shallow courtyard in Figure 12.10. The square courtyard has the proportions 3 units width to 2.5 units height, therefore

$$\text{aspect ratio} = \frac{3 \times 3}{2.5 \times 2.5} = 1.38$$

Use the "top floor" (T) range, and the "50% windows" lower line; the three dark arches and the tree will not be reflecting much daylight! According to Figure 12.11, within the 2.5H floor area, the average DF = about 4.2. The DF in the arcade will be more; the DF within the room itself will be less than 4.

21 Light-colored courtyard surfaces diffuse daylight to the surrounding arcades and spaces.

The courtyard admits, absorbs, and reflects daylight according to its proportions and surface colors. When the courtyard floor is very light in color, a substantial amount of reflected light is cast onto walls and ceilings of the arcade. Thus, elaborately carved ceilings can be appreciated for their subtlety and complexity, as in the courtyards of the Alhambra and the Alcazar at Seville (Figure 12.12a).

22 Provide daylight openings with filtering options.

When a light floor surface is also specular (as with white marble), the sheen of light can become glare. White walls quickly become glare when direct sun strikes them, because they are directly in one's field of vision. In the Museo Arqueológico in Córdoba, an ancient glare-mitigation technique from Islam, the *mashrabiya* breaks the sheet of glare into many sparkling components (Figure 12.12). It also provides privacy along with the filtered view, and the wood conducts heat slowly, tending to keep the heat on the outer surface where winds might better carry it away.

23 The interior surfaces around daylight openings can ameliorate glare.

(Examples: plans in Figure 1.4, and Figures 1.2, 1.10, 2.3, 2.12, 3.4, 3.12, 4.2, 5.3, 7.3, 10.8, 11.9, 12.6.)

Glare is excessive contrast, as between a bright window and dark surfaces in a room. One strategy for glare reduction is to work with the surfaces immediately adjacent to the bright window. In the thick-walled courtyard buildings of Seville, most windows and doors are surrounded by surfaces placed diagonally in the wall; that is, the opening on the interior surface is much wider and taller than the opening in the exterior surface. Such surfaces not only help "spread" the daylight to the interior, but become a "brightness mediator" between the window and the interior wall surface, as in Figure 12.13.

Courtyards and Cooling

If radiation is the primary means of courtyard cooling, then a relationship between aspect ratio and courtyard temperatures, cooler than the official "design condition" temperatures, should become evident. (The "design condition" is the temperature that engineers use when sizing cooling equipment. It typically represents a maximum—but not extreme—temperature, such as one that is surpassed by only a few percent of the summertime hours in a typical season for a given city.)

FIG. 12.13
To reduce glare (excessive contrast), the surfaces around this courtyard window in Córdoba, Argentina are "splayed," exposing more surface area and mediating between the bright window and the darker interior wall surfaces.

In Table 12. 2 and Figure 12.14, these differences in temperature are shown for five courtyards in Andalucía. In each case, three consecutive hot, dry days at summer design conditions were monitored. The air temperatures at (or near) the center of each courtyard are compared with the "official" high and low temperatures for those same three days.

Two kinds of temperature differences are presented here:

The C° difference in *daily temperature range* of the courtyard, compared to official daily temperature range, and

The C° difference in the *highest daily temperature* of the courtyard, compared to official highest daily temperature.

All five courtyards have appeared in previous chapters. The highest aspect ratio (greatest sky exposure) belongs to Encarnación #12, courtyard #36 in Table 7.1, also shown in Figure 9.2. Next is the nearby front courtyard at Osio #4, courtyard #38 in Table 7.1, shown in Figure 9.4. Then the courtyard of the Casa Alta, Bornos is examined, courtyard #39 in Table 7.1, shown in Figure 10.2. The next courtyard is Arenillas #28, courtyard #40 in Table 7.1, shown in Figure 8.4. Finally, the least sky exposure belongs to Armas #14, courtyard #41 in Table 7.1, shown in Figure 8.6.

TABLE 12.2. TEMPERATURE RANGES OVER THREE HOT, DRY DAYS

Location	Aspect Ratio	Courtyard Number, Table 7.1	Dates	Day # One		Day # Two		Day # Three	
				Official °C (ΔC°)	Center Courty'd °C (ΔC°)	Official °C (ΔC°)	Center Courty'd °C (ΔC°)	Official °C (ΔC°)	Center Courty'd °C (ΔC°)
Encarnación #12, Córdoba	0.64	36	8/25–8/27 1995	18–37 (19 C°)	25–31 (6 C°)	19–38 (19 C°)	25–32 (7 C°)	21–39 (18 C°)	27–35 (8 C°)
Osio #4 (front) Córdoba	0.60	38	8/25–8/27 1995	18–37 (19 C°)	22–29 (7 C°)	19–38 (19 C°)	23–29 (6 C°)	21–39 (18 C°)	24–34 (10 C°)
Casa Alta, Bornos (Cádiz)	0.58	39	7/27–7/29 1995	17–42 (25 C°)	21–37 (16 C°)	17–39 (22 C°)	24–35 (11 C°)	21–39 (18 C°)	23–34 (11 C°)
Arenillas #28, Córdoba	0.57	40	8/30–9/1 1995	22–35 (13 C°)	25–32 (7 C°)	23–35 (13 C°)	25–31 (6 C°)	21–38 (17 C°)	24–31 (7 C°)
Armas #14, Córdoba	0.53	41	8/30–9/1 1995	22–35 (13 C°)	26–28 (2 C°)	23–35 (13 C°)	27–28 (1 C°)	21–38 (17 C°)	26–29 (3 C°)

Official Córdoba temperatures from the municipal airport, about 7 km distance
Official Bornos temperatures from Campo de Villamartin, about 8 km distance
ASHRAE 2 percent design dry-bulb temperature, Seville: 36.1° C (Handbook of Fundamentals, 1997)

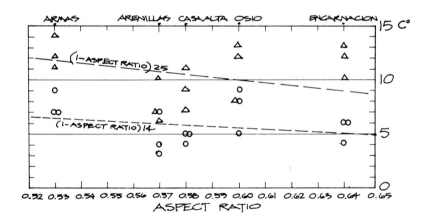

FIG. 12.14
Relating courtyard aspect ratio to differences between courtyard and official temperatures over three hot, dry days in five Andalusian courtyards.
Δ: difference in daily temperature range
o: difference in daily highest temperature

These preliminary design guidelines, at summer design conditions, emerge (shown as dashed lines in Figure 12.14):

24 The C° difference in *daily temperature range* of courtyard, compared to official temperature daily range, is approximately 25 (1 - aspect ratio) C°.

(Theoretical maximum difference = official daily range; in such a case the courtyard range is zero, that is, no temperature change at all.)

25 The C° difference in the *highest daily temperature* of the courtyard, compared to official highest daily temperature, is approximately 14 (1 - aspect ratio) C°.

(Theoretical minimum courtyard high = average official; in such a case the courtyard's highest temperature only reaches the daily average official temperature.)

These five courtyards have similar aspect ratios, so the resulting design guideline must be considered quite preliminary, and subject to these warnings:

1. There are far too few examples, over too small a range of aspect ratio, to draw final, firm conclusions for all courtyards.

2. An aspect ratio of more than 1.0 suggests higher courtyard temperatures than the official temperatures. (But consider that summer direct sun readily enters such courtyards and, indeed, sol-air temperatures are higher than air temperatures).

3. This is only applicable to hot, dry climates at about 36° north (or south) latitude. (This includes northern New Mexico and Arizona and southern Nevada).

4. Official temperatures are usually from a more rural location, outside the urban heat island.

5. Aspect ratio is a simple number, but sky exposure is more complex; Figure 12.15 compares the sun-path sky charts for these five courtyards. (But the simple aspect ratio is an easier concept that is more readily applied at the initial design stage.)

Design Example: A Sacramento, California architect is considering a square courtyard 7 meters wide and 8 meters deep. The aspect ratio is $(7 \times 7)/(8)^2 = 49/64 = 0.766$. The design condition for Sacramento is 37° C, with a mean daily temperature range of 20C°.

On such a day, the C° difference in the *highest daily temperature* of the courtyard, compared to official highest daily temperature, is approximately

14 (1 - aspect ratio) C°:

14 (1 - 0.766) = 3.28 C°.

With Sacramento's high at 37° C, the courtyard's high would be about 37 − 3.28 = about 33.7° C.

On such a day, the *daily temperature range* of courtyard, compared to official temperature daily range, is approximately

25 (1 - aspect ratio) C°

25 (1 - 0.766) = 5.85 C°.

With Sacramento's daily range of 20 C°, the courtyard's range would be about 20 - 5.85 = about 14.2 C°.

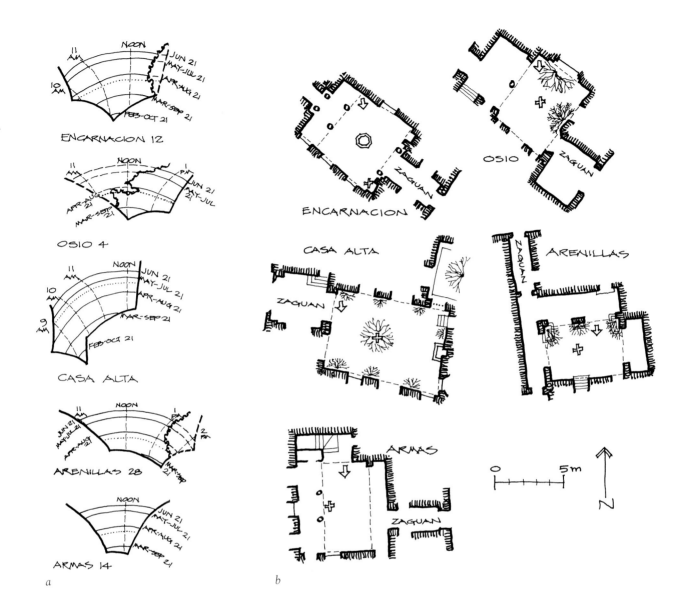

ENCARNACION 12

OSIO 4

CASA ALTA

ARENILLAS 28

ARMAS 14

a

ENCARNACION

OSIO

CASA ALTA

ARENILLAS

ARMAS

ZAGUAN

0   5m

N

b

Summary: Sacramento ranges from 37° to 17° C, while this courtyard ranges from 33.7° to 19.5° C, under design conditions.

26 Provide for thermal sailing: watering, shading, and ventilation.

Courtyard cooling is even more complex than sky exposure, especially given the influence of evaporation in the hot-dry climate of southern Spain. Opening windows can facilitate ventilative cooling as well. Further, radiation can be significantly influenced by *toldos*: of these five courtyards, two (Encarnación #12, and Arenillas #28) had no *toldo*.

Evaporative cooling through the watering of plants and surfaces, moveable shading, and the opening and closing of windows all depends on human intervention. This proactive approach to cooling is also called thermal sailing. It may well be more influential than courtyard proportion in cooling a building.

FIG. 12.15
The five Andalusian courtyards of Figure 12.14. (*a*) Sun-path sky charts, from the northernmost corner at seated eye level (about 1 meter above the floor). Dashed lines are sun filtered through leaves. Dotted line is the sun-path during the monitoring period shown in Table 12. 2. (*b*) Plans of the courtyards, at same scale with north toward top of page.

Ventilation nearly always increases courtyard comfort in hot humid climates, but in hot arid ones, it is far more a friend at night when temperatures are much lower. (See Brown and DeKay 2001, page 209 for estimates of wind speeds as a percentage of free, unobstructed incident wind, for a variety of courtyard proportions.)

27 Consider adjustable shading for the entire courtyard and for its individual openings.

The horizontal *toldo* can cover all or part of the courtyard (Figure 12.16). As explained in Chapters 4 and 5, and detailed in Chapters 8, 9, and 10, a *toldo* is used most often in hot dry climates, to keep sun out during the hours when the sun is highest in the sky. It is left open all night, and as long as possible each day, to maximize exposure to the cold summer sky.

Moveable shades are particularly useful, allowing considerable choice of how and when any part of an arcade might be used. Awnings or roll-down shades are sometimes used in arcades and are more common at windows (Figure 12.17). These smaller, individual shading devices brighten the courtyard, adding color and variety.

28 Consider additional roles for a *toldo*.

Theoretically, such an overall courtyard shade might be used to ward off rain, or to keep in heat on a cold winter night, because when closed it cuts off both the courtyard's radiant heat loss to the cold sky, and wind. But rain, along with wind, are a *toldo*'s great enemies, causing it to collapse with accumulated weight, or to be torn apart. The risk of either wind or rain during a cold night, while the owners are asleep or away, may be too great.

A new addition to the role for the *toldo* might be to generate electricity. When photovoltaic cells (PV) are available in fabric-like material, it is conceivable that a *toldo* could produce clean DC power by day, then be folded back near dusk to expose the courtyard to the cold night sky. At present, a "foldable" PV product is described by its manufacturer:

> Solar modules for remote applications must be tough, lightweight and easy to transport. UNI-SOLAR UNI-PACs are designed for the challenge of the field. They provide power even with bullet holes or in partial shade. The UNI-PAC can be dropped, stepped on, packed and re-deployed, and will continue to operate. Field-proven as dependable and easy to use for military units, trekkers, climbers and professional photographers depend on the UNI-PAC for field communications, emergency power and battery maintenance.

At the very least, such a *toldo* would be resistant to hail!

29 An absorbent floor helps cool the courtyard.

(Examples: Figures 1.2, 1.10, 2.8, 2.15, 2.16, 3.6, 4.3, 4.5, 5.7, 8.3, 8.4, 9.6, 10.1, 11.2, 12.1)

In a hot, dry climate, evaporation is a powerful cooling technique. A damp floor, wicking up moisture from the soil below, can provide cooling throughout the hottest hours of the day or night. This was most evident in Chapter 9, where the twentieth century's hottest days challenged a courtyard in Bornos, Spain.

FIG. 12.16
Looking down into a hotel courtyard at Las Casas de la Juderia, Seville, served by a white translucent *toldo*. (*a*) Open, as in early morning, late evening, or all night. (*b*) Closed, as during sunny hours of a hot day. (*c*) Seen from below, this courtyard with its *toldo* open; note how the blue sky emphasizes the tiles. (*d*) *Toldo* closed, note the diffused, yellow cast of the daylight.

Courtyards and Winter Sun

The solar shadow index was defined in Chapter 1, and applied to courtyards in Chapters 8 and 9. The skyline chart (as seen in Figure 12.15) tells a more detailed story about winter solar access, but requires considerably greater effort to obtain. Again, a simple number is needed at the early stages of design, hence the solar shadow index.

30 In colder climates, provide a lower solar shadow index by lowering the courtyard's south wall.

Table 12.3 relates the solar shadow index to latitude and accessibility to the "best four hours" of winter solstice sun. This table is most accurately applied where one entire wall (rather than only one corner) of the courtyard faces the equator.

For courtyard buildings that need winter heating, limiting the south (or toward-the-equator) wall to minimum height is strongly recommended. Not only will more winter sun enter the courtyard, but more daylight as well. Except on heavily (uniformly) overcast days, the area near the sun will be a bit brighter on cloudy days, and the sun spends its brightest hours in the southern sky. This double benefit of winter sun and daylight will usually be welcome.

FIG. 12.17
The view through the *zaguán* need not violate a courtyard's privacy if blinds or awnings are used at the edge of a courtyard's arcade. Delicate ferns are also shaded. Calle Constitución, Colima.

31 The lower the solar shadow index, the greater the need for summer shading.

Of course, more summer sun will also enter over this lower equatorial wall, but shading over or within the courtyard can mitigate this potential disadvantage.

In the wet-winter, dry-summer climate of Eugene, Oregon, the Emerald People's Utility District offices occupy three sides of a courtyard (Figure 12.18). On the east side is the employee's lunch room, which also acts as a meeting room available to the public after office hours. The courtyard serves as an outdoor break area for employees by day, and as an entry forecourt for the meeting room on evenings and weekends. The courtyard, and the deciduous vines that shade its two-story north-side windows, are so inviting that the meeting room is fully booked months in advance. This 44° north latitude courtyard was designed to allow winter sun (a rare and welcome event in Oregon) to nearly fill the courtyard's north wall.

This courtyard's aspect ratio is 5.14; its solar shadow index is 0.38 (Table 12.3 shows 0.34 as the maximum solar shadow index for sun covering the south wall at 44° north latitude). This is more exposed than most of the Colima and all of the Andalucía examples. In summer, nights are so cool that overheating typically occurs only by midafternoon. Rather than shade the entire courtyard with a *toldo*, the vines on trellises protect the south-facing windows and west-facing doors in summer.

TABLE 12.3 COURTYARDS AND WINTER SUN
SOLAR EXPOSURE FROM 10 AM TO 2 PM AT WINTER SOLSTICE

Latitude ° from Equator	Profile Angle[a]	Maximum Solar Shadow Index[b] for Sun Covering the: S. Wall+ 1/3 floor	Only the S. Wall	Northern Hemisphere	Southern Hemisphere	Latitude ° from Equator
20	43	0.62	0.93	Colima, Mexico City, Veracruz, Campecha, Santiago de Cuba, Port Sudan, Bombay, Hanoi, Haikou, Honolulu	Iquique, Potosí, Belo Horizonte, Bulawayo, Antananarivo, Port Hedland, Papeete	20
24	39	0.57	0.81	La Paz, Mazatlán, Durango, Havana, Western Sahara, Aswan, Riyadh, Karachi, Dacca, Taipei	Antofogasta, Asunción, Sao Paulo, Windhoek, Toliara, Gibson Desert	24
28	35	0.47	0.70	Hermosillo, Chihuahua, Corpus Christi, Orlando, Tenerife, El Minya, Kuwait, Shiraz, Delhi, Chongqing	Santiago del Estero, Florianopolis, Bloemfontein, Brisbane	28
32	31	0.40	0.60	San Diego, El Paso, Savannah, Bermuda, Marraketch, Tripoli, Tel Aviv, Isfahan, Lahore, Shanghai, Nagasaki	Valparaiso, Córdoba, De Aar, Perth, Newcastle	32
36	27	0.34	0.51	Las Vegas, Santa Fe, Raleigh, Gibraltar, Tunis, Malta, Rhodes, Aleppo, Tehran, Tashkent, Lanzhou, Tokyo	Concepción, La Plata, Cape Agulhas (S. Africa), Canberra, Auckland	36
40	23	0.28	0.42	Reno, Denver, Philadelphia, Madrid, Majorca, Taranto, Mt. Athos, Ankara, Baku, Beijing, Morioka (Japan)	Neuquen, Bahia Blanca, Wanganui (N.Z.)	40
44	19	0.23	0.34	Eugene, Milwaukee, Toronto, Halifax, Avignon, Florence, Sarajevo, Bucharest, Sevastopol	Comodoro Rivadávia, Hobart, Christchurch	44
48	16	0.19	0.29	Seattle, Duluth, Quebec, Orleans, Munich, Vienna, Volgograd	Cerro S. Lorenzo (Chile-Argentina)	48
52	12	0.14	0.21	Red Deer, Saskatoon, Cork, Milton Keynes, Rotterdam, Berlin, Warsaw, Kiev, Irkutsk	Rio Gallegos (Argentina)	52

[a] *The profile angle is the altitude of the sun projected onto a north-south plane, at 10 AM and 2 PM solar time, at the winter solstice (Dec. 21 in northern hemisphere, June 21 in southern hemisphere).*

[b] *The solar shadow index =* $\dfrac{height\ of\ south\ wall}{width\ north-south\ of\ floor}$

FIG. 12.18
The courtyard at the Emerald People's Utility District offices, Eugene, Oregon. (a) Looking southeast just after solar noon, late spring. Note the absorbent floor, and translucent green leaves on the trellis. (b) Section north-south, looking east.

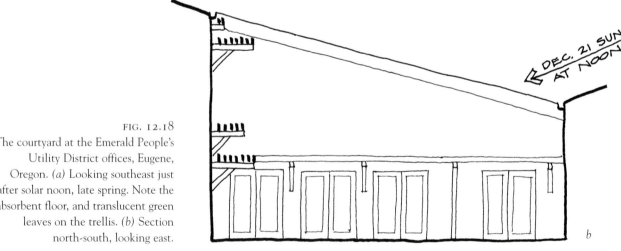

Courtyards and Arcades

32 The arcade can be both "path" and "place."

(Examples: Figures 2.12, 3.4, 3.8, 3.12, 3.15, 4.2, 5.3, 5.4, 7.3, 8.7, 9.5, 11.6, 12.2)

We return now to the question of why the arcades, rather than the rooms around a courtyard, are so often chosen as places for work and social contact. Might it be as simple as avoiding glare? Rooms with daylight openings on only one side (typical of urban courtyard buildings) often suffer from the "cave effect," with an uncomfortably strong contrast between light levels in the room and the light streaming in through the rather small openings in only one wall. The lighter the courtyard surfaces, the more pervasive this daylight. The arcades are not as deep as the rooms beyond, and their daylit side usually has more opening area than opaque surface area. Thus the contrast between the arcade and the courtyard is much lower than between the room and the courtyard.

33 Design for migration: Each arcade may be used at a different time of day.

Arcades modify the extremes of light, wind, and temperature in the courtyard; they mediate between inside and outside. This is another reason why they often seem the most desirable places to be. As the day progresses, different facades and their arcades are exposed to sun (Figure 12.19). The parts still in shade are coolest; the parts now shaded but recently sunny will have considerable residual warmth. Depending on the desired use and the air temperature, almost any part of an arcade might be useful at a particular time.

Moreover, in climates with distinct seasons, some rooms are used mainly in summer and others mainly in winter. This seasonal migration, or nomadism, was discussed in Chapter Two.

34 Occupy the center.

(Examples: Figures 1.2, 1.8, 1.10, 2.2a, 2.4, 2.8, 2.9, 2.15, 3.3, 3.6, 3.10, 3.12, 4.4, 5.9, 6.6, 8.2, 8.10, 8.11, 9.2, 9.4, 10.1)

Most of the courtyards I observed feature some object at or near their center; fountain, well, pond, tree, statue, large potted plant, table with chairs, hammock—something that draws the eye, and that may invite you to stay. This is particularly important when the *zaguán* aims the visitor's eye at this center. But it also helps the courtyard to fulfill its role as the social center of a building.

35 Rehearse a variety of roles for the courtyard.

(Examples: Figures 3.8, 6.3, 6.6, 11.5, 11.8, 11.9)

So many activities benefit from an occasional move outdoors, particularly when surrounded by the beauty and privacy of a courtyard. Looking ahead to possible changes in building function, how versatile can you make the courtyard for a future commercial or institutional use? In Chapter 11, a residence became an art gallery; another became a restaurant.

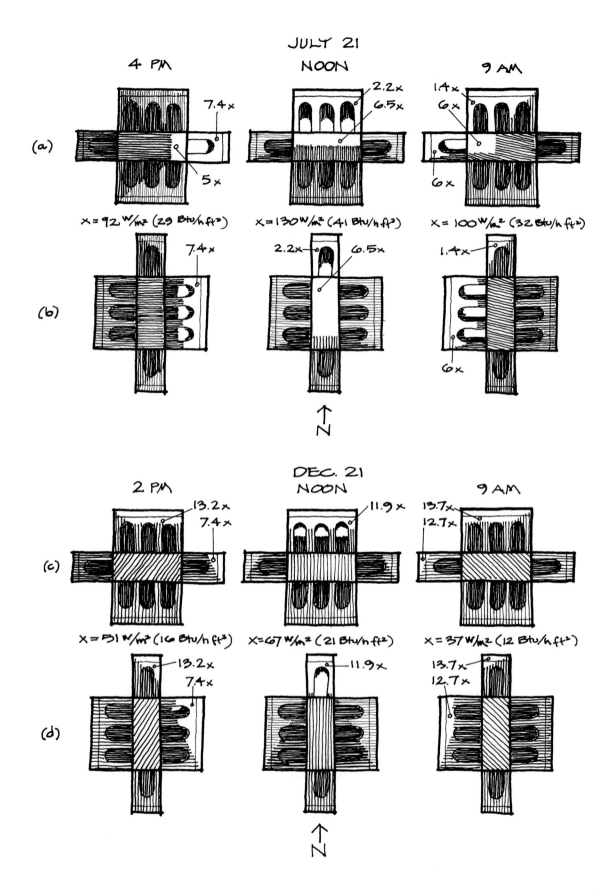

JULY 21

4 PM   NOON   9 AM

(a)

7.4x   2.2x   1.4x
5x   6.5x   6x
                    6x

$x = 92 \text{ W/m}^2$ (29 Btu/h ft²) $x = 130 \text{ W/m}^2$ (41 Btu/h ft²) $x = 100 \text{ W/m}^2$ (32 Btu/h ft²)

(b)

7.4x   2.2x   6.5x   1.4x
                           6x

↑
N

DEC. 21

2 PM   NOON   9 AM

(c)

13.2x   11.9x   13.7x
7.4x   12.7x

$x = 51 \text{ W/m}^2$ (16 Btu/h ft²) $x = 67 \text{ W/m}^2$ (21 Btu/h ft²) $x = 37 \text{ W/m}^2$ (12 Btu/h ft²)

(d)

13.2x   11.9x   13.7x
7.4x   12.7x

↑
N

Part III: Courtyard Design

FIG. 12.19

Relative hourly solar heat gains on sunny courtyard surfaces (on a clear day at 36° north latitude, including Córdoba, Spain). "X" represents the approximate hourly gains on all surfaces in shade or shadow or just grazed by the sun. Units of X are W/m^2 ($Btu/h\ ft^2$). For reference: A typical wintertime floor radiant heating system is designed to deliver about 158 W/m^2 (50 $Btu/h\ ft^2$).

On July 21, *(a)* rectangular courtyards elongated east-west are compared to *(b)* those elongated north-south at (sun time) 9 AM, noon, and 4 PM. July is the time of the hottest temperatures, when sun is an enemy. (The shadow lines on the courtyard floor show the sun's direction [azimuth].)

(a) Elongated east-west:

9 AM: Note the concentration of heat in the northwest corner. Ambient air temperature has probably climbed into the comfort zone by this hour, erasing memories of the cool air at dawn. But all the shaded courtyard surfaces are still quite cool.

NOON: The north side gets a lot of heat, and the ambient air temperature is near or above the top of the comfort zone. The south side is still a bit cool from overnight low temperatures. But even the shaded surfaces are receiving solar heat at a rate almost as great as that produced by wintertime radiant heating systems.

4 PM: The east end gets a concentration of sun, while the ambient air temperature has just passed its highest point, well above the comfort zone. But there are by now no cool surfaces remaining, even in the shade.

(b) Elongated north-south:

9 AM: The shaded floor lessens the concentration of heat in the northwest corner.

NOON: The hot floor and north face create a real heat concentration there. Again, even the shaded surfaces are receiving solar heat at a rate almost as great as that produced by wintertime radiant heating systems.

4 PM: Again, the shaded floor lessens the concentration of solar heat, welcome at this hottest hour.

(See Brown and DeKay 2001, p. 211, for courtyard shaded/unshaded fractions, June through August.)

On December 21, *(c)* rectangular courtyards elongated east-west are compared to *(d)* those elongated north-south at (sun time) 9 AM, noon and 2 PM. December is the time of the coldest temperatures, when sun is a friend. (The shadow lines on the courtyard floor show the sun's direction [azimuth].)

(c) Elongated east-west:

9 AM: Almost all is in shadow, and the air is quite cold. Sun is too high on the walls to contribute much warmth. Almost all surfaces are very cold.

NOON: Standing against the north side, head and shoulders get strong solar exposure. The ambient air temperature is well below the comfort zone, and the shaded surfaces are still very cold.

2 PM: In the northeast corner, the sun's warmth is tantalizingly close, but shadow lines are moving farther upward. The ambient air temperature is at its highest for the day, but still below the bottom comfort zone. Most courtyard surfaces remain very cold.

(d) Elongated north-south:

9 AM: Intensely warmer sun is too high on the walls to contribute much warmth.

NOON: The short north side gets a full dose of very warm sun.

2 PM: The northeast corner of the courtyard will feel very warm—above the waist.

36 Consider the role of the courtyard's silhouette: parapet or eave?

The frame for the courtyard's opening to the sky presents another design decision: roof eave or parapet (Figure 12.20). When the eave provides this frame (often in shallow courtyards), the sky contrasts with the rippled edge of roof tiles. The wider the courtyard, the more the roof tile surface can be seen from the opposite side of the courtyard. This kind of frame emphasizes both the expanse of the sky and the role of the roof as a shelter. It also promotes the collection of rain water within the courtyard and allows night air, cooled by the roof surface radiating to the cold sky, to flow slowly into the courtyard. It connects the courtyard to nature.

When the walls provide the frame (often in deeper courtyards), parapets may be sculpted to emphasize one or more walls, or to accent a major axis at the center of a wall. This frame emphasizes the courtyard as a stage set, where the contents of the courtyard, not the sky, are the center of attention. It is a more inward-looking design.

Parapets might result from other design decisions, especially when the roof over the arcades is used as a terrace. The parapet then serves both as a safety railing and a privacy screen for summer night sleeping. Parapet walls also intercept some of the sun that would otherwise heat the roof surface; this intercepted heat can then be radiated or carried away by the wind.

FIG. 12.20
(a) Where the sky meets the courtyard, roof tile channels rain, cold night air, and the sky itself into the courtyard. The Cabildo, Salta, Argentina. (b) A shallow courtyard gains apparent height with this parapet; the unusual wall and gate within the courtyard provide a separate entrance for a second family unit. Calle Allende, Colima, Mexico.

37 The stair as a stage.

(Examples: Figures 1.12, 3.5)

A stair within a courtyard invites a display of plants along its rising diagonal, and offers a potential stage at the landing. It also invites climbing, which may be welcome in a hotel or office building, but unwelcome in a residence where the upstairs rooms are the most private. Stairs within courtyards take up space, but in return provide a wealth of views from multiple levels, and chances to smell and touch vines that would otherwise be overhead, out of reach.

38 Delight all the senses.

Fountains, fires, stages for performers, blooming and fruiting plants—courtyards can enrich sight, smell, sound, taste, and touch. In such a controlled landscape, sounds and aromas linger. At least two walls are always in shadow, the better against which to display a sunlit centerpiece. Too hot? Drink from, or dip your hands in, a fountain. Too cold? Smell the smoke, hear the crackle, feel the heat of a fireplace or oven. Design for the opportunities that delight all the senses in this surrounded, private yet outdoor space.

39 Plants in pots encourage flexibility in a courtyard.

(Examples: Figures 2.7, 2.14, 2.16, 2.17, and 4.3)

Potted plants were likened to family pets in Chapter 4, demanding care and returning rewards. They are the soft, organic foil to the hard, geometric courtyard. They can serve in many ways: attract attention, provide food or bouquets, perfume the courtyard. They can be moved as needed to direct traffic, provide a privacy screen, shade a resting place. A flotilla of pots adds color and texture to a plain whitewashed wall. Potted plants, stored on a roof terrace or in a service courtyard, can be brought into the main courtyard when they are in season, bringing out the best characteristics of spring blossoms, summer fragrance, or fall color. Very few courtyards contain no potted plants; it almost seems that a lack of potted plants indicates a lack of concern.

40 Vines and trees can celebrate seasonal change.

(Examples: Figures 1.8, 2.1, 2.15, 4.3 through 4.5, 5.3, 5.7, 5.8 and 5.10)

Large rooted plants that provide significant shade require careful design attention. The sky is important to the courtyard's role; trees and vines both frame and filter the sky. Color and scent and swaying leaves add to summer delight, while maintenance and winter shade are likely less welcome. In temperate climates, deciduous vines and trees provide a dramatic seasonal change, often including a change in the color, as well as the quantity, of daylight through their leaves and branches. Before specifying such large and permanent plants for a courtyard, consider the recommendations in Appendix C; pollen allergies may be an issue.

41 Consider masking sound.

Recall the observation (Chapter 3) that a courtyard building has a very hard time concealing secrets between its rooms. "Masking sounds" (sometimes called acoustic perfume) are intended to cover up conversation or other unwanted sounds that echo in the hard surfaces of the courtyard. Masking sound sources include trickling water, birdsong, wind through leaves, wind chimes; of these, only trickling water is reliably continuous. Water also conveys a message about cooling, most welcome in summer when windows are wide open by night.

42 Give water a place.

(Examples: Figures 1.2, 2.2 through 2.4, 2.9, 3.1, 3.6, 3.9, 3.15, 3.16, 4.1, 4.4, 6.6, 8.2, 8.3, 8.10, 8.11, 9.2, 10.6, 10.8, 11.3, 11.5, 11.7, 11.8)

Water was praised in Chapter 2 as representing things cool, fresh, and pure. Water is often (but not always) at the center of the courtyard, where exposure to the sky (and its rain) is at maximum. Even if valued only for its evaporative cooling potential, water is a courtyard treasure.

43 Provide a means to celebrate, rather than conceal, rainwater.

In dry climates, the roofs are often arranged to drain toward the courtyard, which then becomes the collecting place for all the site's rainwater (Figure 12.21). The opening to a cistern below the courtyard might be as simple as a grate in the floor, or it may be the basin around a central fountain. When eaves are the edges of the courtyard's aperture, gutters and downspouts are prominent and often painted in bright colors. When parapets are the edges, horizontal spouts, or *cannales*, shoot water out and down to the courtyard during a storm.

44 Collect and use rainwater.

Rainwater is good for plants because it contains no chlorine or other chemical additives. Sizing the cistern depends both upon the monthly rainfall and the daily usage, as well as upon the total collection area available. Where the monthly rainfall is about the same year-round, a smaller cistern will suffice. Appendix B provides a method for calculating a cistern's size.

FIG. 12.21
Courtyards as rainwater collectors.
(a) Courtyard on Calle Zarco, Córdoba,
features a central grate. (b) At the
Hacienda San Gabriel, Marfil
(Guanajuato), Mexico, a large grate
leads to a cistern for watering the plants
of an extensive garden. (Photo by
Alfredo Fernández Gonzales.)

CHAPTER 13

Thermal qualities—warm, cool, humid, airy, radiant, cozy—are an important part of our experience of a space; they not only influence what we choose to do there but also how we feel about the space. An analogy might be drawn with the use of light quality as a design element, truly a venerable old architectural tradition. The light quality—direct, indirect, natural, artificial, diffuse, dappled, focused—can be subtly manipulated in the design of a space to achieve the desired effect. Thermal qualities might also be included in the architect's initial conception and could influence all phases of design. Instead, thermal conditions are commonly standardized with the use of modern mechanical systems that can be specified, installed, and left to function independently of the overall design concept. Indeed, environmental control systems tend to be treated rather like the Cinderella of architecture; given only the plainest clothes to wear, they are relegated to a back room to do the ordinary drudgery that maintains the elegant life-style of the other sisters: light, form, structure, and so forth.

Lisa Heschong
Thermal Delight in Architecture

Design Examples

Many of the design guidelines in Chapter 12 concern the environmental control aspects of the courtyard—daylight, cooling, and solar access in particular. But others remind designers that people *enjoy* courtyards and their arcades, and that these gardens within buildings create environments that are unmatched by any indoor, covered space. Yes, there are times when courtyards are uninhabitable. But there are times when they are the habitation of choice as well.

The examples in this chapter propose new courtyard buildings in close proximity, rather than as isolated structures on separate lots. Mindful of both old-world traditions and new-world suburban expectations, these design proposals attempt to balance housing density with access to light, sun, wind, and sky. Public open space is as important to these schemes as is the private open courtyard.

For his design proposal for residential neighborhoods in three climates in Turkey, Can Elmas won the $7,000 first prize in the International Sustainable Design Competition in 1992, cosponsored by the American Institute of Architects and the International Union of Architects. In two of those Turkish climates, where summer cooling was as much as or more of an issue than winter heating, the dwellings were designed with courtyards. Elmas designed both interior and exterior spaces with an emphasis appropriate to the climate: thermal mass, southern exposure, moveable shading for hot-arid, vine shading and ample cross ventilation for hot-humid.

Details of this design proposal, complete with their daylighting, passive solar heating, and passive cooling performance predictions, are found in Elmas' Master of Architecture thesis at the University of Oregon (1992).

Hot and Arid

FIG. 13.1
Housing proposal for hot and dry Urfa, Turkey. Partial housing cluster, with plan and section through courtyards. (From Elmas 1992.)

In hot and dry Urfa, inland and about 270 km northeast of Aleppo, Syria, winters are cool, and summer is hot by day and cool by night. Each cluster of houses is arranged around a large common "courtyard" that serves as a street (Figure 13.1). Each private courtyard opens, through a courtyard wall, to this common courtyard-street.

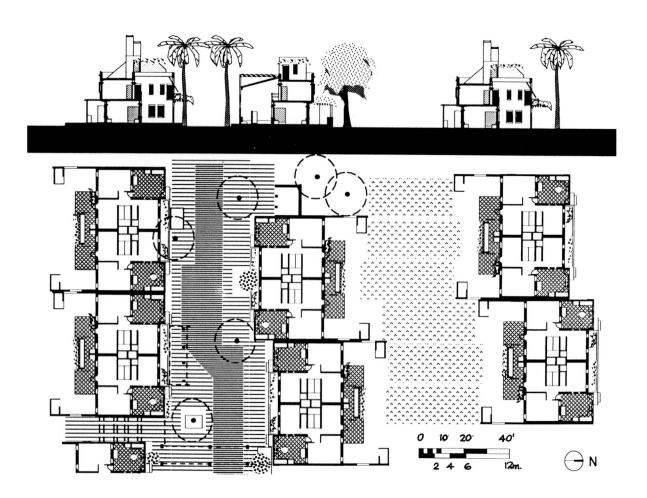

The street is enhanced with different height and colored units, their projections and courtyard entrances. Shaded common areas with small pools provide small oases in the heat of summer. There are also narrow passages from street to the vegetable gardens between the clusters. (Elmas 1992).

The L-shaped plan of each row house results in each courtyard having two sides in common with the residence, and one side (with no openings) adjoining the courtyard next door. The fourth side adjoins the "street" (large common courtyard). The courtyard is enjoyed by the living room, dining-multipurpose room and upstairs bedrooms (Figures 13.2, 13.3). For privacy (also to define the boundaries of the house), the courtyard is elevated 30 cm above the street; the living room is then elevated another 30 cm above the courtyard.

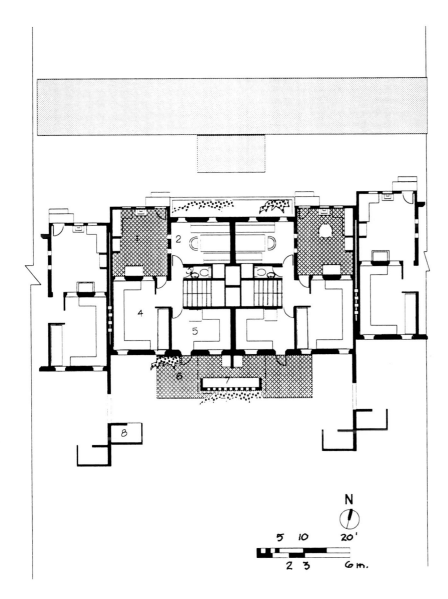

N

5 10   20'

2 3   6 m.

FIG. 13.2
Housing proposal for hot and dry Urfa, Turkey. Ground-floor plan.
1: Courtyard   2: Dining
3: WC   4: Living
5: Kitchen   6: Rear patio
7: Outdoor cooking 8: Storage
(From Elmas 1992.)

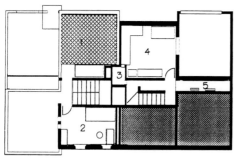

a

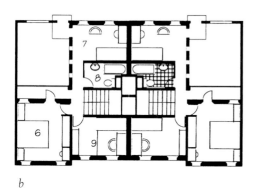

b

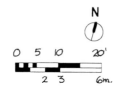

FIG. 13.3
Housing proposal for hot and dry Urfa, Turkey. (*a*) Plans of roof (left side) and basement (right side). (*b*) Second-floor plan.

1: Roof terrace   2: Bedroom-study
3: Cooltower   4: Basement room
5: Cool air registers   6: Master bedroom
7: Bedroom   8: Bathroom
9: Bedroom

(From Elmas 1992.)

The courtyards that face the street to the south are provided with large sloped, pivoting canvas shutters (Figure 13.4), light on one side, dark on the other:

> There are built-in sitting and storage areas in the courtyard. A small pool with sprinkler provides evaporative and psychological cooling and buffers street noise. There are lattice screens in the openings to the street for privacy. The courtyard is shaded with canvas during summer days. During summer nights the canvas is rolled back and surfaces radiate to the cold sky. High courtyard walls provide shading to the street. The pivoting shutter's darker surface faces the house in the summer for minimum reflection. In winter its white surface is turned to reflect sunlight into the courtyard and to the house. (Elmas 1992).

Roof terraces are provided for sleeping, with parapet walls and lattice screens for added privacy. Above the terrace rises an evaporative cooling tower ("cooltower"), shared between each pair of row houses, that provides a passive, gentle flow of cool moist air to a basement room below the living room. This traditional basement refuge from the daytime heat has a small daylight opening to the courtyard, as well as grilles to the living room above that allow a subsequent flow of cooled air, pushed by air from the cooltower, up to that space. With attention both to nighttime rooftop and to daytime underground refuge, this house is designed with daily migration in mind.

Hot and Humid

In hot and humid Adana, only about 500 km west of Urfa but at lower elevation and near the Mediterranean, the housing clusters are more loosely joined to facilitate ventilation (Figure 13.5).

The aim is to get the best ventilation with mid-density, rather than decreasing the density to maximize the use of prevailing wind. . . . The long buildings are broken into smaller parts and oriented obliquely to the wind. Large open areas used as vegetable gardens or recreation fields also maximize air speed at ground level. Accommodating a number of family sizes will produce varying building heights that will enhance the skyline and provide wind turbulence at ground level. (Elmas 1992.)

The vine-shaded courtyards might be more comfortable at any hour than the interior, given the influence of breezes under humid conditions. Therefore, the courtyards are intended to serve as living, cooking, working, sleeping, and play areas. They open on one side to the street, on the other to a more narrow outdoor space, this one shared with the adjacent unit's courtyard and partially overhung by upstairs bedrooms. The courtyards are thus arranged to cross-ventilate, maximizing wind speed through both the courtyard and the house.

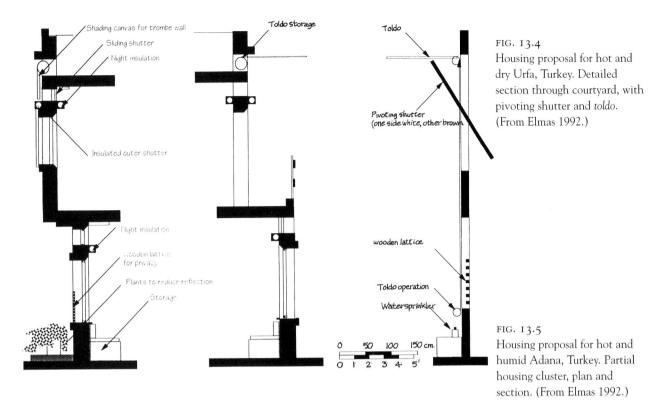

Shading canvas for trombe wall
Sliding shutter
Night insulation

Insulated outer shutter

Night insulation

Wooden lattice
for privacy

Plants to reduce reflection

Storage

Toldo storage

Toldo

Pivoting shutter
(one side white, other brown)

wooden lattice

Toldo operation

Watersprinkler

0   50   100   150 cm.

0 1 2 3 4 5'

FIG. 13.4
Housing proposal for hot and
dry Urfa, Turkey. Detailed
section through courtyard, with
pivoting shutter and *toldo*.
(From Elmas 1992.)

FIG. 13.5
Housing proposal for hot and
humid Adana, Turkey. Partial
housing cluster, plan and
section. (From Elmas 1992.)

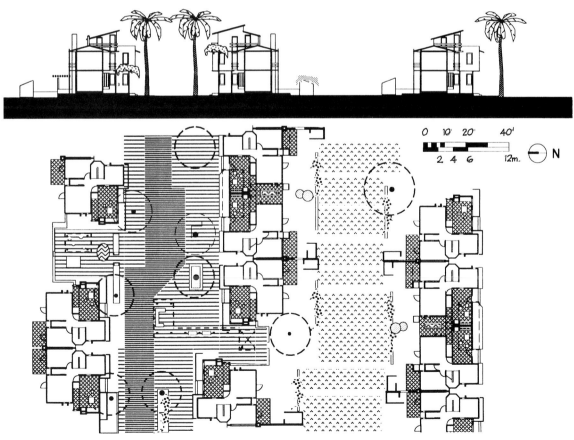

0   10'   20"   40'

2 4 6   12m.   ⊕ N

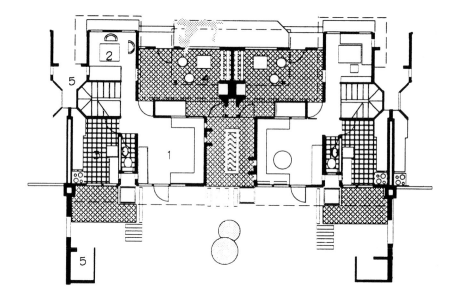

FIG. 13.6

Housing proposal for hot and humid Adana, Turkey. Ground-floor plan.

1: Living   2: Dining

3: Kitchen   4: Courtyard

5: Storage

(From Elmas 1992.)

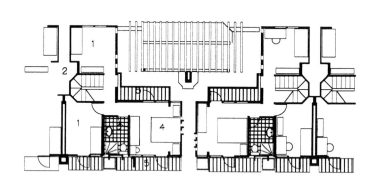

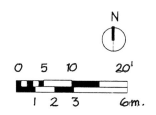

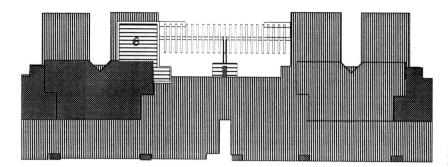

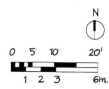

FIG. 13.7

Housing proposal for hot and humid Adana, Turkey. Second-floor plan and roof plan.

1: Bedroom   2: Ventilation well

3: Bathroom   4: Master bedroom

5: Balcony   6: Roof terrace

(From Elmas 1992.)

Part III: Courtyard Design

The living room and master bedroom have openings on three sides, while the smaller bedrooms have openings on two (Figures 13.6, 13.7). The living and dining rooms face opposite directions (north or south), as do upper balconies, to encourage migration during the day, avoiding the sunny side of the residence.

> Due to their importance, sitting and sleeping areas receive cross ventilation. Partition walls and furniture are arranged to utilize and not block air flow.... The kitchen is isolated from the living areas with circulation and service zones around it. Cooking is encouraged to move either to the courtyard or to the patio. The kitchen is naturally ventilated to a small utility courtyard. The humidity-producing bathroom is ventilated to that courtyard also. The staircase is used for stack ventilation during night time when wind speed is lowest. (Elmas 1992).

The details of this design specify shading devices and attention to window heights and how they open, all with maximum ventilation in mind. Even the built-in courtyard benches are ventilated under the seat.

A City Block of Courtyard Row Houses

This courtyard row-house scheme is organized around a large, car-free commons (Figure 13.8). It puts the parked car on a level lower than the courtyard, yet keeps the courtyard in contact with the earth to encourage evaporative cooling and growth of large plants.

FIG. 13.8
Site plan, proposed courtyard row housing filling a city block. Housing units face north and south. Parking off the side streets is below a balcony-level bedroom wing. Courtyards can be shaded by a *toldo*, and earth below each courtyard supports larger trees and vines. (© John S. Reynolds, A.I.A. Reprinted by permission.)

5 Resolve the location of parked cars relative to the courtyard as an initial design decision.

6 Consider putting the carport behind or below the courtyard, rather than between courtyard and street.

29 An absorbent floor helps cool the courtyard.

40 Vines and trees can celebrate seasonal change.

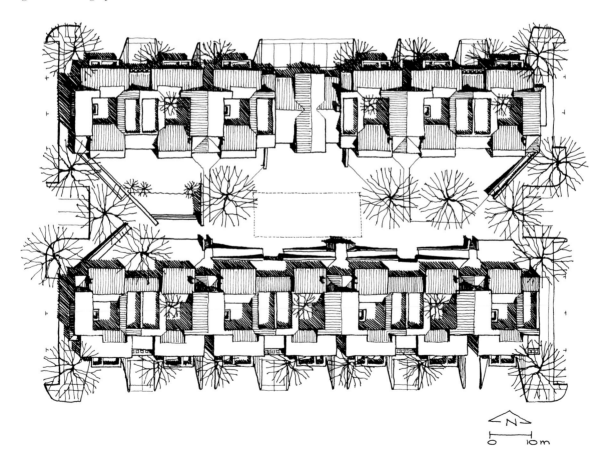

This city block (to centerlines of streets) measures 100 meters (north-south) by 136 meters (east-west). This provides housing for 13 fairly large families and a large indoor space for gatherings (such as a dining/meeting area in a cohousing arrangement). The housing units at the four corners are adapted to include small retail shops or professional offices. This represents a density of 13 families/13,600 m², or 10 families per hectare.

The houses share a commons that pedestrians enter from major streets (running north-south) at either end. The minor streets (running east-west) provide access to parking that slopes down to one meter below the average grade, while the courtyards are elevated one meter above average grade. The main streets (with continuous, non-sloping sidewalks) are thus far more pedestrian-friendly than are the minor streets, where sidewalks are scarce and constantly interrupted by driveways. Skateboarders, however, might find these alternating up- and down-slopes irresistible (for better or worse).

Grade changes can be playful within the commons. However, wheelchair access dictates ramps of no more than 1 in 12 slope, which is also maintained for the sloping driveways. The minor streets and the commons, elongated east-west, provide winter solar access for the living rooms of all the housing.

3 A typical zoning regulation for courtyard-type neighborhoods is that 25 percent of the site must be open to the sky, whether in one large or several smaller courtyards.

Each courtyard house has a total enclosed floor area of up to 214 m², and a footprint of 280 m² (Figure 13.9). Each open courtyard is 44.9 m², less than 25 percent of the footprint, but the generous commons (and roof terraces) compensate. Each courtyard has an exposed floor area of 6.7 x 6.7 meters. The eaves are 4.5 meters above this floor level (except 3 meters at the living room).

Initially, this produces an aspect ratio of $\dfrac{6.7 \times 6.7}{4.125^2} = 2.64$

an exposure similar to courtyards #15, 16, and 17 (Table 7.1) in Colima, and about equal to the most shallow courtyard (#31) in Córdoba. After the upper room is added on one side (east or west), the aspect ratio is

$$\frac{6.7 \times 6.7}{4.5^2} = 2.19$$

20 Aspect ratio influences the available DF.

These fairly high aspect ratios reveal the designer's bias in favor of more daylight and winter sun, and less concern about cooling. This approach is shaped by the warm-dry Pacific Northwest summer, where cooling is easy. East- and west-facing openings are minimized in this scheme, to alleviate summer solar gains. But thermal concern is more about winter solar access than summer cooling.

The solar shadow index (SSI), unchanged by the upper room additions on the east (or west) side, varies with the orientation of the living room. When the living room is on the north side of the courtyard, the SSI is

$$\frac{4.5}{6.7} = 0.67$$

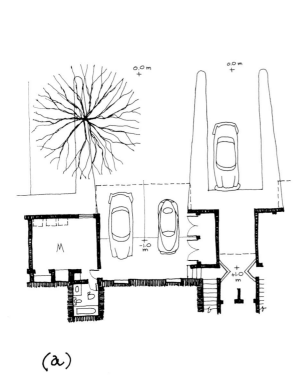

(a)

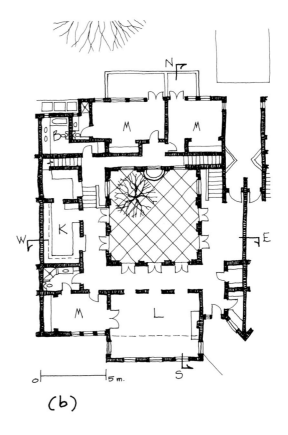

(b)

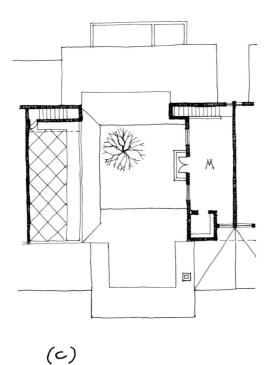

(c)

FIG. 13.9 FLOOR PLANS, TYPICAL COURTYARD ROW HOUSE.

> Key:
> M=Multipurpose rooms: bedroom, study, dining, etc.
> L=Living room with fireplace
> K=Kitchen and utility room
> B=Bathrooms

(a) Parking level. The wheel-chair accessible multipurpose room, with completely separate entrance, could be rented out, used as an office, workroom, or store room, or as a bedroom for a relative or older child. The extra-wide parking slot, shared with the adjacent unit, serves as a delivery ramp up to the courtyard level, or for wheelchair-vehicle parking.

(b) Main level. Most rooms around the courtyard are wheelchair accessible.

(c) Upstairs level. The large multipurpose room can be added later, atop an initially flat terrace. This room could be subdivided. The other roof terrace has complete visual privacy, for sunbathing, clothes drying or other recreation. (© John S. Reynolds, A.I.A. Reprinted by permission.)

30 In colder climates, provide a lower
    solar shadow index by lowering the
    courtyard's south wall.

From Table 12.3, this scheme would provide winter sun over the courtyard's
north side up to 28° north (or south) latitude. At higher latitudes, winter sun
will arrive higher on that wall, providing less exposure for winter heating.

When the living room is on the south side of the courtyard, its lower eave
height will improve winter solar access. In this case, SSI is

$$\frac{3.0}{6.7} = 0.45,$$

providing winter sun over the courtyard's north side up to 38° north (or south)
latitude.

10 Keep the building in touch with life
    on the street.

11 Within the *zaguán*, solid doors and
    iron grille *rejas* are "switches" that
    give occupants a degree of control
    over privacy.

12 Where the facade can or must be set
    back from the street, more of a priva-
    cy screen can be developed within
    this setback.

13 The *zaguán* can be the public eye on
    the courtyard.

4   Consider more than one courtyard to
    serve differing needs.

17 The rooms that face the courtyard
    ideally are wider along the courtyard
    than they are deep.

Each *zaguán* is aimed not at its courtyard's center, but rather at a side arcade that
directly links the front and rear entrances. This defines one more "public"
arcade, leaving the remainder of the courtyard and other arcades out of any public view. Distances from street to courtyard also offer increased privacy. One
exception to this seclusion, however, is the low opening from courtyard to carport (Figure 13.10). This allows ventilation into the courtyard at floor level,
and a view from the courtyard to the stored cars—and vice versa. Clearly,
switches are necessary here—both view and ventilation need the opportunity to
connect or disconnect.

A roof terrace (rather than the traditional second, utilitarian courtyard) provides additional outdoor but private space for drying clothes, gardening, sunbathing, sleeping, or play. This terrace floor is protected behind walls of at least
1 meter height.

The main living room, L, between the courtyard and the commons, has a length
(facing the courtyard) to depth ratio of 1.4:1. This might seem to be too wide,
but it is daylit on both sides, as well as by a south-facing clerestory. The upstairs
multipurpose room has a ratio of 3:1.

Each house has up to five rooms, on four levels, that could serve one of several
purposes; bedroom, study, dining, playroom, or workshop. In each house, two
such multipurpose rooms (each with bath), as well as the living room, kitchen,
utility room, and courtyard, are wheelchair accessible. This variety of room sizes
and levels could appeal to less traditional occupancies—unrelated adults, families with in-laws, home offices, small retail boutiques, or cottage industries.

To accommodate such usages, each house has parking for three automobiles,
perpendicular to the minor street. One space is at street level; two are covered
and slope down to the lowest level. (Two more cars could be temporarily parked
between these cars and the street.) In addition, each pair of units shares an
extra-wide parking space for deliveries (or guests, with wheelchair access) that
slopes up to the rear doors at courtyard level. Additional guest parking is available at both ends of the commons (on the main streets), as well as at the mid-
block meeting room. On- and off-street parking spaces total 70, serving 13 families and up to four home businesses.

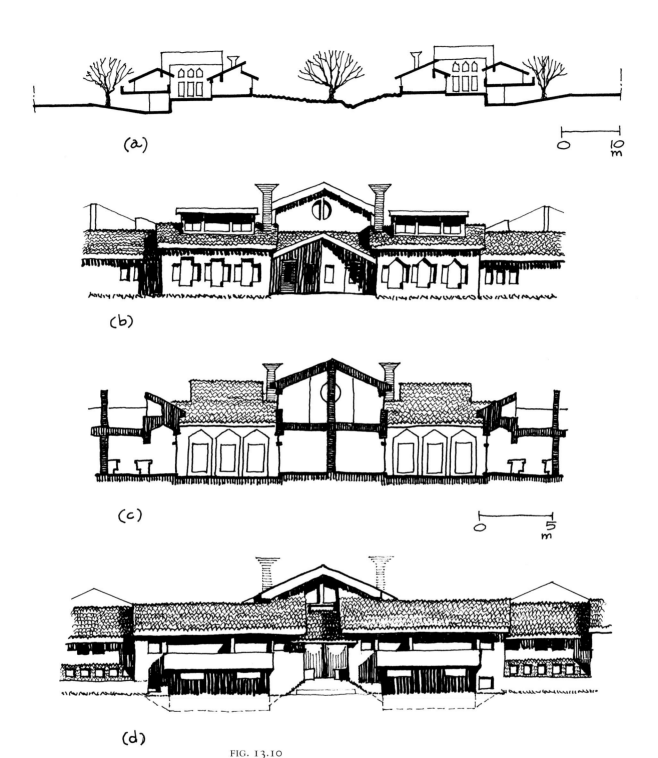

FIG. 13.10

Typical courtyard row houses' sections and facades. (a) Site section north-south.
The courtyard provides light and air to the rear of the lowered, covered parking area.
Almost all spaces in each house are cross-ventilated. (b) Facade, adjacent houses,
seen from the commons, looking north. (c) Section east-west. Taken through adjacent houses, looking toward the living rooms. (d) Facade, adjacent houses, seen
from the minor street. (© John S. Reynolds, A.I.A. Reprinted by permission.)

37 The stair as a stage.

38 Delight all the senses.

39 Plants in pots encourage flexibility
    in a courtyard.

32 The arcade can be both "path" and
    "place."

33 Design for migration: Each arcade
    may be used at a different time of day.

41 Consider masking sound.

42 Give water a place.

43 Provide a means to celebrate, rather
    than conceal, rainwater.

44 Collect and use rainwater.

35 Rehearse a variety of roles for the
    courtyard.

Within the courtyard, one side (north or south, the one with bedrooms) is raised one meter above the courtyard floor. Its arcade thus serves as a kind of balcony that could become a stage, and where rows of potted plants can be enjoyed from courtyard eye level. Against and below this raised passage (between low windows to the carport) is a fountain. Because the courtyard floor has earth beneath, larger trees and vines can be grown. Also, a cistern could easily be included to both celebrate and collect rainwater. The "public" arcade is wider than the others, serving as a kind of greeting place where visitors might be entertained without entering the remainder of the residence.

The confinement of the courtyard provides privacy, but curtails some outdoor activities that suburban life is expected to offer, such as ball games and bicycling. Thus the commons, with stretches of open space unthreatened by cars and directly accessible from every house, is an important feature that helps to visually and socially unify this group of residences. This unity is reinforced by the large indoor meeting/celebration space near the center (Figure 13.11a). This space is served by a rather large kitchen. The commons has a central flat lawn 10m x 30m, with raised embankments that could seat spectators. A pond contributes standing water to this landscape, and also serves for stormwater retention. South-facing grassy slopes invite sunbathing.

City corners are especially promising places for retail. Each of the four corner units can be adapted for such a purpose, however modest its size (Figure 13.11b). When the courtyard can contribute to the product appeal, the residence-retail mix is especially appropriate. Examples: a sculptor exhibits his work, or an outdoor furniture maker displays her folding canvas chairs, in the arcades and the courtyard.

An earlier version of this design appeared in Reynolds and Lowry (1996).

Courtyards invite the designer's detailed attention to a relationship of plants, animals and people; to the juxtaposition of outdoor variation and indoor consistency; to a controlled connection with the community from within the privacy of the courtyard. The surrounding covered yet exposed arcades are not only delightful paths, but places as well, for virtually any activity that might be transported from the indoor rooms, as conditions invite. The geometry of the courtyard is softened by the organic presence of plants, adding that sensual stimuli that architecture by itself cannot provide. It is the dwelling space that most celebrates change, both with the seasons and with age. The courtyard, with its modest area requirements, can return enormous benefits to the surrounding building, allowing a site to be covered with more building than open space, yet still in contact with sun, wind, rain, earth, and stars.

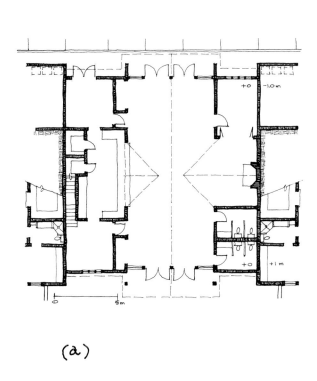

(a)

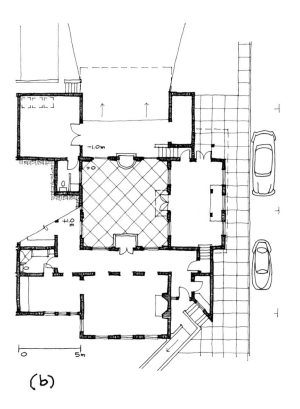

(b)

FIG. 13.11
(a) Plan of the meeting/celebration room
near the center of the north side of the site.
Occupying the same site area as would a housing
unit, this feature is most likely when the entire
block is a co-housing development. (b) Plan of
a courtyard row house at one corner, adapted to
take advantage of the commercial possibilities in
such a location. Courtyard and sales room are at
street level, encouraging their use for retail. The
living room, kitchen, etc. are elevated one meter
as in the other housing units, providing some
privacy. The downstairs space is a likely invento-
ry storage room. (© John S. Reynolds, A.I.A.
Reprinted by permission.)

APPENDIX A
EVAPORATION AND TRANSPIRATION

In hot and dry climates, evaporative cooling can contribute significantly to courtyard cooling. To what extent do the plants in courtyards provide this cooling, in addition to their useful shade? I give transpiration from plants little credit for evaporative cooling in courtyards, and instead consider plants to be more useful as catalysts for watering. Once the hose is flowing for the plants, it is natural to also soak the surfaces, especially the courtyard floor. These large-area moist surfaces provide most of the evaporative cooling.

The courtyard at Córdoba's Calle Osio #4 (rear) serves as a test. See Figure A.1 (also Table 7.1, # 33, and Figures 9.6 and 9.7).

This courtyard's opening to the sky is about 8 m x 7 m = 56 m² . Half this opening is available for solar radiation to plants; the other half is shaded by the *toldo*. Some simplifying assumptions will shorten the calculations; the results of these assumptions are shown in Table A.1.

FIG. A.I
The opening at roof level for the rear courtyard at Calle Osio #4, Córdoba, Spain. In the foreground, supporting wires for the *toldo*; in the background, citrus trees.

TABLE A.1 SOLAR RADIATION AND TRANSPIRATION, COURTYARD #33

Hour(s)	Insolation[*] W/m²	Air Temp. °C	Relative Humidity	Approximate Transpiration Rate[**]	
				gm/10⁶ cm² sec	L/h m²[****]
NOON	889	30	20	4.1	0.15
11 AM, 1 PM	860	28	27	3.9	0.14
10 AM, 2 PM	775	26	35	3.7	0.13
9 AM, 3 PM	646	24	43	2.0	0.07
8 AM, 4 PM	472	22	50	0.9	0.03
7 AM, 5 PM	274			none	none

[*] *From Lunde 1980.*
Data for clear day at 40° north latitude, August 21, horizontal surface.
[**]*From Gates, David M., and L.E. Papian, Atlas of Energy Budgets of Plant Leaves. Academic Press, London, 1971: graph on page 176. Note that 1000 W/m² is equal to 1.0 ergs/10⁶ cm² sec .*
[****]*[gm/10⁶ cm² sec] [kg/ 10³ gm] [3600 sec/h] [10⁴ cm² /m²] [L/kg] = .036 L/h m²*

Assumptions:

- all radiation not blocked by the *toldo* will be used to drive transpiration during the nine hours of strongest sunlight;

- no transpiration will occur in the other 15 hours (after all, if no solar heat gains occur, then no cooling of the leaf by transpiration is necessary);

- there is a very low wind speed in the courtyard (10 cm/sec [0.22 mph] is the minimum in the reference); note that at higher wind speeds, less transpiration occurs;

- the total leaf area of 28 m² (the half aperture area that is open to the sun) consists of 5 x 5 cm (2 x 2 in.) leaves with relatively high resistance (10 sec/cm), typical of plants in a hot dry environment;

- typical clear-day solar radiation is assumed. Temperature and relative humidity is based on measured results at the center of the courtyard, near the floor; for convenience, maximum temperature was assumed coincident with maximum insolation.

On the August day of Table A.1, the total water added by transpiration is:

1 hour (centered around noon)	@ 0.15 L/m² x 28 m² =	4.2 L
2 hours (centered around 11 AM, 1 PM)	@ 0.14 L/m² x 28 m² =	7.8 L
2 hours (centered around 10 AM, 2 PM)	@ 0.13 L/m² x 28 m² =	7.3 L
2 hours (centered around 9 AM, 3 PM)	@ 0.07 L/m² x 28 m² =	3.9 L
2 hours (centered around 8 AM, 4 PM)	@ 0.03 L/m² x 28 m² =	1.7 L
9 hours total	=	**24.9 L**

So, about 25L of water is released in this courtyard by transpiration on a hot day.

For a typical garden hose, the minimum flow rate is 0.21 L/sec, and the average about 0.4 L/sec (Stein and Reynolds, 2000). Thus, at typical flow rates the hose delivers in one minute (0.4 L/sec x 60 sec/min = 24 L) what the 28 m² of leaves transpire in the nine most sunlit hours of the day.

Clearly, compared to about 10 minutes of watering with a hose, the transpirational cooling has a minor role. It is, however, a reliable and continuous one.

I. Using rainwater in the building.

Rain on the roof and courtyard floor can be collected and serve nonpotable uses such as watering the courtyard plants. Year-round, rainwater could be used for flushing toilets. A rough approximation of catchment area and cistern storage volume follows:

1. Find the quantity of rainwater to be used daily:

   [L/capita-day] x [population] = L/d
   (gal/capita-day x population = gal/d)

2. Convert this quantity to the yearly need for water:

   [L/d] x [365 days] = L/yr
   (gal/d x 365 days = gal/yr)

3. Assume, conservatively, that a "dry" year will have two-thirds the precipitation of an average year; this measurement is the "design precipitation." (Average yearly precipitation in the U.S. is available from National Oceanic and Atmospheric Administration [NOAA] annual summaries.)

   [Average yearly precipitation] x [2/3] = yearly design precipitation

4. Determine the catchment area required,

   [needed L / yr] / [L/m² yearly design precipitation] = m² of catchment required
   (where precipitation is given in depth only, as with NOAA, use Figure B.1)

Sloping roofs contribute plentiful rainfall to this courtyard at the Alcazar, Segovia, Spain.

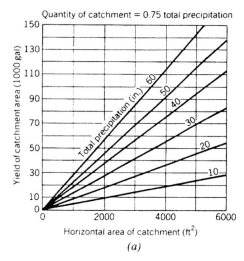

Quantity of catchment = 0.75 total precipitation

(a)

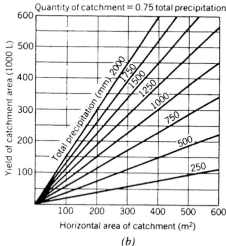

Quantity of catchment = 0.75 total precipitation

(b)

FIG. B.1

Yields of rainfall catchment areas (such as roofs) in terms of total annual precipitation. In these graphs, 75 percent of the total precipitation is assumed to be catchable; the remainder is lost to evaporation or spillage. *(a)* Conventional (inch-pound) units, from the U.S. Environmental Protection Agency's Manual of Individual Water Supply Systems, 1975. *(b)* SI units (1 m^3 = 1000 L). (Reprinted by permission from Stein and Reynolds 2000.)

5. Roughly size the cistern (storage) capacity by finding the longest dry period (in days of negligible rainfall, from NOAA local climatological data):

cistern capacity = [L/d] x [days of dry period]
(gal/d x days of dry period)

6. Convert capacity to volume by the formula

1 m^3 x stores 1000 L water
(1 ft^3 x stores 7.48 gal of water)

EXAMPLE. A courtyard residence in Córdoba, Spain will use roof-collected rainwater to flush its toilets. The total roof area is 130 m^2 *(1,400 ft^2)*. Water-conserving toilets are installed, using 10 L/flush *(2.6 gal/flush)* and serving three residents. If we assume 4 toilet flushes per day per person, we would then need

4 x 10 L = 40 L/capita day
(4 x 2.6 gal = 10.4 gal/ capita day)

1. quantity of rainwater to be used daily:

40 L/capita day x 3 residents = 120 L/d of rainwater needed
(10.4 gal/capita day x 3 residents = 31 gal/d of rainwater needed)

2. Yearly need for rainwater:

120 L/d x 365 days = 43,800 L
(31 gal/d x 365 days = 11,315 gal)

3. Design precipitation:

Córdoba's average annual rainfall is approximately 597 L/m^2 (Domínguez Bascón, 1999).
(Expressed in depth, this is 0.597 m, or 23.5 inches)
Design precipitation is:
2/3 x 597 = 398 L/m^2 in a "dry" year
(2/3 x 23.5 = 15.7 in., "dry" year)

4. Determine the catchment area required:

43,800 L needed / (398 L/m^2 rainfall) = 110 m^2
(or about 85 percent of the residence's roof area of 130 m^2)
(From Figure B.1, to capture 11,315 gal at 15.7 in. rainfall, a catchment area of approximately 1,500 ft^2 is indicated)

5. Roughly size the cistern (storage) capacity:

Córdoba normally has rather dry summers; average monthly rainfall is:

May	35 L/m^2	*(1.38 in.)*
June	17 L/m^2	*(0.67 in.)*
July	3.6 L/m^2	*(0.14 in.)*
August	4.0 L/m^2	*(0.16 in.)*
September	22.5 L/m^2	*(0.89 in.)*

(Domínguez Bascón, 1999).

The dry period, then, runs from June through August—about 90 days.

Thus, capacity $= 120$ L/day $\times$ 90 days $= 10{,}800$ L

$$\text{volume} = \frac{10{,}800 \text{ L}}{1{,}000 \text{ L/m}^3} = 10.8 \text{ m}^3$$

For example, 1 m deep $\times$ 3 m wide $\times$ 3.6 m long = 10.8 m³, a size that readily fits under a typical courtyard floor.

(Thus, capacity = 31 gal/day $\times$ 90 days = 2,790 gal

$$\text{volume} = \frac{2{,}790 \text{ gal}}{7.48 \text{ gal/ft}^3} = 373 \text{ ft}^3$$

For example, 4 ft deep $\times$ 9 ft wide $\times$ 10 ft 4 in. long = 373 ft³, a size that readily fits under a typical courtyard floor.)

For a more detailed sizing procedure for a building's cistern, using monthly totals, see Stein and Reynolds (2000), Chapter 9.

II. Rain gardens: a stormwater management alternative.

Use your courtyard to filter rainwater and recharge the aquifer? It may help you avoid stormwater runoff fees, which for my modest-sized Oregon home cost $85 every year. Of course, the water level is subject to drastic change! What follows is an excerpt from an article in *Landscape Architecture*:

> Rain gardens are small-scale stormwater infiltration devices that may replace conventional stormwater detention basins while providing the benefits of groundwater recharge, beauty, and wildlife habitat. Designed for use in small spaces with small drainage areas, such as a parking lot island, rain gardens are typically two-inch to six-inch deep retention areas planted with native species. These depressions capture runoff, and the plants and soil then filter pollutants in the stormwater, allowing the cleansed water to recharge the water table. Monitoring of installed rain gardens has shown positive results, with pollutant removal rates of 60 to 80 percent for nutrients and 93 to 99 percent for heavy metals. Rain gardens should infiltrate all water into the soil within four to six hours; if the infiltration rate of the native soil is lower than one inch per hour, a soil mix should be substituted. A minimum planting soil depth of two feet will provide adequate soil for root systems. Rain-garden plants should be capable of surviving periodic inundation and drought after the water has infiltrated. Rain gardens can be more cost-effective than traditional stormwater management designs because they require less piping, concrete and excavation.

(Based on *Landscape Architecture*, July 2000, p. 24, by Zolna Russell. Reprinted courtesy of Chris Hammer, *GreenClips* sustainable design news by e-mail.)

FIG. C.1
Abundant *bougainvillea* and an *acacia*
(mimosa) tree grow to a height well
above the roof terrace around the oldest
courtyard in Oaxaca's Hotel Camino
Real, a former convent. This courtyard
is also shown in Figure 1.8.

APPENDIX C
SOME COURTYARD PLANTS

Here are some 125 plants that might grace—or threaten—a courtyard. Vines, ground covers, pond plants, some trees, and a few perennials and annuals are included. I observed many of these in Spanish or Mexican courtyards. Some are personal favorites that would certainly be in my courtyard, whether for their color, texture, fragrance, or edibility. And a few are so allergenic, poisonous, or otherwise dangerous that a warning seems advisable.

The Ogren plant allergy scale, OPALS™, is used here. This index, devised by Thomas Leo Ogren, © 2000, rates plants on a 1 to 10 scale, with 1 the best, most allergy-free and 10 the worst. This scale includes pollen, contact, and odor challenges. The complete listing of some 3,000 plants is found in his *Allergy-Free Gardening: The Revolutionary Guide to Healthy Landscaping* (Ten Speed Press, Berkeley, 2000).

Ogren says "most plants rated 8 to 10 really have no place in a healthy landscape." Alas, this tarnishes the reputations of such potential courtyard dwellers as alder, almond, arborvitae, bay (male), bayberry (male), cascara, castor bean, catalpa, cork (male), cypress, date palm (male), elm, filbert, forsythia, jojoba (male), juniper (male), mango (male), Mediterranean fan palm (male), mesquite, monkey puzzle tree (male), mulberry (male), myrtle, oak, olive, papaya (male), pecan (male), pepper tree (male), privet, Russian olive, sagebrush (*Artemisia*), silk tree, smoke tree (*Cotinus*) (male), sycamore, willow (male), and zelkova. Less surprisingly, it also banishes poison ivy, poison oak, skunk cabbage, and the colorful sumac.

Note the number of male plants with high allergy potential; this is due to the abundant and allergenic pollen they release. While the females of these species are usually far less threatening, remember that they may produce fruits or seeds that litter the courtyard.

Pollen is not the only allergy threat; some people are sensitive to strong fragrances; others get skin rash from contact with leaves or sap; parts of many plants are poisonous if eaten.

Another numbering system refers to the USDA plant zones of cold hardiness. The coldest zone is 1, the warmest (least cold-hardy) is 11. (In Europe, Córdoba and inland Andalucía are zone 9; coastal Andalucía is zone 10. In Mexico, Colima is on the edges of zones 10 and 11.) A map of these zones, including Canada, the United States, and Mexico, can be seen at:

www.ars-grin.gov/ars/Beltsville/na/hardzone

Each entry is reprinted with permission from Tom Ogren's *Allergy-Free Gardening: The Revolutionary Guide to Healthy Landscaping*. The safest plants (rated 1 and 2) are accompanied by the symbol ❊. The most threatening plants (rated 9 and 10) are accompanied by the symbol ☆. Tom Ogren's entries are often followed by my own comments *[in italics within brackets]*.

Acacia.   Shrubs 8, trees ☆10
AUSTRALIAN WILLOW, BLACKWOOD ACACIA, GOLDEN WATTLE, MIMOSA, MULGA, RIVER WATTLE, SILVER WATTLE, WHITETHORN. Common evergreen shrubs and trees from warm areas all over the world, especially Australia. Hardy in zones 9 and 10, they are common in California and Florida. *Acacia* trees cover themselves with thousands of little yellow flowers in early spring. Easy to grow and fast-growing, they cause plenty of allergies. *Acacia* leaves are poisonous. [*They cast a delicate shade, and litter the courtyard floor with long bean-like pods. They also act a bit as would a* toldo, *spreading their tiny leaves wide by day, folding them vertically by night.*]

Acanthus mollis.   ✳1
BEAR'S BREECH, SNAIL'S TRAIL. A big, shade-loving perennial with large leaves; hardy to zone 3 if mulched heavily in the fall. Bear's breech often thrives where nothing else will grow. Tall spikes of white or purple flowers. Must be protected from snails and slugs. [*These leaves are the model for the capital of Corinthian columns.*]

Acer saccharinum.   Males 9, females ✳1
SILVER MAPLE. The silver maples make up a large group of common, fast-growing deciduous trees, hardy in all zones. They will often grow where other maples will not. Their fast growth leads to weak wood, and large broken branches are common. Most varieties should be avoided in the allergy-free landscape, especially "Silver Queen" and "Skinner's Cutleaf Silver Maple," both of which are male. One silver maple can be recommended, however. *A. saccharinum* "Northline" is a variety that produces no pollen, grows slower than most, has a wide-spreading habit, and is among the hardiest of all maples. "Northline" turns a bright yellow color in the fall. [*But just try to grow many courtyard plants in the shade underneath any maple—and beware those falling limbs.*]

Agave.   4
CENTURY PLANT, RHINO'S HORN. Big, bold succulents hardy only in the warmest areas, or grown as houseplants for sunny rooms. Some *Agave* species grow far too large for the average landscape, and many have stiff leaves tipped with very sharp, dangerous spines. Do not use the spine-tipped species near walkways or where children play. Plants may not flower for many years and then usually die after blooming. The attractive *A. attenuata*, or rhino's horn, is spineless and makes a fine and unusual houseplant for a sunny room. The sap of certain *Agave*, especially *A. americana* (century plant) can cause severe contact skin rash. Landscapers removing old century plants often contract this blistering rash. All parts of some species of *Agave* are poisonous. [*Given the threats, it is surprising to find this so widely used in Hispanic courtyards. Perhaps it is the very symbol of hot-aridity; or maybe it's the by-product of* A. tequiliana?]

Albizia julibrissin.   8
MIMOSA, SILK TREE. A hardy Japanese native common in California; it thrives in areas with high summer heat. Leaves are poisonous. [*Bees love its pink flowers; like Acacia, it casts a delicate shade and folds its leaves by night.*]

ALMOND, see *Prunus communis.*

Aponogeton distachyus.   ✳2
CAPE PONDWEED, WATER LILY, WATER HAWTHORN. Aquatic plants for lakes, ponds, and small pools.

APPLE, see *Malus.*
APRICOT, see *Prunus armeniaca.*

Araucaria.   8
BUNYA-BUNYA, MONKEY PUZZLE TREE. Large group of nonnative evergreen trees; some hardy into zone 5. *A. heterophylla*, the Norfolk Island pine, is often grown as a houseplant. Kept in a container, most *Araucaria* will never bloom or cause allergies. Planted in the ground, however, they are not good choices for allergy-free landscapes. Some species are separate-sexed, and in the future, female-only plants may be available. Because young *Araucaria* trees do not bloom, a small Norfolk Island pine can be a good substitute for a real Christmas tree for those with odor and perfume allergy to pine.

ARBORVITAE, see *Thuja.*
ARTICHOKE, see *Cynara.*
AVOCADO, see *Persea.*
AZALEA, see *Rhododendron.*

BAMBOO.   ✳2
Giant grasses. Many people are allergic to grass pollen, and allergies to bamboo pollen are not unusual in the tropics; however, bamboo does not flower when grown in the United States (except Hawaii). (I had a planting of golden bamboo, a 3-foot-tall variety, that grew many years and never flowered.) There are many varieties of bamboo and most can be cut to the ground every year; they will regrow without flowering. Some of the more exotic and expensive species, such as black bamboo, are usually kept confined to a large pot. [*Woe to those courtyard dwellers who don't confine any bamboo in a pot, preferably with no direct access to the ground below! The rhizomes spread relentlessly and are hard as iron to dig up. I've seen bamboo come up through the asphalt of my driveway.*]

BANANA, see *Musa paradisiaca.*
BAY, see *Laurus nobilus.*

Beaumontia grandiflora.   ✳2
EASTER LILY VINE, HERALD'S TRUMPET. Evergreen vine for zones 9 and 10 with large, fragrant, trumpet-shaped white flowers with bright green veins. Needs good soil and plenty of water. Flowers on old wood only, so do not prune too heavily. Protect from wind.

Begonia.   Fibrous 4, tuberous 3
Annual and perennial shade-loving flowers. *Begonias* from seed are called FIBROUS BEGONIAS. TUBEROUS BEGONIAS are grown from the fleshy tubers. *Begonias* are monoecious, but the male flowers are situated above the female blooms. The petals are large, richly colored, and attractive to insects. The small fibrous *begonias* shed more pollen than the large tuberous kinds. In large-flowered *Begonias*, the female flowers are often single while the male are usually fully double. *Begonias* are not high allergy plants, but they expose the gardener to more incidental pollen than would *Impatiens*. Good for hanging baskets in all but the hottest areas.

BE-STILL PLANT, see *Thevetia.*

Betula.   7
BIRCH. Although airborne birch pollen causes allergy, the actual bloom time of most birch trees is not long, usually finished within a few days. An occasional tree in the landscape (planted far from doors or windows) does not pose too much of a problem. However, people who are allergic to ALDER (*Alnus*) may also become allergic to birch . Birch trees rate better than alders because birch usually mature to be smaller trees, shed less pollen, and have a shorter pollen season. Birch trees bloom early in the spring and occasionally again in late summer or fall. These shallow-rooted trees need plenty of water. [*Lovely leaves and branch structure, but avoid these in courtyards! Pollen allergy or no, aphids love birch leaves and their sticky secretions on the fallen leaves can plaster your courtyard floor and stick to your feet. Ugh.*]

BIRD-OF-PARADISE, see *Strelitzia.*
BLACK LOCUST, see *Robinia.*
BOSTON IVY, see *Parthenocissus.*

Bougainvillea.   ✳1
Popular flowering evergreen vines and shrubs for zones 9 and 10; used in colder zones as container plants. Most commonly seen with red or purple flowers, but dozens of new colors are available. The plants need warmth, and the roots are especially sensitive to being moved, so transplant carefully. The color in *Bougainvillea* comes mostly from colored leaves, called bracts, not from the actual flowers themselves, which are small and usually yellow. A fine choice for an allergy-free landscape where it will grow, or as a good, sunny window houseplant elsewhere. In Japan, *Bougainvillea* is trained into stunning bonsai plants. [*See Figure C.1. What a relief to find that this widespread courtyard-beautifier is allergy-free! Yes, there's lots of litter, and what lovely litter it is. But watch those thorns; some people plant* Bougainvillea *under windows to discourage burglars.*]

BOXWOOD, see *Buxus*.
BRADFORD PEAR, see *Pyrus*.
BRIDAL WREATH, see *Spiraea*.

Brugmansia. 4
ANGEL TRUMPET, DATURA. An evergreen sub shrub that can be trained as a small tree. For zone 10 or greenhouse; houseplant with good light. It bears large, night-fragrant, trumpet-shaped flowers of white, salmon, pink, or orange. Provide shelter from the wind, which can damage large, soft leaves. Very easy to grow from cuttings. Do not plant angel trumpet under bedroom windows. All parts of these plants are mildly poisonous and contain a powerful, unpleasant hallucinogenic drug. *[Bedroom windows are hard to avoid in a residential courtyard. But what spectacular flowers these bear.]*

Buddleia. 5
BUTTERFLY BUSH. Tall, fast-growing perennial, shrub, or small tree, hardy in all zones. Some species are poisonous. *[These readily adopt a kind of weeping habit, so give them room to droop.]*

BULRUSH, see *Scirpus*.

Buxus. 7
BOX, BOXWOOD. Numerous species of evergreen shrubs and small trees, often used for low hedges. The very small, rounded leaves and dense growth habit make boxwood a good hedge plant. Boxwood flowers are small, greenish, and inconspicuous; however, they do cause allergies. Boxwood flowers on old wood, so if hedges are kept closely sheared, the plants will not flower. All parts of the plant are highly poisonous if eaten.

CALLA LILLIES, see *Zantedeschia*.

Camellia. Double-flowered ✳1, single-flowered 3
Of the many species, the most common and popular is *C. japonica*, an evergreen shrub or small tree. *Camellia* flowers are white, red, pink, or mixed and resemble tuberous begonias. Hardy into zone 6, *Camellias* are grown in cool greenhouses worldwide. Culture is exacting; they need acid soil, rich in humus; perfect drainage, but also constant moisture; lots of iron. Keep a deep mulch of leaf litter around the base. *Camellia* flowers may be singles, semidoubles, or full doubles. In some fully double varieties, the flowers have no stamens (the male parts) and so have no potential to release pollen. *Camellias* belong to the TEA family and, although sometimes difficult to grow, they're worth the effort. The full doubles, known as formal doubles, are excellent choices for the allergy-free landscape; the single-flowered varieties only slightly less so. *[The plentiful, browning litter of camelia petals has never appealed to me, especially in a small courtyard.]*

Canna. 3
Hardy in all zones, but the tuberous roots should be lifted and stored in the coldest climates. Tall, broad-leafed plants with terminal flower clusters of many colors. Easy to grow, but does best with full sun and good moisture. *[Spectacular candidates for that center-of-the-courtyard display.]*

Carica papaya.   Males 8, females ✳1
PAPAYA. Tropical evergreen fruit tree. Separate-sexed trees with airborne pollen. Females are excellent, pollen-free trees.

CATTAIL, see *Typha*.
CENTURY PLANT, see *Agave*.

Cercis. 5
REDBUD. Some species hardy into zone 5. Deciduous flowering tree with reddish flowers. The bark is occasionally used to relieve diarrhea, usually as a tea. *[Lovely, perfect heart-shaped leaves make this a favorite even after the blooming has ended.]*

Chaenomeles. ✳2
FLOWERING QUINCE, QUINCE. Deciduous shrub hardy in all zones. Quince is one of the first shrubs to bloom in early spring, with showy bright pink, white, or red blossoms. Most have thorns but a few varieties are thornless. (FRUITING QUINCE is *Cydonia*.) *[One of the better shrubs from which to force blooms indoors in very early spring. And hummingbirds love it, thorns or not.]*

Chamaerops humilis. Males ★9, females ✳1
MEDITERRANEAN FAN PALM. The only palm tree native to Europe, this is among the hardiest of all palms. Short, with a very thick trunk, this tree grows as far north as Seattle, Washington. Propagated from clumps that develop at the base. Almost all fan palms are insect-pollinated and do not pose allergy problems. The Mediterranean fan palm is, however, an exception: it is a separate-sexed, wind-pollinated tree that, when mature, may cause allergy. Female trees bear no pollen and are good choices in the allergy-free landscape.

CHINESE ELM, see *Ulmus*.

Chrysanthemum.   Double-flowered 4, single-flowered 7
COSTMARY, DUSTY MILLER, FEVERFEW, FLORIST'S CHRYSANTHEMUM, GARDEN CHRYSANTHEMUMS, MARGUERITES, OXEYE DAISY, PAINTED DAISY, SHASTA DAISY. A large group of over 200 species of annuals and perennials, including some of our most common garden flowers. Allergy to *Chrysanthemum* is common. Allergy to the insecticide *pyrethrum*, made from a type of *Chrysanthemum*, is also common. A few people are sensitive to the leaves of *Chrysanthemums* and may get skin rashes from handling the plants.

Some people may also be allergic to their fragrance. *[These extend the courtyard's color season well into the fall.]*

Citrus. 4–5
CITRONS, GRAPEFRUITS, KUMQUATS, LEMONS, LIMES, ORANGES, TANGERINES. Long-lived, handsome evergreen trees for zones 9 and 10 in favored locations with good frost drainage. *Citrus* needs good soil drainage and summer irrigation to thrive. Most also need high summer heat to produce sweet fruit, especially grapefruit. Mature trees bear fragrant, white blossoms during most of the year and most allergy to *Citrus* is in response to the heavy fragrance. Allergy to the pollen is less common. People living in or next to *Citrus* groves are more likely to develop sensitivity. The flowers of most tangerines and kumquats are smaller and much less fragrant, making them better choices for individuals with fragrance sensitivities. Allergy to *Citrus* is neither particularly common nor severe. On rare occasions, however, some people develop *photodermatitis* from contact with *Citrus* plants or fruit. Photodermatitis is a rash caused by exposure to sunlight after contact with an allergen. *[Most Andalusian courtyards have at least one member of the citrus family. Memorable fragrance.]*

Clematis. 3
Several hundred species of evergreen or deciduous hardy flowering vines. *Clematis* are among the most beautiful vines for winding up the trunks of trees, climbing on a trellis, or growing up and through climbing roses. *Clematis* does best when the roots are kept cool (mulch) and the tops have warmth and sunlight. They should have fast-draining soil and do well in large pots. Acid soil should be limed before planting. There are some well-documented cases of skin rashes caused by contact with *Clematis* foliage. Slow-growing at first and hard to establish, *Clematis* is worth the effort. Poisonous if eaten. *[Keep roots cool, give the tops warmth and sunlight? Sounds like the definition of the courtyard microclimate!]*

Cornus. 5
CORNELIAN CHERRY, CRACKERBERRY, DOGWOOD, FLOWERING DOGWOOD, OSIER, RED OSIER. Large group of hardy deciduous shrubs and trees, many native to the United States. On rare occasions implicated in allergy. Avoid direct contact with flowers. *[Makes a lovely courtyard centerpiece, leaves almost as attractive as the flowers.]*

Cotinus. 8
SMOKE BUSH, SMOKE TREE. Two species of unusual but attractive deciduous shrubs or small trees, hardy in all zones. A relative of POISON IVY, *Cotinus* has highly allergenic pollen, but because the smoky-colored flowers are borne on old wood, the pollen can be avoided by hard yearly pruning. Contact with the sap of this plant is known to

cause skin rashes. [*Hard yearly pruning is also needed to keep this a small, dense shrub rather than a rather rangy tree. The purple variety has a delightful coppery color, especially when its leaves and seed clusters (the "smoke") are backlit by the sun.*]

CRABAPPLE, see *Malus.*

Crocosmia (Montbretia).

Hardy corm grows into zone 6, if mulched in winter. Will naturalize in mild areas. Orange, red, or yellow blooms make long-lasting cut flowers. [*Another word for "naturalize" is "invade," pushing all else aside. But the stalks of blooms are lovely, if unfragrant.*]

Cynara. 3

ARTICHOKE, CARDOON. Perennial vegetables of the THISTLE family. Artichokes are hardy in zones 9 and 10. Cardoon is grown for its edible leaf stalks; hardy zones 8–10. [*Spectacular blue-green foliage, but perhaps not a plant that invites close contact.*]

DATE PLUM, see *Phoenix dactylifera.*
DATURA, see *Brugmansia.*
DAYLILY, see *Hemerocallis.*

Dieffenbachia. 5

DUMB CANE. Large evergreen houseplant with big, often variegated leaves. Needs good light and should not be overwatered. Dumb canes get their name because the sap, if ingested, irritates the tongue, mouth, and throat, making speech difficult. The effect can last up to 20 hours. The sap or juice can also cause skin rash. When grown as houseplants, these plants seldom bloom, but if they do the flowers have good capacity for allergy. In a greenhouse they are more likely to flower and present allergy problems.

Diospyros. 3

PERSIMMON. Many species of evergreen and deciduous trees in the EBONY family. Two species of deciduous fruit trees are used in the United States. Beautiful landscape trees, *Diospyros* is Latin for *two fires*, referring to the bright fiery color of the ripe fruits and also to the unusually good scarlet-orange fall color of the leaves. *D. virginiana*, the AMERICAN PERSIMMON, is a tall fruiting tree, native to the southeastern United States and hardy in zones 3–10. In zones 6 or 7, with good soil and regular water, this persimmon may reach 100 feet, although 50 feet is average. *D. kaki*, the JAPANESE PERSIMMON, is a shorter, rounder tree. The cultivar "Fuyu" has orange fruits, flattened rather than round, which can be eaten any time after they turn orange. The fruits of the American persimmon must be dead ripe before eating; otherwise they are inedibly astringent. "Fuyu" grows slowly but matures to a handsome, spreading small tree with netted bark and excellent fall color. Ornamental in all seasons.

[*One of my late fall favorites, when bright orange fruit clings to by-now-leafless branches.*]

Distictis. 5

TRUMPET VINES. Evergreen vines for zones 8–10. Several related species, all producing large flowers on fast-growing vines. All may cause contact skin allergies, so use caution when pruning.

DOGWOOD, see *Cornus.*
Doxantha, see *Macfadyena unguis-cati.*

Dracaena. ✳2

CORDYLINE, CORN PLANT, DRAGON TREE. Outside in zone 10; houseplants elsewhere. Palm-like trees and strap-shaped leafed, erect houseplants. *Dracaenas* (Latin for "little dragon") are superb for cleaning up indoor air pollutants such as carbon monoxide, benzene, and formaldehyde.

DUMB CANE, see *Dieffenbachia.*

Elaeagnus angustifolia. ☆9

RUSSIAN OLIVE. Small deciduous tree commonly planted in the Midwest as a windbreak. Not a true olive. Small yellow flowers in early summer are the cause of much allergy in some areas.

ELM, see *Ulmus.*
ENGLISH IVY, see *Hedera helix.*

Eucalyptus. 6–8

GUM TREES, IRONBARK, MALLEE, PEPPERMINT WILLOW, SALLY, YATE. A very large group of evergreen shrubs and trees native to Australia and widely planted throughout mild areas of the world. All *Eucalyptus* cause some allergy, but some species cause far more problems than others. The odor of fresh or dried *Eucalyptus* leaves and flowers is offensive to certain individuals and may cause an allergic odor response. There are over 500 species of *Eucalyptus* in Australia, and well over 100 species are grown in the United States. Overplanted in California, Arizona, and Florida, *Eucalyptus* shed profuse amounts of pollen. *Eucalyptus* flowers are pollinated by insects but imperfectly so, and each flower has an unusually high number of pollen-producing stamens. Several species, such as the FUCHSIA GUM, the SQUARE-FRUITED MALLEE, and the CORAL GUM pose a constant problem because they flower throughout the year. In areas directly below large BLUE GUM trees, the fall of pollen goes on for weeks and covers everything with a persistent dust. Some of the *Eucalyptus* such as *E. ficifolia*, the RED-FLOWERED GUM, have sticky pollen mixed with nectar, and these do not cause nearly as much allergy. (Some claim that they have gained a measure of allergy protection by eating *Eucalyptus* honey.) [*Perhaps the king of trees that litter.*]

Euphorbia. Rating varies by species

BASEBALL PLANT, CROWN-OF-THORNS, GOPHER PLANT, MILK BARREL, MILKBUSH, PENCIL TREE, POINTSETTIA, SNOW-ON-THE-MOUNTAIN, SPURGE. Very large group of evergreen shrubs, perennials, biennials, vines, succulents, and annuals. With well over 1,000 different species, *Euphorbia* is a complex genus, all members of which have potential for allergy. The milky sap or latex from many is often poisonous and usually has potential to cause skin rash. The white sap of the annual ground cover SNOW-ON-THE-MOUNTAIN (*E. marginata*), can cause severe skin burns even on people who are not allergic. This same highly caustic sap was once used to brand cattle. Certain of the succulent, leafless *Euphorbias* release a potent gas when cut that may be carcinogenic. Take care when making cuttings; a worker at the University of California, Davis, became violently ill while making *Euphorbia* cuttings in a small enclosed greenhouse. Pollen from various *Euphorbias* is suspect because none have complete flowers, and all may bear separate male (pollen-producing) flowers. Many *Euphorbias* are "short day" plants and only bloom in the autumn when the days are short. The most famous and popular of all *Euphorbias* is the POINSETTIA. Native to Mexico, poinsettias may reach 10 feet when planted outdoors. The red "flowers," which often appear around the Christmas season, are composed not of petals but of colored leaf-like structures called *bracts*. The actual flowers are inconspicuous yellow structures near the center of the rosette of bracts. These flowers are unisexual and shed pollen, especially at midday, although it is not normally airborne. Given their many noxious relatives, it would not be wise to inhale this pollen. Those with allergy to rubber would be wise not to get the white latex milky sap of poinsettia on their skin. The many *Euphorbias* that are completely separate-sexed plants can be counted on to contribute to inhalant allergy. (See also *Hevea brasilensis.*)

FERN. 4–7

A very large group of spore-bearing plants. Most grow best in moist, shady situations and they vary greatly by species in ability to withstand cold and frost. All ferns produce spores on the undersides of the leaves and, because these spores are airborne, can cause allergy. People who are already allergic to molds (or more precisely, to the spores of molds) may well find themselves allergic to ferns. CLUB MOSS (*Lycopodium*) is a related species that also bears spores; allergy to club moss spores is common and often severe, and cross-allergic reactions between ferns and club moss is also common. In the garden, and if not overused, most small ferns do not present a great allergy problem. Hanging ferns and large TREE FERNS, however, may drop spores on tables, chairs, pets, and people below them and should be used with care. [*Hanging ferns are indeed plentiful in the arcades of Hispanic courtyards, often over one's favorite chair.*]

Ficus. ✳2

FIG. Evergreen or deciduous vines, shrubs, house-plants, or trees, hardy to zone 6. Although related to MULBERRY, a known allergen producer, most *Ficus* are relatively benign, although all are capable of provoking skin rash from their milky sap. *F. benjamina* is a common indoor tree that normally never flowers and so presents few problems. The edible fig, *F. carica*, has its flowers inside the fruits and presents little problem, except that the fuzzy, slightly hairy leaves of edible fig can cause a contact rash in people with sensitive skin. The milky sap from fresh domestic figs also can cause contact skin rash. The huge evergreen MORTON BAY FIG, with great spreading heavy branches and large, leathery leaves, also makes tiny figs, and does not pose an allergy problem. A Morton Bay fig, one of the largest fig trees in the United States, grows beside the freeway on the west side of United States 101 in the heart of Santa Barbara, California, near the train station. Local lore has it that a sailor gave the seedling to a Santa Barbara girl and she planted it in 1876. *F. microcarpa*, the INDIAN LAUREL FIG, is a common street tree in California and Florida. It presents a low allergy risk, but its roots are famous for breaking up sidewalks. The RUBBER PLANT, *F. elastica decora*, also makes tiny figs and as a houseplant almost never blooms. The same can be said for the huge-leaved *F. lyrata*, the FIDDLELEAF FIG. Although once used for rubber production, *F. elastica*, the common rubber tree is no longer commercially grown. Rubber is commercially produced from *Hevea brasiliensis*.

Forsythia. 8

GOLDEN BELLS. Several species of deciduous, hardy shrubs grown for their early, bright yellow flowers. Related to olives. [*Give this weeping-habit shrub room to spread.*]

FRANGIPANI, see *Plumeria*.

Fraxinus.

ASH, BLACK ASH, FLOWERING ASH, WHITE ASH. Related to the olives, ash are large, native, deciduous trees that produce copious amounts of potent pollen. In some countries, ash is a primary allergy plant. Various ash species are hardy in almost any zone. Luckily, most ash are separate-sexed trees; females are easy to identify by their drooping clusters of winged seeds. Commercial budded or grafted varieties sold as SEEDLESS ASH are male trees that produce pollen. The inconspicuous flowers appear early in the year, often before the leaves. Ash are handsome, large, fast-growing shade trees, and their strong wood makes good firewood and fine lumber. White ash is used to make professional baseball bats.

Fuchsia. 3

Evergreen in zones 9 and 10, and houseplants or summer annuals elsewhere. Hanging, tubular flowers with brightly colored petals and sepals. Easily grown from cuttings, *Fuchsia* flowers attract hummingbirds. They grow best in filtered sunlight with good soil, plenty of moisture, and regular feeding. Plants are occasionally bothered by aphids or whiteflies; these can be controlled with a soap spray. In California, a tiny insect called the *fuchsia gall mite* has infested many *Fuchsia*, causing distorted leaves and branches. Cut off diseased portions well below the affected parts and dispose of them. *F. magellanica* is hardier than other species and can be grown outside into zones 4 or 5 if the roots are heavily mulched. Tops die back in autumn and resprout from crowns in spring.

Gardenia. 4

Evergreen shrubs with shiny, dark-green leaves and large, highly fragrant white flowers. An extremely attractive plant when well grown. *Gardenia* is hardy to zone 8 and is often grown as a greenhouse or container plant in all zones. They thrive in rich, acid, moist soil with fast drainage and plenty of humus, in full sun close to the coast or partial shade further inland. Heavy feeders, requiring acid-based fertilizers, *Gardenias* may become chlorotic in soil that is too alkaline. Low-growing *G. Radicans* is occasionally used as a ground cover for a small area. The heavy fragrance of *Gardenia*, so pleasant to many, may be too much for some who are odor-sensitive.

Geranium. 3

CRANESBILL, TRUE GERANIUMS. Low-growing, spreading perennials hardy into zone 3. Not to be confused with the showier related pot-plant or greenhouse GERANIUM (*Pelargonium*), true geraniums produce many small flowers in shades of rose, purple, white, red, or blue, and their leaves lack the strong scent of the *Pelargonium*. Fine plants for the perennial border or rock garden, *Geraniums* require constant moisture and do best in cool summer climates.

Ginkgo biloba.   Males 7, females ✳2

CHINESE MAIDENHAIR TREE. Deciduous trees hardy into zone 4. *Ginkgos* are separate-sexed trees; mature female trees produce large, malodorous fruits which contain an edible pit. Oil from these seeds can cause skin rash, as can handling the ripe fruit. Because most find the fruit objectionable, male trees are commonly used in landscaping. The female *Ginkgo* trees grow broader than the males and are often more handsome. A good tree for large landscapes where it can be planted far from the house. There are at least three female cultivars sold: "Golden Girl" has outstanding bright yellow fall color, "Liberty Splendor" is a tall, wide tree of perfect form, and "Santa Cruz" is a low spreading tree. *Ginkgo* extract is used to improve memory and also for certain heart conditions. [*At the first hint of frost, Ginkos drop all their bright yellow leaves at once, creating a truly magical carpet.*]

GOLDEN CHAIN TREE, see *Laburnum*.
GRAPE, see *Vitis*.
GRAPEFRUIT, see *Citrus*.

Hedera helix. 7

ENGLISH IVY. The hardiest, most common, and most popular of the ivies, used as a ground cover, houseplant, or hanging basket plant. *H. helix* 'Baltica' is the hardiest of all small-leafed English ivies. All *Hedera* pose serious allergy potential unless kept small and grown in containers. The sap is known to cause occasional severe skin rash and the pollen can bring on sudden, intense allergic reactions. Ivy usually blooms only on old wood, so that if it is pruned hard each year there is much less chance of exposure to the pollen. Occasionally ivy grows up the trunks of trees, eventually killing them, and in rare cases forming an "ivy tree." The leaves are poisonous if eaten and the black seed heads are especially toxic. Birds, however, especially robins, will eat ivy fruit in early spring when there is little else to consume. A good substitute for *Hedera* is perennial *Vinca*. [*Ivy also climbs walls quite easily, leaving an unsightly row of dried rootlike fibers when it is removed. Gives lots of dark green that needs very little care—but forget growing anything else in the beds that it invades.*]

Hemerocallis. 3

DAYLILY. Hardy, easy-to-grow perennial. Many possible flower colors. Thrives in sun or partial shade, with ample moisture. Poisonous.

Hevea brasiliensis.   ✶10

RUBBER TREE. A large tropical tree grown commercially for the production of rubber. Both the pollen and the sap are highly allergenic for many people. *Hevea* is a member of the SPURGE or *Euphorbia* family, a large group infamous for causing many serious contact allergies, including swelling, rash, itching, burning, and in some cases, death. Allergy to rubber (also called PARA RUBBER), or latex, is on the rise because of the increased use of latex gloves by medical personnel, food service personnel, police, and emergency workers. The allergy often takes months or years of repeated exposure to emerge. Reaction can then be swift and often severe; there are reported cases of fatalities occurring when rubber dental implements, catheters, and other medical devices have been placed in contact with sensitive individuals. Severe rashes and other allergic responses to the wearing of latex gloves, or from inhaling the powdery dust found on gloves, are also possible. In addition to *Hevea*, *Parthenium argentatum*, or GUAYULE, is occasionally used in the production of natural rubber. This desert shrub is related to RAGWEED, and it is quite possible that cross-allergic reactions will occur with increased use of guayule-based natural rubber. This is especially true because guayule rubber is being touted as a safe alternative to rubber from *Hevea brasiliensis*.

Hibiscus. 4

ALTHEA, MALLOW, ROSE-OF-SHARON. A large group of over 200 species of annuals, perennials, herbs, shrubs, and trees mostly grown as ornamentals. Common *Hibiscus* relatives are HOLLYHOCKS and COTTON. Most members of this group have large, highly-colored flower petals that are well-designed by nature for pollen transfer by insects; thus, although most *Hibiscus* flowers have exposed pollen, few if any members of this group cause allergy. *H. syriacus*, rose-of-sharon or shrub althea, is a tall, hardy shrub. *H. moscheutos*, the ROSE MALLOW, is a large-flowered perennial that dies back in winter but regrows from a fleshy hardy rootstock. *H. rosasinensis*, the CHINESE HIBISCUS, is a popular shrub in zone 10, with many beautiful hybrids in a wide array of colors. All *Hibiscus* are easy-to-grow plants in good sun with average soil and ample water.

HONEYSUCKLE, see *Lonicera*.

Hosta. ✳1

PLANTAIN LILY. Very hardy perennials, members of the lily family, grown for their large, ornamental leaves. *Hostas* grow best in rich, moist soil in partial shade, and are especially beautiful when planted under trees. The large leaves are frequently damaged by snails and slugs. Many hybrid varieties are available. White, pink, or pale lavender, sometimes fragrant flowers are held up above foliage on long, slender stalks. *[Shady courtyards are welcoming environments for these huge leaves.]*

Hydrangea macrophylla. 3

BIG-LEAF HYDRANGEA. May reach 12 feet outdoors in mild climates. Most often sold as a potted plant. Broad leaves and large, flat flower heads in pink, blue, or white. *Hydrangea* flowers are pH sensitive—rather like a natural litmus paper. Blue flowers can be changed to pink with the addition of limestone to sweeten or raise the pH of the soil. Conversely, pink flowers can be changed to blue by lowering the pH or acidifying the soil with sulfur.

Hypericum. 5

SAINT JOHN'S-WORT. Hardy perennial that is often used as a drought-tolerant ground cover that will grow in either sun or shade. In the Pacific Northwest this plant has naturalized and is known as KLAMATHWEED. It is the bane of livestock who eat it, because it causes photosensitivity; many cattle die from the resulting sunburn. Saint John's-wort also contains natural calmative compounds and is used in herbal medicine as a mood enhancer. *[Expect lots of bees when it flowers.]*

Ilex. Males 7, females ✳1

HOLLY. Many species; most are hardy evergreen shrubs or small trees, although some are deciduous. All hollies are separate-sexed, and the male plants present potential for some airborne allergy. A great number of named, sexed cultivars are available for sale. To produce their characteristic red, white, yellow, or black berries, female hollies must be pollinated; one male plant can pollinate many females. Landscapers frequently use all-male varieties as hedge plants, and in this situation they pose serious allergy potential. Allergy from holly pollen is not well documented, but is worthy of further research. Fruit is poisonous but not fatal. *[I'd expect to find this only in the courtyard of the Addams family. Those who have trod barefoot on holly leaves, or even attempted to pick one up, know better than to allow this in a courtyard! On the other hand, unarmed leaves are available on some cultivars—Ogren recommends Ilex cornuta "Bufordii".]*

Impatiens. ✳1

BALSAM, BUSY LIZZY, TOUCH-ME-NOTS. A tender annual for all zones, with shade and ample moisture. All *Impatiens* were once tall and white-flowered, but through selective breeding, there are hundreds of compact, dwarf, multiflowered, and multicolored varieties available at almost any nursery. *Impatiens* are easy to root from cuttings stuck in small pots of potting soil and kept well watered in the shade for a few weeks. As an annual for shady areas *Impatiens* are the top bedding plants used in the United States, easy to grow and dependable. From an allergy point of view *Impatiens* is one of our best annual flowers. The petals are large and highly colored, and the pollen-producing parts are few and deeply hidden well inside the flower. They are not known to cause any rashes nor do they have any close allergenic relatives. The yellow- and orange-flowered *Impatiens* grows along the margins of woodlands in much of North America. The juice from its soft stems is a time-honored remedy for rashes caused by stinging nettle and poison ivy, which usually thrive under similar cultural conditions. But the Latin name *Impatiens* and the common name of touch-me-not refer to the fact that the ripe, oval-shaped seed pods eject their seeds forcefully when even lightly touched or slightly squeezed.

Ipomoea (Calonyction, Quamoclit). 4

MORNING GLORY. Perennial or annual vines for full sun or partial shade. Very fast-growing when well adapted. In zones 9 and 10, morning glory can become rampant and overgrow fences, shrubs, and sheds. Annual varieties reseed readily. Flowers come in many colors, but perhaps the most impressive is the very large-flowered annual "Heavenly Blue." All morning glory leaves are capable of causing skin rash in sensitive individuals. The individual flowers of the morning glory have little exposed pollen and do not present much problem as an inhalant allergen. However, when growing strongly, the sheer mass of blooms may present an overwhelming fragrance for perfume-sensitive individuals; will often reseed and can indeed become weedy. The seeds of *Ipomoea* contain a powerful hallucinogen similar to the drug LSD.

IVY, see *Hedera helix*.

Jacaranda mimosifolia. 4

JACARANDA. A large deciduous tree from Brazil which puts on a glorious display of small, tubular, sky-blue flowers. Cold-hardy only to about 20 degrees, *Jacaranda* is grown in mild winter areas around the world.

Jasminum. 7

JASMINE. Several hundred species of evergreen or deciduous flowering vines and shrubs. Members of the olive family. Flowers, usually strongly fragrant, are white, yellow, or pink. The flowers present allergy potential both for their intense fragrance and for their pollen, which is similar to that of olives, a well-known and potent allergen. *[Córdoba on a warm evening is awash in this fragrance. It would seem that Andalucia, with jasmine in nearly every courtyard and olives covering the hills, could be a very difficult place for pollen allergy sufferers.]*

JOSHUA TREE, see *Yucca*.

Juniperus. Males ✶10, females ✳1, monoecious plants ✶9

CEDAR, HABBEL, JUNIPER, MOUNTAIN CEDAR, OZARK WHITE CEDAR, RED CEDAR, WHITE CEDAR. Hardy, drought-tolerant, easy-to-grow, common coniferous evergreen shrubs and trees, which are related to CYPRESS, not CEDAR. Juniper is the cause of allergies in many parts of the world. In certain areas of the United States, juniper is the primary cause of asthma and hay fever. Cross-allergenic reactions are common between juniper and cypress. The different species bloom in different ways: the very worst are the males of the separate-sexed species (dioecious); monoecious species always present allergy problems as well; the female plants of separate-sexed species, however, are fine for allergy-free landscapes. Most junipers bloom from early winter into late spring, sometimes releasing so much pollen that the shrubs appear to smoke. A few species of mostly western junipers bloom from September to November. Other species bloom sporadically throughout the year, creating an almost constant level of airborne pollen in many areas. In zones 8–10 in particular, junipers, especially male plants, may bloom several times each year. In Arkansas, Missouri, Oklahoma, Texas, and parts of Mexico the most common juniper is *J. Ashei*, the OZARK WHITE CEDAR, which is a juniper, despite its name. All of these are separate-sexed. In New Mexico, Arizona, parts of Texas, and into Mexico the most common species is the alligator juniper, *J. Deppeana*, also separate-sexed. In the eastern United States the most common species is the red cedar, *J. virginiana*, again a separate-sexed species. In much of the Rocky Mountain area the predominant juniper is the COLORADO RED CEDAR, *J. scopulorum*, another separate-sexed species. In parts of California, there is a common monoecious juniper, the CALIFORNIA JUNIPER, *J. occidentalis*. This species is sometimes separate-sexed. Other JUNIPERS native to California are separate-sexed. In separate-sexed juniper species, only the pollen-free female plants produce the round juniper berries. Plants without berries are male. Each male juniper bush or tree produces enough pollen to fertilize thousands of female plants. In some areas of the United States, during the early spring or fall months of the juniper bloom, there is so much male pollen in the air that every person living there is inhaling hundreds of juniper pollen grains with every breath. The relative humidity of an area has much to do with the actual amount of allergy to juniper pollen. In humid areas there is less allergy but in warm, dry areas, typical of much of the western United States, juniper pollen floats easily in the air, causing a great deal of allergy. Juniper pollen can also irritate the skin and is capable of causing contact dermatitis as well as severe inhalant allergy. In certain geographical locations where cities are surrounded by hills full of wild junipers, the only effective measure may be to selectively remove many of the wild male junipers growing close to the urban areas; males are easy to identify since they are the ones with no berries. Throughout America there are many millions of imported juniper trees, shrubs, and ground covers, most of which are separate-sexed; the female plants of these species can be used in allergy-free landscapes. One notable exception is the HIMALAYAN JUNIPER (*J. recurva*), which is monoecious and, like all plants bearing flowers of both sexes on the same tree, sheds allergenic pollen. Over the years landscapers have preferred to plant junipers without berries to reduce the amount of litter produced by each plant, and wholesale nurseries have propagated many millions of these pollen-producing male selections, all of which cause allergy. The net result has been a steady increase in urban *Juniperus* pollen and related allergic reactions. The answer is to identify and use female-only junipers in all future landscaping applications. [*So beware! But Ogren's book lists a number of sexed junipers, including many female clones.*]

KUMQUAT, see *Citrus*.

Laburnum. 7

GOLDENCHAIN TREE. Deciduous tree, hardy to zone 4. Produces long chains of pea-like yellow flowers. The three-lobed leaflets resemble CLOVER leaves. Often confused with another yellow flowering deciduous tree, *Koelreuteria paniculata*, the GOLDENRAIN TREE. The trees produce a quantity of seeds and pods, and this seed is very poisonous if eaten. All parts of the *Laburnum* are highly toxic. Children have been poisoned from simply sucking on the fresh *Laburnum* flowers. [*A dangerous and messy choice for the courtyard.*]

Laurus nobilus. Males ☆9, females ❊2

BAY, GRECIAN LAUREL, ROMAN LAUREL, ROYAL BAY, SWEET BAY, SWEET LAUREL. A large, slow-growing evergreen tree with aromatic leaves that are used in cooking. Hardy into zone 6, the sweet bay is a popular large container plant. The males of these separate-sexed trees produce abundant allergenic pollen. Allergy to the pollen is fairly common, and cross-reaction allergies caused by eating foods flavored with the leaves are also not uncommon. *Laurus* is not usually sold sexed except for the cultivar "Saratoga," which is a male and should not be used.

Lavandula. 6

LAVENDAR. Several species of evergreen, gray-leafed shrubby plants with fragrant leaves and flowers used in sachets and for perfumes. Although the pollen is rarely allergenic, lavenders are a common cause of allergy in those who are sensitive to perfumes and other strong odors. Oil of lavender, made from the fresh flowers and leaves, is known to cause skin rash.

LEMON, see *Citrus*.

Ligustrum. 8

PRIVET. Deciduous or evergreen shrubs or small trees, often used as hedges in all parts of the United States. Privet is among our most common landscape shrubs, but as a member of the olive family, it presents several allergy problems. The fragrance of the many small white flowers may cause allergy in odor-sensitive people, and the pollen from the flowers also causes an often severe reaction, especially in people already allergic to olive pollen. Keep privet hedges low and well-pruned to discourage blooming. Plants and seeds are poisonous. [*If a hedge is needed, consider the fragrant* Myrtus communis (Myrtle).]

LILAC, see *Syringa*.

Lilium. 4

LILLIES. Numerous varieties of bulbous perennials, hardy in most zones. Like most bulbs, they require fertile, well-drained soil to thrive. Allergy to lily pollen is not common, despite the fact that it is held on exposed stamens and easily contacted. The pollen is heavy and not designed by nature to travel far in the air, and the petals of all lilies are large, highly colored, and attractive to insect pollinators. People handling large numbers of lily bulbs, especially those working in fields or packing houses, frequently develop contact rashes from the bulbs. Many lilies are poisonous if eaten.

LIME, see *Citrus*.
LINDEN, see *Tilia*.

Liquidambar. 7

SWEET GUM. Large, deciduous trees, native to the eastern United States and Asia. Very popular street trees in many cities, sweet gums are hardy in zones 5–10. They are prized for their brilliant scarlet autumn color, in which they resemble MAPLES; but unlike maples, sweet gums produce a quantity of small, prickly round seed capsules in late summer. The trees are monoecious, having both sexes on the same tree but not in the same flowers, and thus relying on the wind for pollination. Allergic reaction to *Liquidambar* pollen is usually not severe. Sap from the Asian sweet gum is used to make aromatic *storax*, which is used in incense and perfumes. Allergy to storax itself is not uncommon. [*If you want a deciduous tree that allows sun through its branches in winter, this is not the choice. Holds onto its leaves well into February in western Oregon. Seed pods are not kind to bare feet.*]

Lonicera. 5

HONEYSUCKLE. Many species of evergreen and deciduous shrubs and vines, some hardy into zone 3. Because it is such a common landscape plant, and large numbers of people have long been exposed to the sweet pervasive scent, allergy to the fragrance is not uncommon. Pollen from honeysuckle has occasionally been implicated in allergy but is fairly rare. In some southern states *L. japonica*, JAPANESE HONEYSUCKLE, has naturalized and is rapidly taking over large areas of native woodland plants. This evergreen honeysuckle has a slightly higher potential for allergy than other species. [*With its strong sweet fragrance, it may be a good colder-climate substitute for jasmine.*]

Macfadyena unguis-cati (Doxantha). 3

CAT'S CLAW, YELLOW TRUMPET VINE. Drought-tolerant perennial vine for zones 8–10 that grows best with good summer heat. Bears bright yellow, trumpet-shaped flowers and large, round, deep-green leaves. Claw-shaped tendrils make it able to cling to masonry. Can grow to 30 feet.

Magnolia. Deciduous 6, evergreen 5

Evergreen or deciduous trees and shrubs, for zones 3–10, depending on species. M. *acuminata*, the CUCUMBER TREE or SWEET BAY, is a very large, tall, common deciduous shade tree hardy in zones 4–10. M. *denudata*, the large CHINESE WHITE MAGNOLIA or LILY TREE, bears very large white flowers, and is hardy in zones 3–10. M. *grandiflora*, the COMMON BULL BAY or SOUTHERN MAGNOLIA TREE, is a common evergreen tree that gets quite tall and wide and bears large cup-shaped fragrant white flowers. It is hardy in zones 5–10. M. *soulangiana*, the SAUCER MAGNOLIA or

TULIP TREE, is a deciduous, often shrubby tree that puts on a big display of flowers early in spring before the leaves appear. It is good for areas where late frosts are a problem. Allergy to *Magnolia* is only occasional and allergic response to the pollen is usually moderate, not severe. Those who live on a block lined with big *Magnolias*, or who have a large *Magnolia* in their own yard, have a much greater chance of becoming hypersensitive than others. Because deciduous *Magnolias* produce most of their flowers abundantly early in the year, their total bloom is much heavier than that of the evergreen varieties, which bloom off and on throughout much of the year. The fragrance from some of the deciduous *Magnolias*, especially the cucumber tree, may cause negative odor challenges for some individuals. *[Those who have a large Magnolia in their own courtyard will also sweep up considerable litter in blooming season.]*

Malus.   4

APPLE, CRABAPPLE. Apples and crabapples are hardy in most zones and make handsome additions to the landscape. Apple trees are not known to cause much allergy, but those living in or next to orchards may well develop hypersensitivity to the pollen. People who are allergic to roses have a greater chance of developing an allergy to apple blossom pollen because they are both in the rose or *Rosa* family. Apple pollen is heavy and does not travel far from the tree, so if planted away from the house, apples and crabapples present few allergy problems. Leaves and seeds are poisonous. *[Courtyards put apple trees in very close proximity, but they are indeed beautiful in flower, can be shaped in pruning, and of course reward with fruit.]*

Mangifera indica.   ☆10

MANGO. A tropical fruit tree for the mildest frost-free coastal areas of zone 10. It produces large, attractive, sweet fruit. Mango is an especially interesting allergy plant; the trees bear three kinds of flowers—male only, female only, and complete flowers with both male and female parts in the same flower. As a result of this system, some highly allergenic pollen becomes airborne. A relative of poison ivy and poison sumac, mango has sap that may cause a rash. Typical of the allergic reactions to members of this group (*Anacardiaceae*), the onset of symptoms is delayed for several hours after exposure. Those who have been overexposed to poison ivy or poison oak may develop a cross-allergic reaction to eating mango. *[I well remember when my three young children threw mangoes at one another in a Colima garden. Swellings yielding unspeakable disfigurement lasted several days!]*

MAPLE, SILVER, see *Acer saccharinum*.
MEDITERRANEAN FAN PALM, see *Chamaerops humilis*.

MESQUITE, see *Prosopis*.
MIMOSA, see *Acacia*; *Albizia julibrissin*.
MONKEY PUZZLE TREE, see *Araucaria*.

Monstera.   4

SPLIT-LEAF PHILODENDRON, SWISS CHEESE PLANT. (Also known as *Philodendron pertusum*.) Frost-tender evergreen tropical and subtropical vines for shady, protected areas of zones 9 and 10, and as houseplants elsewhere. Easy to grow, these large-leaved plants rarely flower indoors, but when they do, their pollen may trigger reactions. Outside these plants present little allergy potential. The sap of these big-leaved tropicals may also cause contact rash. All parts are poisonous.

MONTBRETIA, see *Crocosmia*.
MORNING GLORY, see *Ipomoea* (*Calonyction*, *Quamoclit*).
MOUNTAIN ASH, see *Sorbus*.

Musa paradisiaca.   5

BANANA, PLANTAIN. Tall, frost-tender evergreen trees that produce bananas. To grow best they need ample water, fertile soil, warmth, and protection from wind. In cooler areas, bananas are grown in large pots and then moved inside when frost threatens. The flowers are eaten in many areas, usually boiled. The fruit should be left on the trees until almost ripe, and then picked and brought inside to ripen off the tree; bananas left to ripen on the tree often cause indigestion.

Myrtus communis.   3

True myrtle. An easy-to-grow, drought-tolerant evergreen shrub or small tree (to about 16 feet), for zones 8–10. Very small, dark green leaves and small, white flowers make this an attractive plant for full sun, but it may get leggy in the shade. Because it is easily shaped by shearing, it is often used for foundation plants, screens, tub plants, topiary, and hedges. *[They give off a fragrance when brushed against, giving them a special presence in a tightly organized garden.]*

NASTURTIUM, see *Tropaeolum*.

Nerium oleander.   6

OLEANDER. Very common evergreen landscape shrubs and small trees in zones 8–10. All parts of the oleander are very poisonous, as is the smoke from them when burned. In recent years a virus has been killing off many oleander hedges in southern California, especially in some desert areas. There is no known cure for this virus and it is expected to spread. Oleanders are tough, drought-resistant, and flower well if pruned back occasionally. Pollen from oleander is not a well-documented allergy factor, despite the fact that the plants bloom profusely and the pollen-bearing stamens are well exposed. The sap is known to cause rash, and the odd fragrance is allergenic for some individuals.

Nymphaea.   ✳1

WATER LILY. Blooming aquatic plants hardy in all zones. *[Good to know that this favorite pond-dweller poses absolutely no allergy threat.]*

Olea europaea.   ☆10

OLIVE. Evergreen trees hardy in zones 8–10. Olives need good summer heat to make best fruit. Olive trees are easy to transplant and, as urban sprawl has taken over orchards, many have been moved into city landscapes. This is unfortunate, because olive blossoms are a primary cause of severe allergy. The bloom on olives is heavy, and the trees often are in bloom from April through June. The pollen is exceptionally light and buoyant and often becomes airborne. In many southern and western cities olives produce the worst early summer pollen. If olive trees are pruned hard each winter they will not bloom, but this is difficult if the trees are allowed to grow tall. One variety, "Swan Hill Olive," never flowers, making it an acceptable tree. Also worth noting is the fact that olive trees will grow perfectly well in the tropics and subtropics but will almost never flower in these climates. *[So if you really want an olive in your courtyard, prune it well and often.]*

OLEANDER, see *Nerium oleander*.
OLIVE, see *Olea europaea*.
ORANGE, see *Citrus*.

ORCHIDS.   ✳1
The largest group of plants in the world, orchids come in many sizes, shapes, and colors. Some are hardy into the coldest zones while others thrive only in frost-free jungles. Many orchids, called *epiphytic*, live in trees and need no soil. Other terrestrial orchids grow in the ground. All orchids need good moisture, and most potted orchids are planted in containers of pure tree bark, or a mix of bark and sand; these require regular fertilizing every two weeks during the growing season. Most orchids do best in partial shade, and a lath house is a popular place in which to grow them. Because orchids often have some of the world's fanciest flowers, well designed to attract insect pollinators, they rarely cause allergy.

OSIER, see *Cornus*; *Salix*.

Osmanthus.   5

SWEET OLIVE. About 15 species of slow-growing, evergreen tall shrubs and small trees, some hardy to zone 6. *Osmanthus* grows best in partial shade with ample moisture. The tiny flowers have a powerful fragrance, suggestive of apricot, and this scent may trigger allergenic reaction in odor-sensitive individuals. Some species are separate-sexed, but the male plants do not release much airborne pollen. *Osmanthus* is related to olive and ash, but unlike them, *Osmanthus* flowers have very few and very small male stamens.

PAINTED DAISY, see *Chrysanthemum*.
PALM, see *Chamaerops humilis*; *Phoenix dactylifera*; *Sabal*.
PAPAYA, see *Carica papaya*.

Parthenocissus.   4

BOSTON IVY, VIRGINIA CREEPER, WOODBINE. Several species of deciduous, long-lived clinging vines, some native to the United States and others to Asia. Allergies to Boston ivy or Virginia creeper are uncommon. Members of the GRAPE family, the grape-like fruits are mildly toxic if consumed. *[One of my favorites for summer window-shading deciduous vines, because its seasonal color change is spectacular; translucent chartreuse in spring, nearly opaque dark-green in summer, translucent blood-red in fall, and red twigs with tiny dark-blue berries in winter.]*

Passiflora.   3

MAYPOP, PASSION FLOWER, PASSION FRUIT. Mostly evergreen, some deciduous vines for zones 8–10. *P. edulis* produces a rich, sweet, flavorful fruit that is said to be an aphrodisiac. The vines are easy to grow, easily propagated from cuttings, and have very unusual large flowers, the parts of which are said to represent the Passion of Jesus Christ. The best fruit is produced when there are several plants for cross-pollination. Leaves and unripe fruit are poisonous. *[With a resume like that, who could resist it?]*

PEAR, see *Pyrus*.

Pelargonium.   5

GERANIUM. These are the tender, showy-flowered houseplants and warm-climate perennials that most people know as geraniums. They thrive in full sun and are remarkably drought-resistant. The large, soft, slightly fuzzy leaves have a characteristic pungent odor and are occasionally zoned with dark-green or purple or variegated. *Pelargoniums* release little pollen, but their fragrance and the smell of their leaves may affect odor-sensitive individuals. IVY-LEAF GERANIUMS have waxy leaves without the characteristic odor. They tolerate some shade, and because of their lack of scent, are a better choice for the allergy-free garden. *[Every self-respecting courtyard in Córdoba flaunts these easy-to-care-for plants.]*

PERIWINKLE, see *Vinca*.

Persea.   3

AVOCADO. A large group of tender evergreen trees for zones 9–10. *P. americana*, the common edible avocado, is not frost-resistant and is most commonly grown as a houseplant outside of the warmest zones; "Bacon" is among the hardiest cultivars. In fertile soil in areas with little frost, a mature avocado tree can grow to 70 feet. Because of its shallow roots, avocado requires summer irrigation and year-round mulch. The pollen is rarely implicated in allergy. *P. borbonia*, the RED BAY, SHORE BAY, or SWAMP BAY, is a large tree, native to the southeastern United States, which can reach 80 feet, although it is usually much smaller. It thrives in moist to wet soils in zones 8–10. *P. indica* is a smaller evergreen tree used mostly in California. *Persea* leaves are poisonous.

PERSIMMON, see *Diospyros*.

Phoenix dactylifera.   Males ✦9, females ✳1

DATE PALM. The date palm of commerce is a tall, thin-trunked tree, cold-hardy to 10 degrees. Of the approximately 15 other species of date palms, none else is cold-hardy below 20 degrees. All members of this genus are separate-sexed, but no attempt has been made to sell them sexed, despite the fact that the trees are easy to propagate from root suckers, which produce young trees of the same sex as the parent. As with all separate-sexed trees, the males produce quantities of potent, airborne pollen. CANARY ISLAND DATE PALMS are very common street trees in California, Florida, and all along the Gulf Coast, creating a corridor of allergy when they bloom. The pollen of male Canary Island palms is occasionally used to pollinate female *P. dactylifera* but results in smaller fruit.

Photinia.   4

The deciduous *P. villosa* is hardy in zones 3–10. *P. x Fraseri* is a common evergreen shrub or small tree hardy in zones 9–10. *Photinia* flowers are usually white, occasionally pink, showy, and, like the blossoms of the related PEAR, malodorous. When pruned hard, the new leaves grow back a bright red color, which slowly turn green as they mature. Despite its offensive smell, *Photinia* blossom is not a great contributor of allergenic pollen. *[I love the red leaves in spring, but that odor, confined to a courtyard, could be a real problem.]*

Pinus   4

PINE, PIÑON, PIÑON NUT TREE. Evergreen coniferous trees and shrubs that are native to most temperate parts of the world, including Asia, Europe, and America. Some species are hardy into the coldest zones. In urban landscaping large pine trees often overwhelm the area in which they are planted. Pines shed enormous quantities of pollen, but because it is waxy and not highly irritative to mucous membranes, their potential for allergy is rather low, and when it occurs, not usually severe. Allergic reactions to the scent of cut pine are reported but are also rare. On the central coast of California most of the native MONTEREY PINES have died off recently. The small, low-growing varieties such as the MUGO PINE present even less allergy potential than larger types and are good choices for the allergy-free landscape. One *Pinus* species, *P. contorta*, the LODGEPOLE PINE from Colorado, is known to cause asthma. Use of the lodgepole pine in landscaping should be discouraged.

Pistache.   Males 8, females ✳1

A group of deciduous and evergreen trees and shrubs from the southwestern United States, Mexico, the Mediterranean region, and the Canary Islands. All species are separate-sexed, and the male plants have very high potential for causing allergy. *Pistache* is in the *Anacardiaceae* family of plants that includes POISON IVY, POISON OAK, and POISON SUMAC. Because of this close familial connection, it is probable that those with hypersensitivity to poison ivy or poison oak may develop a severe allergy to either pistachio nuts, their pollen, or both. *P. atlantica*, the MOUNT ATLAS PISTACHE, is a large, briefly deciduous separate-sexed tree for zones 8–10. *P. chinensis*, the CHINESE PISTACHE TREE, is a deciduous tree to 60 feet, prized for its orange and red autumn color in zones 8–10, and for the ornamental, glossy, half-red, half-blue-green fruit of the female trees. A popular street tree in California, the cultivar "Keith Davey" is a male and should never be used. *P. vera* is a small- to medium-sized deciduous nut tree for hot summer areas of zones 8–10. Both sexes needed to produce the edible nuts.

PLANE TREE, see *Platanus*.
PLANTAIN LILY, see *Hosta*.
PLANTAIN, see *Musa paradisiaca*.

Platanus.   ✦9

BUTTONBALL TREE, PLANE TREE, SYCAMORE. Big, fast-growing deciduous trees, some native, with attractive, peeling bark. Sycamore trees are used throughout the world, and they cause allergy everywhere they're cultivated. Several species grown in zones 3–10. The fuzzy leaves may cause contact rash in sensitive individuals. When they bloom in early spring, sycamores produce large amounts of airborne pollen, and allergy to sycamore is common. *[Its favorable points include gorgeous patchy colors of bark, resistance to smog, and those seed pods that give its bare branches such character through the long winter months. But at close range in a courtyard . . .]*

Plumeria.   4

FRANGIPANI. Frost-tender evergreen and deciduous shrubs, and small trees for sheltered locations of zone 10, or as greenhouse plants. *Plumeria* are easy to propagate from cuttings and make good container plants. Their extremely fragrant flowers may affect those with odor sensitivity. Flowers and leaves are poisonous.

POINSETTIA, see *Euphorbia*.
POISON IVY, POISON OAK, and POISON SUMAC, see *Rhus*.
POMEGRANATE, see *Punica granatum*.

Populus. Males ✭9, females ✳1

ASPEN, COTTONWOOD, and POPLAR. More than 30 species of large, fast-growing, deciduous trees, members of the WILLOW family, hardy in all zones and under conditions ranging from arid deserts to wetlands, depending on species. Almost all species of *Populus* are separate-sexed; male trees often cause widespread and severe allergy, and in many areas, poplar pollen is the primary cause of springtime allergy. Female trees cause no allergy but are often maligned for the "cotton," seeds, and fruit that they shed. Because they shed their seeds, each with its parachute of highly visible cotton at the same time that ragweeds, coyote bush, Chinese elm, and other highly allergenic plants are shedding their pollen, female poplars are unfairly blamed for the resulting allergy. (Female trees often mature to larger, longer-lived, rounder specimens than do male trees.) Trees sold as COTTONLESS COTTONWOODS or COTTONLESS POPLARS are males, and highly suspect in the allergy-free landscape. The following named cultivars are all males and should be avoided: "Androscoggin," "Concordiensis," "Majestic," "Mojave Hybrid," "N.E. 17," "N.E. 308," "Wheeler," as should *P. songarica* (*P. manchurica*). *P.* "Volunteer" is a highly rated female RUSSIAN POPLAR, and *P. wilsoni* is a large female tree with reddish twigs and leaves that are bluish above and white below. *P.* "Noreaster" is one of the best, a sterile female. All three are excellent choices for the allergy-free landscape. [*My experiences with poplars/cottonwoods have been tainted by the sticky secretions of thousands of aphids, not to mention mounds of cotton that pile up in spring and are impossible to sweep up, as they merely drift away from the broom or rake. Maybe those sterile females are the answer, but I'd not risk one in a courtyard.*]

PRIVET, see *Ligustrum.*

Prosopis. ✭9

MESQUITE, SCREW BEAN, TORNILLO. Twenty or more species of summer-deciduous or evergreen thorny shrubs or trees, native to desert areas of the southwestern United States and Mexico. With its fernlike foliage and numerous pollen-shedding small yellow flowers, mesquite is a major allergy plant in some areas.

Prunus armeniaca. ✳2

APRICOTS are hardy in most zones, but do not fruit regularly in any but the mildest winter areas. Good trees often can be grown from seed, although they may take three or more years to fruit. They are especially beautiful when in bloom, and many have excellent fall color. Allergy to apricots is usually confined to those living in or near orchards; as the occasional yard tree, apricots are a very good choice for the allergy-free landscape. *P. glandulosa* is the FLOWERING APRICOT.

Prunus communis. ✭10

ALMONDS. In allergy studies almonds stand out as the cause of severe allergy. People living in or close to almond orchards are most likely to develop allergy. Although there is occasionally a cross-over allergic reaction to eating almonds, this is less common.

Punica granatum. ✳2

POMEGRANATE. Deciduous shrubs or small trees, hardy to zone 7, but growing best in full sun, in hot summer areas of zones 8–9. Good heat is required to ripen sweet fruit. The large, orange flowers are followed by round fruits that require heat and adequate moisture to ripen fully. Although occasionally grown as an ornamental, pomegranates are good fruit trees, with the variety "Wonderful" producing the largest fruit. *Punica* is easy to propagate from dormant cuttings.

PUSSY WILLOW, see *Salix.*

Pyrus. Ornamentals 4, fruiting varieties 3

BRADFORD PEAR, PEAR. Deciduous fruit trees hardy to zone 4 but growing best in zones 7–9. PEAR blossoms are attractive but malodorous, although the strong smell does not carry far in the air. The pollen is not usually an allergen. Among the many ornamental, flowering, non-fruiting pears grown, the most common and popular is the pyramidal Bradford pear. ASIAN PEARS, which have large sweet fruit, rounder than the common pear, are also prized for their good autumn color. Pears often suffer from fireblight, a bacterial disease that can kill entire branches or even whole trees. Fireblight is spread through airborne spores and direct contact, so diseased branches should be burned, not composted. It is worst during cool, damp weather. Excessive growth encourages fireblight, so use of nitrogen fertilizers is not advised. [*In a small courtyard that odor is likely to be a problem.*]

Quercus. Deciduous 8, evergreen ✭9

OAK. With over 400 species of deciduous or evergreen hardy shrubs or trees worldwide, oaks are important timber and landscape plants in much of the temperate world. All oaks make acorns, the usually large, capped oak seeds. Acorns are eaten by many wild animals and in the past were sometimes used as food by native peoples. Oaks are pollinated by the wind, and they produce abundant pollen that provokes a great deal of allergy in areas with many oaks. In some cities, planted landscape oaks are the most common street trees, and these in turn contribute to frequent allergic attacks. The large deciduous trees usually flower while the branches are still bare of leaves or as the new leaves are budding out. The evergreen oaks often bloom later; in California they are often at their peak around the first of June. (In California there are so many kinds of oaks, both native and planted, all of them

blooming at different times, that parts of the state have a perennial oak pollen allergy season.) Some oaks produce much more pollen than others, and an occasional oak tree does not ever bloom. It is hoped that in the future, nurserymen will seek out nonblooming oaks and graft them onto oak seedlings. The literature on oak allergy suggests there are distinct differences in severity between the allergy potentials of different species of oaks, but as yet we are forced to group them into two oversimplified groups, evergreen and deciduous. Some bright graduate student could do us all a wonderful service by sorting out the actual allergy potential of each kind of oak, how much pollen each releases, and exactly how allergenic each kind of pollen is. Allergy to oak pollen is such that if someone is allergic to the pollen of RED OAK, for example, he will usually also be allergic to pollen of WHITE OAK or any other oak. The actual degree of allergy to each species varies greatly and as yet is something of a mystery. Most oaks produce heavy pollen loads, but the evergreen or LIVE OAKS often produce the most pollen and produce it for a longer time. In California, *Q. agrifolia*, the COASTAL LIVE OAK, is a major allergy tree. A large, spreading oak tree may be the centerpiece of a landscape, and most people would be reluctant to remove it. If someone with allergies has a big oak, he or she would be wise to get skin-tested for oak pollen, and if positive, undergo desensitizing shots for oak. For oaks that are not too large in height, it is hoped that the future will bring us some sort of nontoxic spray that could be used to knock down the huge amount of male flowers before they can release their pollen. Pollen from all types of oak is also known to sometimes cause skin rashes from contact. [*Slipping on acorns, sneezing from pollen, waiting well into winter for the leaves to fall— I would avoid an oak in a courtyard.*]

QUINCE, see *Chaenomeles.*
REDBUD, see *Cercis.*

Rhododendron. Azalea 3, rhododendron 4

AZALEA, RHODODENDRON. A very large group of about 800 species of deciduous and evergreen shrubs or small trees. In general azaleas are lower-growing than rhododendrons, but all have colorful, extremely showy flowers, often in large, impressive clusters. They thrive in the partial shade of large deciduous trees, in deep, peaty, well-drained acid soil with a steady supply of moisture. Because they are completely unforgiving as far as drought is concerned, it is advisable to keep these plants deeply mulched at all times. *Rhododendron* pollen is relatively heavy and not usually airborne; the male stamens are exposed, however, and direct contact with the pollen is possible. Tall plants should be used at the back of the garden, where the danger from dropping pollen is lessened. All parts of azalea and rhododendron are poisonous.

Rhus. Males ★10, females 7

AFRICAN SUMACH, CHINESE VARNISH TREE, FRA-GRANT SUMAC, LAUREL SUMAC, LEMONADE BERRY, NUTGALL TREE, POISON ELDER, POISON IVY, POISON OAK, POLECAT BUSH, SMOOTH SUMAC, SUGAR BUSH, SUMAC, VINEGAR TREE, WILLOW SUMACH. About 150 species of evergreen or deciduous shrubs and trees, from many regions. Most are separate-sexed, and the light, buoyant pollen produced by males of the species presents a distinctly serious allergy potential. The most well-known of the allergenic *Rhus* are poison sumac (*R. vernix*), poison ivy (*R. radicans*), and poison oak (*R. toxicodendron*), and cross-allergic reactions to the pollen of other *Rhus* species are a distinct possibility for those already hypersensitive to these three noxious weeds. Although several of the *Rhus* species are prized as landscape shrubs because of their ease of growth and their good fall color, no members of this genus are recommended for allergy-free landscapes, because even the female plants present a host of allergy problems from contact rashes to odor allergies. In southern Italy, *R. coriaria*, the TANNER'S SUMAC, is grown as a source of tannin for leather making. In Japan, *R. orientalis*, is a vine with similar properties to our native poison ivy. In east Asia, Japan, and India, *R. succedanea*, the WAX TREE, is used to make both a commercial wax and a lacquer. Both the wax and the lacquer may cause allergy. In Japan the native *R. verniciflua*, or VARNISH TREE, which is often described as poisonous to touch, is used to make varnish or lacquer. It is occasionally grown in the United States in zones 9–10, even though varnish or lacquer produced from the sap of this tree has been implicated as causing severe contact rash in individuals who handle furniture coated with this lacquer. *R. integrifolia*, a California native, has berries that are occasionally used as a substitute for lemons in lemonade; those who suffer allergy to any *Rhus* species should not drink this beverage. *R. ovata*, or SUGARBUSH, is a large, drought-tolerant evergreen shrub native to the southwestern United States. Female plants (with red berries) are rated at 4, while males are rated at 9. Since *Rhus* species are separate-sexed, only the female plants have fruit. Because *Rhus* males produce allergenic pollen in addition to all the other potential problems, the males should never be used. Cross-reactive responses between all different species of *Rhus* are well known, and since allergy to poison ivy and poison oak is so common, none of these plants can be recommended. Even the volatile organic compounds (VOCs) released into the air when the plants are pruned are capable of causing allergy. Lastly, it is important to realize that allergic response to *Rhus* species is almost always a delayed reaction. The actual allergy may not occur until hours, or even days, after the initial exposure. *[But it has such a lovely branch structure, and such vivid red in the fall! Want to risk it? Then get a female.]*

Robinia. 5

BLACK LOCUST, FALSE ACACIA, GUMMY ACACIA, LOCUST, SILVER CHAIN TREE, SMOOTH ROSE ACACIA, WHYA TREE. *Robinia* is a group of several species of large, fast-growing deciduous, often thorny, flowering trees of the LEGUME family. All have very hard, durable wood and are well adapted to growing in hot, dry summer areas; some species are cold-hardy to zone 3. Because they cast a light, filtered shade, they are prized lawn trees. Some named cultivars are spineless. All *Robinias* have seeds, flowers, and leaves that are poisonous if eaten (see also *Laburnum*). *[That light, filtered shade could be prized for a courtyard as well.]*

Rosa. Varies by variety.

ROSES. A large group of over 100 species, hardy in all zones, according to species. Allergy to the fragrance of roses is more common than is allergy to the pollen, and any allergic response is usually low to moderate. Fully double roses release far less pollen than single-flowered varieties.

Roses grow best in full sun to partial shade and require fertile, well-drained soil and ample moisture to thrive. Many roses are easy to grow from dormant cuttings, which can often be rooted simply by using long cuttings, direct-stuck in a partially shaded spot. Roses are best purchased bare root in spring. Because they are susceptible to many diseases including mildew, rust, and black spot, many garden roses are heavily sprayed. Both the spores of rose diseases and the chemicals used to control them may trigger allergic responses. Remove and replace disease-prone varieties with disease-resistant ones (a process rosarians refer to as shovel-pruning). When insects or diseases are a problem a soapwater spray is usually enough to afford control. The botanical product *Neem* is nontoxic and also controls both insects and disease. The very best roses for an allergy-free garden are highly disease resistant, have either light or absent fragrance, and are fully double. Good choices for the allergy-free garden include "Sally Holmes," a disease-resistant single that is a very low pollen producer; "Iceberg," a semidouble white that releases almost no pollen (I've found that "Iceberg" is also the best all-around white garden rose); "New Day," a yellow; "Olympiad," a red; "Gene Boerner," a pink; "Singing in the Rain," a salmon-colored rose; "Honor," another good white; and "Touch of Class," a rosy-coral hybrid tea that produces minimal amounts of pollen and has won many a blue ribbon. Miniature roses are also a good choice, because they release small amounts of pollen. There is little point in trying to rate roses as a group, because of their incredible diversity. Very lightly scented or unscented roses with fully double blooms and many petals, combined with disease resistance, would rate at 2. Multiflora roses with many highly fragrant, small flowers would rate as high as 5. Double roses with very high fragrance, such as "Double

Delight" or "Fragrant Cloud," rate 4, unless they are cut and brought into the house. In that case, depending on the season, they could rate as high as 6, as roses are more fragrant in warm weather. (To reduce the amount of pollen released by your roses, do not destroy earwigs, a common albeit minor pest of roses. Earwigs usually eat only the pollen-producing stamens and don't bother with the petals. Cucumber beetles also happily dine on rose pollen.)

ROSE-OF-SHARON, see *Hibiscus*.

Rosmarinus officinalis. 6

ROSEMARY. Evergreen erect or prostrate shrubby herbs for zones 8–10, with small, highly aromatic leaves and numerous small, sky-blue flowers. Rosemary is very drought-resistant and grows best in well-drained soil, in full sun. The fragrance is objectionable to many and allergenic to some. *[For those fond of its aroma, brushing with the hands yields a nice reward.]*

RUBBER TREE, see *Hevea brasiliensis*.
RUSSIAN OLIVE, see *Elaeagnus angustifolia*.

Sabal. 5

BERMUDA PALM, BUSH PALM, CABBAGE PALMETTO, DWARF PALM, OAXACA PALMETTO, PALMETTO, PUERTO RICAN HAT PALM, SCRUB PALMETTO, SONORAN PALM, TEXAS PALM. A group of about 20 species of closely related small, fan-leaved palms, some to over 60 feet. This group of palms has complete flowers that are insect-pollinated, but still produce some airborne pollen. Common in zones 8–10 and hardier than most palms, the SABAL PALMETTO causes allergy only in those areas where it is extremely common. A few of these in a garden should pose little threat.

SAINT JOHN'S-WORT, see *Hypericum*.

Salix.

OSIER, PUSSY WILLOW, SALLOW, WEEPING WILLOW, WILLOW. A large genus of mostly deciduous shrubs and trees, with over 500 species worldwide. Various species are adapted to grow anywhere from desert washes to frozen tundras, and are native to every continent except Australia. The common willows and weeping willow are useful in damp spots where most trees fail to flourish. They grow quickly and may be used to form a quick-growing tall hedge. Low-growing willow shrubs are used as ground covers. Because most willows are easily propagated from cuttings, a number of clones exist. Willows are often mentioned as potent allergen-producing plants, but because they are separate-sexed, the females of the species are excellent choices in the allergy-free landscape. *[Willows are infamous for invading sewer lines, so use in a courtyard with care.]*

Some Courtyard Plants

Santolina. 7

GREEN SANTOLINA, GRAY SANTOLINA, LAVENDER COTTON. A shrubby perennial for full sun in zones 7–10. *Santolina* bears small, daisy-like yellow flowers; the bruised leaves release a pungent odor. [*Despite the aroma, this is said to be one of famed landscape architect Gertrude Jekyll's favorites, and I can see why.*]

Scirpus. 5

LOW BULRUSH. A tall reedy plant for wetlands or to edge ponds. [*A particularly useful plant for cleaning waste water, if you care to try such strategies in a courtyard!*]

Senecio (Jacobaea, Kleinea). 7 to ★10, depending on species.

CALIFORNIA GERANIUM, CANDLE PLANT, CINERARIA, DUSTY MILLER, FLAME VINE, GERMAN IVY, GOLDEN RAGWORT, HOT-DOG CACTUS, INCHWORM, KENYA IVY, LEOPARD'S BANE, NATAL IVY, PARLOR IVY, PURPLE RAGWORT, SPEARHEAD, STRING OF BEADS, TANSY RAGWORT, TAPE WORM, VELVET GROUNDSEL, WATER IVY, WAX VINE, also known as *Kleinia repens.* A very large genus of nearly 3,000 species of annuals, biennials, perennials, vines, and shrubs, with worldwide distribution. Forming a group of plants whose uses range from flower garden herbs to landscape plants to weeds, all are implicated in causing some degree of allergy. Because of the close relationship between *Senecio* and ragweed, *Senecio* pollen is a cause of airborne allergy and, in areas where they are numerous, may be the primary cause of summer and fall allergies. Most *Senecio* species bear small yellow flowers, but a few, like the cineraria, bear larger, more colorful flowers that do not release as much pollen as the small-flowered species. With many members of the genus, there is a distinct chance of contact skin rash from the leaves and flowers. The flowers and leaves of most *Senecio* are poisonous if eaten.

SHASTA DAISY, see *Chrysanthemum.*
SILK TREE, see *Albizia julibrissin.*
SMOKE TREE, see *Cotinus.*
SNAKE PLANT, see *Sansevieria trifasciata.*
SNOW-ON-THE-MOUNTAIN, see *Euphorbia.*

Sorbus. 4

MOUNTAIN ASH. A group of about 80 species of deciduous trees and large shrubs, producing small, edible fruits, hardy to zone 3. Mountain ash has leaves resembling true ash, but it is a member of the rose family. They are beautiful trees when in full bloom and are also attractive when heavy with small red or orange fruit, which is used to make the sweetener Sorbitol. The pollen of *Sorbus* may cause limited allergy.

Spiraea. 6

BRIDAL WREATH. Many species of mostly deciduous shrubs of the northern hemisphere, most bearing heavy panicles of small, bright white flowers. Allergy to *Spiraea* is not common, but may be severe when it does occur. It is best planted far from doors and windows. [*Sounds like only the largest courtyard should harbor spiraea.*]

SPLIT-LEAF PHILODENDRON, see *Monstera.*

Stevia. ★9

A large group of perennial herbs and shrubs native to the tropics of North and South America. *S. serrata* is common in zones 8–10 and in Mexico. *S. rebaudiana* is used to make a strong natural sweetener. Another plant called STEVIA is *Piqueria trinervia*, another highly allergenic perennial flower.

Strelitzia. ✳1

BIRD-OF-PARADISE. *S. regina*, the bird-of-paradise, is the official flower of the city of Los Angeles, despite the fact that it is native to South Africa and the tropics. The long-stemmed orange and blue flowers are popular in floral arrangements. *S. Nicolai*, the GIANT BIRD-OF-PARADISE, grows much larger and taller, resembling a banana tree. The flowers are very large and more unusual than beautiful. These tree-like plants are often used with good effect in indoor shopping mall landscaping. The birds-of-paradise are not known to cause allergy, and the design of their flowers keeps pollen inside. Because it produces no airborne pollen and lacks the insect needed to pollinate it, bird-of-paradise rarely sets seed in the United States. The flowers can be hand-pollinated, and the resulting seeds are large and black, with a small, fuzzy orange tuft.

SWEET GUM, see *Liquidambar.*
SYCAMORE, see *Platanus.*

Syringa. 6

LILAC. Deciduous shrubs or small trees, hardy to zone 3. *S. vulgaris*, the common lilac, is a tall shrub bearing clusters of highly fragrant flowers in early spring. The intensely sweet fragrance may produce allergic reactions in those with odor sensitivities. As a member of the olive family, lilac has allergenic pollen, but because it is rarely airborne, it does not present much allergy potential. Lilacs should be planted away from doors and windows. [*Another candidate for only the largest courtyards?*]

Tabebuia. 5

TRUMPET VINE TREE. Large evergreen flowering trees from the tropics and subtropics, occasionally used in zone 10. Two species, *T. avellanedae*, and *T. chrysotricha* (the GOLDEN TRUMPET TREE), are hardier than others of this genus. In the United States, these trees rarely get taller than 25 feet, but in the tropics they may grow to 100 feet. They are closely related to the hardy CATALPA TREE, which is known to cause allergy. Because these three trees have many similarities, use *Tabebuia* as a landscape tree with discretion. *Tabebuia* pollen is heavy and does not fall far from the tree; plant these trees away from the house. [*And here's another questionable courtyard dweller.*]

TANGERINE, see *Citrus.*

Tamarindus indica. ✳2

TAMARIND. A large evergreen tree from the tropics, also grown in south Florida for its fine shape, attractive foliage, and sweet fruit, which is very popular in Mexico and Latin America. Tamarind is entirely insect-pollinated and is not known to cause allergy. [*Many Mexican courtyards are graced by the filtered light below wide-spreading tamarinds.*]

Tecomaria capensis. 3

CAPE HONEYSUCKLE. A shrub or vine native to South Africa and common in zones 9–10. It grows best in full sun or partial shade, and can be clipped to form a hedge. *Tecomaria*'s orange tubular flowers are attractive to hummingbirds. There is a yellow-flowering variety that needs more light and heat to thrive. *Tecomaria* is unrelated to COMMON or JAPANESE HONEYSUCKLE (*Lonicera*).

Thevetia. 4

BE-STILL PLANT, LUCKY TREE, YELLOW OLEANDER. A fast-growing small tree or shrub from tropical America and Mexico, used in landscapes in zones 9–10. Its common name derives from the fact that its long green leaves tremble in the slightest breeze. *Thevetia* tolerates a little light frost but does best in hot, frost-free areas. The sap has allergy potential, and all parts of the plant are poisonous. [*Leaves that tremble in the slightest breeze could be useful signals of cooling in a hot-weather courtyard. Not cold-hardy, though, and a cousin of the extremely poisonous oleander.*]

Thuja. 8

ARBORVITAE, THUYA, WESTERN RED CEDAR, WHITE CEDAR. Five species of evergreen coniferous trees native to North America and eastern Asia. Many of these are used as either trees or shrubs in all plant zones in the United States. Many cultivars of *Thuja* are sold as arborvitae. Popular shrub forms of *Thuja* are sold as either "globe" or "pyramid" types. All species of *Thuja* release large amounts of airborne pollen over an extended period of time; those allergic to cypress or juniper have a good chance of cross-allergic reaction to arborvitae.

Thymus. 3

THYME. Perennial ground covers, small shrubs, or culinary herbs for sunny areas of zones 4–10. The fragrance may affect perfume-sensitive individuals. [*One of those ground covers that smells so very good when trod upon.*]

Tilia. 7

BASSWOOD, CRIMEAN LINDEN, FEMALE LINDEN, LIME TREE, LINDEN, LITTLELEAF LINDEN, MALE LINDEN, MONGOLIAN LINDEN, SILVER LINDEN, WHISTLEWOOD, WHITE LINDEN, WHITTLEWOOD. A group of about 30 species of fast-growing, spreading, deciduous trees, native to most of the northern hemisphere and popular as street trees and valuable lumber trees. They thrive only in areas of adequate moisture. Despite some of their common names, no linden is actually either a male- or female-only tree. They produce many small white flowers; although honeybees visit these flowers often, the trees are imperfectly insect-pollinated, and a good deal of pollen becomes airborne. *Tilia* pollen, although often allergenic, is fairly heavy and does not easily travel far from the tree. Exposure to linden pollen is often caused by trees growing in the allergy sufferer's own yard or workplace. [*The leaves of* T. tomentosa *are easily stirred by the wind, turning up silvery undersides. Another useful symbol of the presence of a cooling breeze.*]

Trachelospermum (Rhynchospermum). 6

CONFEDERATE JASMINE, STAR JASMINE. A group of about a dozen species of shrubby, vining evergreen plants with bright, star-shaped, highly fragrant white flowers. These very popular landscape plants are often used as ground covers in sun or shade, in zones 8–10. Star jasmine's milky sap can occasionally cause rash, and the heavy fragrance is allergenic to those who are perfume-sensitive. The fragrance is most intense on still, warm summer nights, and it should not be planted near bedroom windows. It is unrelated to true jasmine (*Jasminum*), and those who cannot tolerate the heavy fragrance of *Jasminum* may not be as affected by *Trachelospermum*. [*For that Córdoban fragrance with less risk of fragrance-allergic reaction.*]

Tropaeolum. 3

NASTURTIUM. Two species of *Tropaeolum* are commonly used in landscaping. *T. majus*, the common garden nasturtium, is a perennial that is used as a fast-growing annual. The large, round leaves and bright yellow or orange flowers are edible and piquant, and are occasionally added to salads. *T. peregrinum*, the climbing nasturtium, can reach 12 feet. It is yellow-flowered. Some individuals may be sensitive to its fragrance. [*A staple of the Hispanic courtyard.*]

TRUMPET VINE, see *Distictis*; *Macfadyena unguis-cati* (*Doxantha*); *Tabebuia*.
TULIP TREE, see *Magnolia*.

Typha. 6

CATTAIL. A common wetland plant. [*Like Scirpus, useful in waste-water treatment.*]

Ulmus. 8

ELM. A group of 18 deciduous or partially evergreen trees native to the United States, Mexico, Europe, and Asia. All the elms are bisexual, having both male and female parts in the same flowers (despite reports that elms possess both unisexual and bisexual flowers). Many plants with bisexual flowers do not release much airborne pollen, but with elms this is not the case: They release significant amounts of pollen into the air. Part of the confusion about the elm flowering systems is probably caused by the fact that some close relatives—*Aphananthe*, *Hemiptelea*, *Holoptelea*, *Planera*, *Trema*, and *Zelkova*—produce unisexual (one-sex) flowers. All elms produce allergenic pollen. DECIDUOUS ELMS produce their pollen in early spring, just before or at the same time as new leaves are appearing. An exception to this is *U. crassifolia*, the cedar elm, which blooms in the fall. It is rated at 8 on the allergy-potential scale. The CHINESE ELM (*U. parvifolia*), which can be found growing throughout zones 6–10, is often evergreen in the warmest winter areas. CHINESE ELM releases its pollen from late summer into early winter. It is rated at ✴ 10. There are also at least three cultivars of elm that never bloom, making them fine allergy-free landscape trees: *U. americana* "Ascendens," a large columnar tree; *U. glabra* "Horizontalis," a weeping selection of SCOTCH ELM; and *U. minor* "Gracilis," a cultivar of the EUROPEAN SMOOTHLEAF ELM. All three of these nonflowering elms are grown by cuttings or are budded onto seedling elm rootstock. They are rated as excellent for the allergy-free landscape. Because Dutch Elm Disease (DED) has killed off millions of elm trees worldwide, the prevalence of elm allergy has dropped considerably. In areas where elms have been replaced by disease-resistant lookalikes like the Chinese elm, however, the replacements may be more potent allergenic trees than the vanished elms. In fact, a strong argument can be made that the huge rise in urban allergy is directly linked to the millions of monoecious and dioecious male trees that were used to replace so many of the dead elms. [*Another reason to avoid Chinese elms: they are very brittle, and can be reduced to an awkward stalk of trunk by an ice storm.*]

Verbena. 5

BLUE VERVAIN, GARDEN VERBENA, VERVAIN, WHITE VERVAIN. A genus of about 200 species, annuals and perennials, some low-growing and others tall and almost shrub-like. *V. hybrida* is the common *Verbena* sold in most nurseries, and is grown as a short-lived perennial or ground cover in zones 9–10, and as an annual in other zones. *Verbenas* are heat-loving plants needing full sun and fast-draining soil for best results. Grown well, they flower profusely. *Verbena* is occasionally implicated in causing skin rash, and the scent of several species, especially when planted en masse, is unpleasant.

Vinca. ✴2

PERIWINKLE, MYRTLE. *V. minor* is a small-leafed, slow-growing, prostrate vine, hardy to zone 3, where it is used as a ground cover. *V. major* is a fast-growing, large-leafed version, not as hardy. Both vines bear five-petaled purple-blue flowers and have attractive dark, leathery leaves. Variegated forms of both species are available. *Vinca* grows well in full sun to full shade, but becomes tall and less compact in deep shade. Drought-tolerant once established, it performs better when provided with adequate water. Vinca sap may cause allergic skin rash, and although this is uncommon, use care when shearing the vines. Because the flowers have almost no exposed pollen, *Vinca* makes a very good substitute for more allergenic ALGERIAN or ENGLISH IVY. The plant known as *V. rosea* or ANNUAL PERRIWINKLE is a fine sun-loving annual flower properly named *Catharanthus roseus*. [*Not only drought-tolerant, but invasive as well.*]

VIRGINIA CREEPER, see *Parthenocissus*.

Vitis. 3

GRAPE. All grape flowers release pollen, but it is not a common allergen. More common is skin rash on those pruning or harvesting grapes: the undersides of the leaves are covered with fine hairs that may cause irritation, although not a classic allergic response. Dander from the small insects, especially aphids, that are common pests of grapes may cause inhalant allergy. The MUSCADINE GRAPE is an exception, in that it is separate-sexed and produces airborne pollen that has been implicated as causing allergy. It is not a good plant for the allergy-free garden. [*The classic grapevine over the courtyard, as in the Italian trattoria; seasonal shade, color change, and a harvest of fruit. But lots of busy bees visit at harvest time.*]

WATER LILY, see *Aponogeton distachyus*; *Nymphaea*.

Weigela. 3

Deciduous shrubs that are widely used in zones 3–8, with many named cultivars. Because they flower on new wood, hard pruning after bloom encourages next season's blossoms. There are about a dozen different species of *Weigela*, usually bearing pink, purple, or carmine-colored flowers. All need ample water to thrive, but are otherwise easy to grow. Not often implicated in allergy, they are related to HONEYSUCKLE, and those with allergy to honeysuckle should avoid inhaling the fragrance of *Weigela*.

WILLOW, see *Salix*.

Wisteria. 4

Less than a dozen species of woody vines native to Asia and the eastern United States.

Two species, *W. floribunda* and *W. sinensis*, are commonly used worldwide. *W. floribunda*, the JAPANESE WISTERIA, is hardy in zones 4–10, long-lived, heavy-flowering, and may grow far up into trees or onto houses. Its fragrant flowers are white, purple, or lavender and are borne in long drooping clusters. The cultivar "Plena" has fully double, deep blue-violet flowers. "Plena" releases almost no pollen and is a fine choice for the allergy-free garden. *W. sinensis*, the CHINESE WISTERIA, has shorter, faintly fragrant, purple flower clusters that open all at once, making them very showy in bloom. "Alba" is a highly fragrant white cultivar. Hardiness is similar to *W. floribunda*. *W. macrostachya* is a native species, found in wet areas of the Southeast, west to Arkansas. It has foot-long clusters of lilac-blue flowers, and its pods are smooth. Another native is *W. frutescens*, also from the Southeast, west to Texas; it produces five-inch-long lilac-colored flower clusters. All species produce long pods filled with poisonous seeds that eject forcefully when ripe, often with a bang like a small firecracker. Frequently as one pod explodes, others quickly join in; it sometimes sounds like the yard has just come under gunfire! *Wisteria* is difficult to propagate from cuttings (as are most members of the *Leguminosae* or PEA family), but it is easy from seed, and good selections can be budded or grafted. Vines often take many years to bloom, and occasionally, if the soil is too rich in nitrogen, the vines grow rampant but never bloom. *[Another seasonal shade favorite, it draws the bees to its blossoms in spring.]*

Yucca. ✳2

ADAM'S NEEDLE, BANANA YUCCA, BLUE YUCCA, DAGGER PLANT, JOSHUA TREE, NEEDLE PALM, PALM LILY, PALMA PITA, ROMAN CANDLE, SOAP TREE, SOAPWELL, SPANISH BAYONET. A group of about 40 species of sharp-spined plants native to the warm areas of North America; some are hardy to zone 4, but few will flower north of zone 4. *Yucca* flowers are usually creamy white, tinged with pink or purple, and borne on tall, stiff stalks that rise well above the foliage. The flowers are entirely insect-pollinated and do not shed pollen. The long, dagger-like leaves are dangerous, however, especially to small children, and placement of these vigorous plants requires good judgment. One species from Florida, *Y. recurvifolia*, lacks the sharp-tipped leaves and makes a better garden plant than most *Yuccas*. Another species, *Y. elephantipes*, the GIANT YUCCA, grows far too large for most gardens and is difficult to remove.

Zantedeschia. 4

CALLA, CALLA LILLY. Tall perennials, with unusually prominent calyxes in white, yellow, pink, or red; they are easy to grow and hardy in zones 8–10. In cooler climates, the roots must be lifted and over-wintered indoors. They thrive in shade or sun, but require ample water. The sap of calla lilies has properties similar to that of DUMB CANE (*Dieffenbachia*), and it may cause contact rash. The pollen, which is prominently displayed on the stiff stamens, may cause allergy if inhaled. All parts of the plant are poisonous if eaten.

GLOSSARY

arcade transition space between courtyard and surrounding rooms, usually with arched openings to the courtyard, and windows and doors opening to the rooms

aspect ratio

$$\frac{\text{area of the courtyard floor}}{(\text{average height, surrounding walls})^2}$$

brocale well head

cal whitewash applied in layers onto masonry walls

centro center, as of a Hispanic city

closed facade a wall enclosing a courtyard with no arcade or colonnade; instead, a common wall separates the courtyard from the adjacent rooms

colonnade like an arcade, but the openings to the courtyard are spaces between columns rather than a series of arches

Concurso de Patios Córdoba's annual contest for the most beautiful courtyards, with monetary prizes, and subsequent listing on maps for tourists

coolth the absence of heat

cooltower passive down-draft tower, in which hot dry air encounters a wet media at the top, gains moisture and a lowered dry-bulb temperature, thereby becoming heavier, and falls to an outlet at the bottom

corredor gallery, porch, corridor (or arcade, colonnade)

galleria arcade or colonnade

loggia a covered space open on one side (or two) to an outdoor space; similar to arcade or colonnade

mesón inn, lodging house

open facade an arcade or colonnade enclosing a courtyard, separating the rooms behind it from the courtyard

portico see "arcade" or "colonnade"

reja an ornamental metal screen, usually serving as a gate within a *zaguán*

sol-air temperature the higher temperature of outside air just above a roof (or courtyard floor) surface that is produced by solar radiation, and radiant exchange between roof (or courtyard floor) and sky

solar shadow index

$$\frac{\text{south wall height}}{\text{north-south floor width}}$$

toldo Moveable horizontal fabric used to cover a courtyard's opening at the roof

vela awning (or sail), a term sometimes applied to a *toldo*

zaguán Covered entranceway from street to courtyard

References

Bagneid, Amr. 1989. "Indigenous Residential Courtyards: Typology, Morphology and Bioclimates." In *The Courtyard as Dwelling*, Traditional Dwellings and Settlements Working Paper Series, volume 6, IASTE WP06-89. Berkeley: Center for Environmental Design Research, Univ. of California.

Baker, N., A. Fanchiotti, and K. Steemers. 1993. *Daylighting in Architecture: A European Reference Book*. London: James & James Science Publishers.

Bicknell, Catherine. 1989. "The Courtyard Houses of Langatha." In *The Courtyard as Dwelling*, Traditional Dwellings and Settlements Working Paper Series, Volume 6, IASTE WP06-89. Berkeley: Center for Environmental Design Research, Univ. of California.

Blaser, Werner. 1985. *Atrium: Five Thousand Years of Open Courtyards*. Translated by D. Q. Stephenson. Basel: Wepf & Co.

Borges, Jorge Luis. 1977. *Obras Poeticas, 1923–1977*. Buenos Aires: Alianza Editorial, Emecé Editores.

———. 1999. *Selected Poems*. New York: Viking Penguin.

Brown, G. Z., and Mark DeKay. 2001. *Sun, Wind and Light*. New York: John Wiley & Sons.

Carrasco, Victor, and John Reynolds. 1996. "Shade, Water and Mass: Passive Cooling in Andalucía." In *Proceedings of the 21st Annual Passive Solar Conference, Asheville N.C.* Boulder, Colo.: American Solar Energy Society.

Collantes de Terán Delorme, Francisco, and Luis Gómez Estern. 1976. *Arquitectura Civil Sevillana*. Seville, Spain: Ayuntamiento de Sevilla.

Domínguez Bascón, Pedro. 1999. *Clima, Medio Ambiente y Urbanismo en Córdoba*. Córdoba, Spain: Colección Estudios Cordobeses, Diputación de Córdoba.

Elmas, Can. 1992. "Energy conscious housing design for three different climatic regions of Turkey." Master of Architecture thesis, University of Oregon, Eugene.

Fardeheb, Fewzi. 1985. *Examination and classification of passive solar cooling strategies in Middle Eastern vernacular architecture*. Univ. of California, Los Angeles. Duplicated.

Fathy, Hassan. 1973. *Architecture for the Poor: An Experiment in Rural Egypt*. Chicago: University of Chicago Press.

———. 1986. *Natural Energy and Vernacular Architecture*. Chicago: University of Chicago Press.

Fathy, Hassan, and J. Steele. 1988. *Hassan Fathy*. New York: St. Martin's Press.

García Márquez, Gabriel. 1988. *Love in the Time of Cholera*. Translated by Edith Grossman. New York: Alfred A Knopf.

———. 1990. *The General in His Labyrinth*. Translated by Edith Grossman. New York: Alfred A. Knopf.

———. 1995. *Of Love and Other Demons*. Translated by Edith Grossman. London: Jonathan Cape.

Gates, David M., and L. E. Papian. 1971. *Atlas of Energy Budgets of Plant Leaves*. London: Academic Press.

Gerlach-Spriggs, Nancy, Richard Enoch Kaufman, and Sam Bass Warner, Jr. 1998. *Restorative Gardens: The Healing Landscape*. New Haven: Yale University Press.

Givoni, Baruch. 1998. *Climate Considerations in Building and Urban Design*. New York: Van Nostrand Reinhold.

Golany, Gideon. 1990. *Design and Thermal Performance: Below-Ground Dwellings in China*. Newark: Univ. of Delaware Press.

Hanna, R. and P. Simpson. 1996. "The Climate and the Social Climate of a Design Stereotype: The Courtyard Paradigm." Traditional Dwellings and Settlements Working Paper Series, volume 88. Berkeley: Center for Environmental Design Research, Univ. of California.

Heschong, Lisa. 1979. *Thermal Delight in Architecture*. Cambridge: MIT Press.

Hinrichs, Craig. 1989. "The Courtyard Housing Form as Traditional Dwelling." In *The Courtyard as Dwelling*, Traditional Dwellings and Settlements Working Paper Series, Volume 6, IASTE WP06-89. Berkeley: Center for Environmental Design Research, Univ. of California.

Knowles, Ralph L. 1998. *Rhythm and Ritual: A Motive for Design*. Los Angeles: Ralph L. Knowles.

Knowles, Ralph and Karen Kensek. 2000. "Interstitium: A Zoning Strategy for Seasonally Adaptive Architecture." In *Architecture, City, Environment: Proceedings of PLEA 2000, Cambridge, England*.

Lowry, William P., and Porter Lowry. 1995. *Fundamentals of Biometeorology: The Biological Environment*. McMinnville, Ore.: Peavine Publications.

Lunde, Peter J. 1980. *Solar Thermal Engineering*. New York: John Wiley & Sons.

Lung, David P. Y. 1991. *Chinese Traditional Vernacular Architecture*. Hong Kong: Regional Council.

Millet, Marietta, and James Bedrick. 1980. *Manual Graphic Daylighting Design Method*. Department of Architecture, University of Washington, Seattle.

Milne, Murray, and Baruch Givoni. 1979. "Architectural Design Based on Climate." In Donald Watson, ed., *Energy Conservation Through Building Design*. New York: McGraw-Hill.

Ogren, Thomas Leo. 2000. *Allergy-Free Gardening: The Revolutionary Guide to Healthy Landscaping*. Berkeley, Calif.: Ten Speed Press.

Perez-de-Lama, Jose, and Jose M. Cabeza. 1998. "A Holistic Approach to the Mediterranean Patio." In *Environmentally Friendly Cities: Proceedings of PLEA '98*. London: James & James Science Publishers.

Polyzoides, Stefanos, Roger Sherwood, and James Tice. 1992. *Courtyard Housing in Los Angeles*. 2d ed. New York: Princeton Architectural Press.

Rapoport, Amos. 1969. *House Form and Culture*. Upper Saddle River, N.J.: Prentice-Hall.

Reynolds, J. 1982. "Passive Cooling and Courtyards in Colima, Mexico." In *Passive and Lower Energy Alternatives: Proceedings at First International PLEA Conference, Bermuda*. Oxford: Pergamon Press.

———. 1996. "Change, Threat and Opportunity: Courtyard Buildings in Colima, Mexico." Traditional Dwellings and Settlements Working Paper Series, Volume 88: pp. 2–16. Berkeley: Center for Environmental Design Research, Univ. of California.

———. 1997. "Adaptation Strategies for Hispanic Courtyard Buildings." In *Symposium on The Courtyard House and the Urban Fabric, Aga Khan Program for Islamic Architecture, MIT*.

———. 2001. "Courtyard Cooling: Proportion vs. Proaction." In *Proceedings of the 26th Passive Solar Conference*. Boulder, Colo.: American Solar Energy Society.

Reynolds, John, and William Lowry. 1996. "The Garden in the Building: Observations of Córdoba's Courtyards." In *Landscape Journal* 15 (no. 2): 123–137.

Sang Hae Lee. 1991. "Continuity and Consistency of the Traditional Courtyard House Plan in Modern Korean Dwellings." In *Traditional Dwellings and Settlements Review* 3 (no. 1). (Published by International Association for the Study of Traditional Environments, Berkeley, Calif.)

Siembieda, William J. 1996. "Walls and Gates: A Latin Perspective." In *Landscape Journal* 15 (no. 2): 113–122.

Sinha, Amita. 1989. "Traditional Rural Settlements and Dwellings in Northern India." In *The Courtyard as Dwelling*. Traditional Dwellings and Settlements Working Paper Series, Volume 6, IASTE WP06-89. Berkeley: Center for Environmental Design Research, University of Calif.

Stein, Benjamin, and John Reynolds. 2000. *Mechanical and Electrical Equipment for Buildings*. 9th ed. New York: John Wiley & Sons.

Warren, John and Ihsan Fethi. 1982. *Traditional Houses in Baghdad*. Horsham, England: Coach Publishing House Ltd.

CREDITS

Blaser, Werner. *Atrium: Five Thousand Years of Open Courtyards*. Introduction by Johannes Spalt; English translation by D. Q. Stephenson. © Wepf & Co. AG, Verlag, Basel, Switzerland 1985. Selections reprinted by permission.

"Patio," from *Jorge Luis Borges Selected Poems 1923–1967* by Jorge Luis Borges, © 1968, 1969, 1970, 1971, 1972 by Jorge Luis Borges, Emece Editores, S. A. and Norman Thomas Di Giovanni. Used by permission of Dell Publishing, a division of Random House, Inc.

"Patio," Jorge Luis Borges. Copyright © 1995 Maria Kodama, reprinted with the permission of the Wiley Agency, Inc.

"The South," translated by W. S. Merwin, from *Selected Poems* of Jorge Luis Borges, © 1999 by Maria Kodama. Used by permission of Viking Penguin, a division of Penguin Putnam Inc.

"El Sur," Jorge Luis Borges. Copyright © 1995 Maria Kodama, reprinted with the permission of the Wiley Agency, Inc.

Fathy, Hassan. *Architecture for the Poor, An Experiment in Rural Egypt*. © 1973, The University of Chicago Press. Selections reprinted by permission.

García Márquez, Gabriel. 1990. *The General in His Labyrinth*. Translation, Edith Grossman. Alfred A. Knopf, Publishers. Selections reprinted by permission.

García Márquez, Gabriel. 1988. *Love in the Time of Cholera*. Translation, Edith Grossman. © 1988 by Alfred A Knopf Inc. Reprinted by permission of Alfred A Knopf, a Division of Random House Inc. Selections reprinted by permission.

García Márquez, Gabriel. 1995. *Of Love and Other Demons*. Translation, Edith Grossman. Jonathan Cape, Publishers, London. Selections reprinted by permission.

Gerlach-Spriggs, Nancy, Richard Enoch Kaufman, and Sam Bass Warner, Jr. *Restorative Gardens: The Healing Landscape*. © 1998, Yale University Press. Selections reprinted by permission.

Heschong, Lisa. *Thermal Delight in Architecture*. The MIT Press, Cambridge, Massachusetts. © 1979 by the Massachusetts Institute of Technology. Selections reprinted by permission.

Knowles, Ralph L. *Rhythm and Ritual: A Motive for Design*. © Ralph L. Knowles, Professor Emeritas, School of Architecture, University of Southern California. Selections reprinted by permission.

Lowry, William P., and Porter P. Lowry II. 1995. *Fundamentals of Biometeorology, The Biological Environment*. Peavine Publications, McMinnville and Portland, OR: in press. Distributed by Missouri Botanical Garden Press, St. Louis. Selection reprinted by permission.

Ogren, Thomas Leo. *Allergy-Free Gardening: The Revolutionary Guide to Healthy Landscaping*. Ten Speed Press, Berkeley. © 2000 by Tom Ogren. Selections reprinted by permission.

Polyzoides, Stefanos; Sherwood, Roger; Tice, James. 1992. *Courtyard Housing in Los Angeles*, 2nd edition. Selections courtesy of Princeton Architectural Press.

Rapoport, Amos. *House Form and Culture*, © 1969. Reprinted by permission of Prentice-Hall, Inc., Upper Saddle River, NJ.

Photographs and drawings, except as otherwise credited: John S. Reynolds, A.I.A.

Whitewash, 41, 145–146, 156, 173, 177, 233. *See also* Cal

Wilson, Matthew, 35, 37

Wind, 26, 29, 40, 57, 66, 67, 75, 79, 80, 84, 88–92, 112, 114–115, 136, 148–149, 163, 165, 178, 186, 194, 196, 199, 202, 210, 214

Wind catcher, 91

Women (in Islam), 48, 53

Wong, Y. C., architect, 170–171

Zaguán (entryway), 1, 4, 24, 46, 48–53, 59, 90, 99, 116, 118, 123, 124, 132–137, 157–165, 188, 191, 208, 233
   cars in, 174–177
   detailed description, 178

Zoning, 167, 173, 174, 206